About Island Press

Since 1984, the nonprofit Island Press has been stimulating, shaping, and communicating the ideas that are essential for solving environmental problems worldwide. With more than 800 titles in print and some 40 new releases each year, we are the nation's leading publisher on environmental issues. We identify innovative thinkers and emerging trends in the environmental field. We work with world-renowned experts and authors to develop cross-disciplinary solutions to environmental challenges.

Island Press designs and implements coordinated book publication campaigns in order to communicate our critical messages in print, in person, and online using the latest technologies, programs, and the media. Our goal: to reach targeted audiences—scientists, policymakers, environmental advocates, the media, and concerned citizens—who can and will take action to protect the plants and animals that enrich our world, the ecosystems we need to survive, the water we drink, and the air we breathe.

Island Press gratefully acknowledges the support of its work by the Agua Fund, Inc., The Margaret A. Cargill Foundation, Betsy and Jesse Fink Foundation, The William and Flora Hewlett Foundation, The Kresge Foundation, The Forrest and Frances Lattner Foundation, The Andrew W. Mellon Foundation, The Curtis and Edith Munson Foundation, The Overbrook Foundation, The David and Lucile Packard Foundation, The Summit Foundation, Trust for Architectural Easements, The Winslow Foundation, and other generous donors.

The opinions expressed in this book are those of the author(s) and do not necessarily reflect the views of our donors.

THE CASE FOR A CARBON TAX

The Case for a Carbon Tax

GETTING PAST OUR HANG-UPS TO EFFECTIVE CLIMATE POLICY

Shi-Ling Hsu

Washington | Covelo | London

ISLAND PRESS is a trademark of the Center for Resource Economics.

Library of Congress Cataloging-in-Publication Data

Hsu, Shi-Ling.
The case for a carbon tax : getting past our hang-ups to effective climate policy / Shi-Ling Hsu. — 1st ed.
p. cm.
Includes bibliographical references and index.
ISBN-13: 978-1-59726-531-7 (cloth : alk. paper)
ISBN-10: 1-59726-531-4 (cloth : alk. paper)
ISBN-13: 978-1-59726-533-1 (pbk. : alk. paper)
ISBN-10: 1-59726-533-0 (pbk. : alk. paper) 1. Carbon taxes. 2. Climatic changes—Government policy. I. Title.
HJ5316.H78 2011
363.738'746—dc23
2011014901

Printed on recycled, acid-free paper

Manufactured in the United States of America

10 9 8 7 6 5 4 3 2 1

Keywords: climate change, environmental policy, cap-and-trade, energy subsidies, renewable energy, Kyoto Protocol, greenhouse gas emissions, global warming, environmental economics, Stern Report

For my children,
Katharine and Allen

CONTENTS

ACKNOWLEDGMENTS

I tease my wife about things that take longer than she initially thinks they would, but to put up a mirror and consider my own projects, this book is really very typical of the things that I have done with some care: it took *much* longer than I thought it would. Along the way, I benefited from the comments, advice, support, and input of many people, including Michael Waggoner, Michael Meurer, David Weisbach, Dan Cole, Scott Schang; and from the many fine faculty and students that have attended workshops at Pace Law School, the James E. Rogers College of Law at the University of Arizona, the Florida State University College of Law, the Boston University School of Law, Boston College Law School, and from my friends and colleagues that have listened to me pontificate at meetings of the Midwestern Law and Economics Association and the Society of Environmental Law and Economics. I am also indebted to Island Press's Emily Davis for her editorial support and from three anonymous reviewers who have helped improve this book immensely. I have benefited from and learned much from my research assistant, Oliver Pulleyblank, who will write something much better than this someday. I have also been aided by the institutional support of the University of British Columbia Faculty of Law. Closer to home, I owe a huge debt of gratitude to my parents, who made everything before and after this book possible by crossing the Pacific Ocean to a strange country in which they did not speak the language. On the other side of the generational divide, I am inspired every day to try and do better by my children, Katharine and Allen, who are the real "game-changers." And finally and most of all, to bring this full circle, I owe my wife, Debby—"big time," as her astute friends have put it—for just putting up with everything.

Chapter 1

Introduction

Global climate change has become the dominant environmental issue of our time. The "greenhouse effect," or the trapping of heat from the sun as it bounces off the Earth's surface, keeps heat within the Earth's atmosphere instead of allowing it to radiate back into space. "Greenhouse gases" such as carbon dioxide trap this heat, and in fact play a vital role in regulating the Earth's temperature. But this regulatory mechanism preserves a delicate balance, one that has been disturbed by the carbon dioxide emissions from the burning of fossil fuels. The Earth can only absorb so much carbon dioxide, it appears, and the excess emissions that have been accumulating since the onset of the Industrial Revolution have increased the Earth's temperature, threatening to disrupt life for an entire planet that has gotten used to very specific climatic conditions.

This theory of global climate change has been around for a long time, dating back to the findings of Swedish chemist Svante Arrhenius, who reported in 1908 that the buildup of "carbonic acid" in the Earth's atmosphere created the possibility that the Earth could gradually grow warmer. He noted that a warmer Earth could improve agricultural yield "for the benefit of rapidly propagating mankind." As a Swede, Arrhenius could be forgiven for finding some comfort in this possibility, but we have long been on notice—since at least the 1970s[1]—that the buildup of atmospheric carbon dioxide could have

1

very dire consequences. As it turns out, the accumulation of greenhouse gases in the Earth's atmosphere will have much more destructive effects than just warmer weather. Changes in weather patterns could bring about prolonged heat waves, prolonged droughts, and resulting water shortages; warmer oceans could produce more frequent and stronger storm events; and rises in sea levels could jeopardize trillions of dollars of real estate worldwide. In simple physical terms, trapping heat means that more energy is staying within the Earth's system, and this excess energy is likely to release itself in disruptive ways. And some effects of climate change pose dangers of positive feedback effects: warmer temperatures could unlock and release methane from cold, hard, frozen tundra and from oceans, unleashing a greenhouse gas twenty-five times more powerful than carbon dioxide. A "burp" of methane from Northern Canada alone could swamp worldwide efforts to reduce carbon dioxide emissions.

More than most environmental problems, global climate change has become a defining social issue. Climate effects will impose particularly high social costs on the equatorial regions of the world. Since the equatorial countries are generally poorer, climate change is a problem that will aggravate global inequalities. Moreover, it is largely the developed world that has created this problem by its prolific combustion of fossil fuels (and prospered from it). As a final insult, the capacity to *adapt* to a climate-changed future, as much as is possible, lies mostly within the developed world. In a climate-changed future, the rich could well be poorer, but the poor stand to be *much* poorer.[2] Extreme weather events such as Hurricane Katrina, which made a mockery of US federal disaster response efforts, will punish developed countries but overwhelm poorer ones.

Against this complicated geopolitical backdrop is the daunting reality that addressing the problem of climate change will in all likelihood require a global response, and will require the engagement of the vast majority of countries. The nature of the greenhouse gas problem is such that unilateral action by one or a few countries is likely to be ineffective. Imagine the United States biting the bullet and dramatically reducing its use of petroleum in its transportation sector. What would be the effect of the world's largest consumer of crude oil reducing its demand by, say, 20 percent? The answer would almost certainly be that the price of crude oil, which is a fungible, globally traded good, would plummet. In the wake of a global price drop, would we not fully expect developing countries to snap up the suddenly plentiful, suddenly cheap crude oil and use it to develop their own economies? The net global effect of a costly unilateral action could well be zero, or perhaps even worse, since developing countries almost certainly burn fossil fuels less efficiently than the United States. This prospect of "leakage," or the offshoring of greenhouse gas emissions, is at the heart of the problem confronting climate negotiators as they try to hammer out an international agreement to reduce greenhouse gas emissions.

And yet there is fierce resistance to a global response. Developing countries, having benefited little from the past combustion of fossil fuels, do not wish to commit to limiting their greenhouse gas emissions, as that would mean they would refrain from doing that which developed countries have already done. Developing countries have largely said to the developed nations of the world: "you created the problem, you fix it." This is an understandable position from the viewpoint of developing countries. A number of "justice" theories have been put forth by academics in support of this course of action. But where does that leave the problem of climate change? If developed countries do not act first for fear of leakage, and developing countries are unwilling to act until developed countries act first, how will there be any kind of agreement, let alone a global response?

Consider the illustrative relationship between the United States and China. These two superpowers are now the two largest emitters in the world, together accounting for more than 40 percent of the world's carbon dioxide emissions in 2006.[3] China became the world's largest carbon dioxide emitter in 2006, emitting 6,240 megatons of carbon dioxide that year, nearly double the 3,228 megatons it emitted in 2001.[4] This *growth* in emissions has its own economic momentum, and will be difficult to check. Even a dramatic slowdown of this growth in emissions would still result in large increases for at least a decade. Yet, China still counts itself as a developing country, and its official position is that it will not accept emissions limitations on the grounds that it would interfere with its development. China has made some moves that signal a slightly greater engagement with the climate change problem, such as the adoption of a climate change program in 2007, an increasing interest in wind energy, and its approval of the Copenhagen Accord.[5] But by and large, unless China reverses itself dramatically, its emissions will continue to grow, making huge contributions to global greenhouse gas levels and driving climate change.

For its part, the United States has contributed more to the *stock* of greenhouse gases in the Earth's atmosphere than any other country:

240 gigatons from 1950 to 2005, 26.5 percent of the world's emissions over that period.[6] And in terms of per-person cumulative emissions from 1950 to the present, the United States averaged 808 Mt per person, more than ten times the figure for China over that period.[7] The annual per person emissions for the United States are still more than four times that of China at current emissions rates and populations. Yet, at the time of writing of this book, the prospect of climate legislation in the United States seemed remote, at least in part because China has yet commit to any meaningful efforts to reduce emissions.[8]

Even if the United States and China somehow manage to bridge their differences and agree to something that would be politically acceptable in both countries, what about the rest of the world? Assuming somewhat generously that the European Union would be supportive of a bilateral arrangement between the United States and China, that would bring the emissions total of three cooperating parties to about 55 percent, still 45 percent short of universality. What about brooding, defiant, natural-gas-rich Russia, which accounts for more than 5 percent? What about India, which also puts itself in the have-not category with China and the developing countries, but itself accounts for another 5 percent? What about the swarm of other developing countries with growing economies, such as Brazil and Vietnam? The nature of the leakage problem is that the greater the efforts to reduce greenhouse gas emissions, the greater the leakage. The more that is done by a group of countries cooperating to reduce the combustion of fossil fuels that lead to climate change, the cheaper those fossil fuels become and the greater the temptation for noncooperating countries to buy and burn those fossil fuels, undoing all of those reductions.

So the big question is exactly how the diverse nations of the world will come together to curtail the emission of greenhouse gases. Burning fossil fuels and emitting carbon dioxide are such inherent parts of economic activity that it is hard to imagine the diverse nations of the world finding agreement on abstaining from something so important to economic growth. This is especially true when developed countries have already emitted and prospered, and developing countries have not. With the developing countries of the world clamoring for a first step on the part of the developed countries, and the developed countries worried about leakage and waiting for developing countries to commit, how will this impasse be resolved?

Some movement is afoot, with most developed countries taking some steps to address climate change. Most developed countries seem to accept that their participation in an agreement to reduce emissions is a necessary, but not a *sufficient* condition to bring about global cooperation in addressing climate change. The only alternative to undertaking costly emissions reductions without knowing whether others will reciprocate is to do nothing. So while it is still possible that the developing nations could undo reduction efforts, for developed nations doing something still seems preferable to doing nothing. The United States does not know that its efforts will be successful, but it does know that without an American push, the world will hurtle toward an historic and frightening climatic experiment.

Moreover, developed countries recognize that climate change poses a security threat: poor countries left with nothing will have nothing to lose by violence, and the sheer numbers of dispossessed could overwhelm the ability of rich countries to insulate themselves from climate-induced unrest. Even the traditionally conservative US Department of Defense has acknowledged the threats to national security that could arise because of humanitarian crises throughout the world brought on by climate change. Defense Secretary Robert Gates has long espoused planning for the security threats that will arise at least partially as a result of climate change:

> Current defense policy must account for . . . the implications of demographic trends. . . . The interaction of these changes with existing and future resource, environmental, and climate pressures may generate new security challenges.[9]

And in its 2010 Quadrennial Defense Review, the Department of Defense noted that a number of new trends, including climate change, could "spark or exacerbate future conflicts," and that it was "developing policies and plans to manage the effects of climate change on its operating environment [and] missions."[10]

But to undertake the fairly radical, economy-wide changes necessary to bring annual emissions levels down, and eventually stabilize atmospheric concentrations at reasonably safe levels, these unilateral baby steps undertaken by developed countries are insufficient. Because of the leakage problem, global engagement with the reduction of greenhouse gases is absolutely necessary, and almost every country, developed or not, has to be a party. What can possibly be proposed, that could satisfy almost every country in the world?

This book explores potential policy options, and argues that a carbon tax is currently the most effective means of reducing emissions. A carbon tax is a tax that is levied on the emission of a quantity of carbon dioxide. In its simplest form, a carbon tax is levied on fossil fuels, at some transaction point before combustion, as essentially a sales tax based on the carbon content of the fuel. Carbon dioxide is the most abundant greenhouse gas, and while ideally a policy instrument would cover all greenhouse gases, the regulation of carbon dioxide emissions from fossil fuels is the most important aspect of controlling greenhouse gas emissions. Because carbon dioxide is the longest-lived greenhouse gas, remaining in the atmosphere for more than 100 years after emission, it is important to start now because humankind will live with the consequences for such a long time. And because it is such a fundamental part of economic activity, it poses the greatest challenges and will take the greatest and most sustained behavior modification efforts to control. This book proposes such a carbon tax on fossil fuels, expanded to include a few other sources of greenhouse gas emissions that can be monitored and measured with relative ease.

No policy is perfect, and the prospects for finding one that satisfies even a bare majority of countries seems dim. Other alternatives have emerged as being more popular and politically palatable, but there is considerable doubt as to whether they will move the world toward the coordinated effort necessary to curb greenhouse gas emissions, as they represent no real commitment on the part of the United States to actually reduce emissions.

Despite its apparent political liabilities, the carbon tax may just fit the bill. A carbon tax presents a number of advantages relative to the heretofore more popular alternatives. These advantages, as well as the disadvantages and the implementation challenges, are explored in this book. A carbon tax, if adopted, should start at a modest level right now and increase in time, to allow time for economies to plan and adjust, and also to at least parallel (if not track) what most economists believe to be a path of increasing marginal damages over time.

There is no time to wait in terms of addressing climate change, as delay will only further complicate the task of stabilizing greenhouse gas levels at an acceptable level. Waiting to see what other countries will do will only drive up the future costs of reducing emissions. It is thus in the self-interest of developed economies to impose a carbon tax now not only because it is the most effective way to reduce emissions, but also because it will begin the important job of re-ordering economies that have long been predicated on low fossil fuel prices. Because time is not on our side, doing something modest right now is vastly preferable to finding just the "right" greenhouse gas policy, assuming adventurously that such a thing exists.

Many other initiatives, governmental and nongovernmental, need to be undertaken. This book does not contend that a carbon tax is the perfect or the only policy that needs to be implemented. In fact, one of its central arguments is that a carbon tax has the great advantage of precluding nothing else. There are no jurisdictional conflicts between the federal government and states or provinces, and there is no problem with imposing a carbon tax along with a cap-and-trade program, or almost any other policy to reduce greenhouse gases. There is no legal downside to a carbon tax. This is important because almost every other policy option will take time, and time is running short. More work will certainly need to be done in addition to a carbon tax, but there is no first step more important, more effective, and more flexible than a carbon tax.

The case for a carbon tax is hardly a novel thesis. Most economists who have waded into the climate change policy debate have argued for a carbon tax over alternatives. A number of academics in other disciplines have also supported this approach. However, nowhere is there a comprehensive treatment of all of the major advantages and disadvantages of a carbon tax. Economists, law professors, and other academics and policy wonks have made a wide variety of points drawing upon a variety of disciplines in arguing for a carbon tax. But lacking is a collection of these arguments (as well as the counterarguments), so that the totality of the case for a carbon tax can be taken in all at once. A myriad of other policy instruments have been proposed and are purported to mimic the effects of a carbon tax or be superior to a carbon tax in various ways. But it is easy to cherry-pick perceived flaws with carbon taxes; the real task is to weigh all of the advantages and disadvantages of a carbon tax against those of other instruments. This book attempts to do this, reducing the most important considerations down to ten basic arguments in favor of carbon taxes and four arguments against.

This book makes an additional contribution. It has never been seriously disputed that a carbon tax is more effective and efficient, as effective and efficient, or nearly so as almost any other broad-based policy instrument to reduce carbon dioxide emissions. A carbon tax is simply easier to design and implement and more effective than almost anything else. This is true for almost every country, every kind of society, and almost every imaginable economic circumstance. Why then do we not see more carbon taxes, or more talk of carbon taxes? Ask any serious policy expert, and at some point, the answer will be that it is somehow "politically infeasible," or "the political third rail." But why? Why is it that a simple, effective, efficient, and common sense prescription is one that is so universally unpopular? What is the cause of this allergy to a sensible policy that happens to have the word "tax" in it?

The deeper answer has to do with group and individual psychology, and with the way that people perceive taxes as compared to the alternatives. This book explores some of the cognitive biases that humans have when processing information and weighing different options, biases that are mutually reinforced by public opinion polls that ask questions that contain a subtle but powerful bias against certain policies. The standard economic assumption that individuals behave rationally in the public policy realm turns out to be as spectacularly false as it is in the economic realm. It is not just that people make irrational choices from time to time. Several entire fields of study have emerged that show how people systemically make choices that are inimical to their self-interest. One of the most puzzling—and important—irrationalities is the widespread tendency for people to have misperceptions and make cognitive misjudgments about matters having to do with taxes. People consistently make mistakes about the real effects of payments and financial benefits that, again, confound rationality assumptions. In these two areas, economic models that treat people as reasonably informed decision-makers (and perhaps very good decision-makers in the aggregate) simply do not hold up under scrutiny. Researchers investigating pathologies in these areas have been clever in searching for the boundaries between rational behavior and systemically mistaken behavior. But psychological research has not, as a general matter, applied very much of this theoretical work to specific policy problems. This book does not attempt to fill these enormous vacuums. It does attempt to summarize some of the research that seems closest to answering these types of questions, and apply it to the question of why people dislike the carbon tax as a way of addressing climate change. Combined with and compounded by a bias in the way that public opinion polls characterize climate policy options, these chronic mistakes skew perceptions of carbon taxes in a way as to make them seem politically infeasible.

The second chapter of this book will describe a typical carbon tax, and reviews three alternative policy instruments: a cap-and-trade program, "command-and-control"–type policies or standards, and government subsidies. Again, this is not to say that the carbon tax should be the only instrument used to combat climate change; this book argues that a carbon tax should be the first and most central policy instrument. The third chapter of this book sets forth ten considerations in choosing from among policy instruments to reduce greenhouse gases. In each of these ten ways, a carbon tax is a superior or equally effective or efficient instrument as all of the other three instruments. The arguments draw on literature in economics, law, and public administration, and together, form the comprehensive case for a carbon tax. The fourth chapter of this book deals with the challenges to carbon taxes, including political barriers. Other instruments enjoy some political advantages in that they can be designed in such a way as to pay off certain industries that are particularly disadvantaged by greenhouse gas regulation, such as the coal industry. This part of the book addresses these arguments, as well as the most compelling political problem with a carbon tax: the problem of its perceived regressiveness. It is true that without adjustments to aid poor households and individuals, a carbon tax will make up a larger fraction of a poor household's budget than a rich one's, and therefore impose an apparently greater hardship on the poor. However, exactly how much regressiveness we should tolerate, and how we might reverse regressiveness through governmental payouts, are complicated questions. Finally, the fifth chapter of this book will address the psychology of carbon taxes, and why they seem to be so unpopular. That our approaches have thus far been so purposefully chosen to hide the real cost of mitigation is a phenomenon worthy of intellectual inquiry. Irrationality in individual, group, and societal behavior is interesting in and of itself, and when laid across the backdrop of the potentially civilization-crushing problem of climate change, it becomes all the more compelling.

This book assumes that the reader is comfortable with economic thinking and familiar with some economic concepts. Only brief reviews of economic concepts such as public good provision are undertaken. The book also takes as its starting point the proposition that global climate change is a serious problem with unacceptably high risks of catastrophic consequences that must be addressed immediately, and that the primary task before us is to begin to make the massive political, economic, social, and legal changes that are required to address this problem. Although there is still a great deal of uncertainty with respect to the climatic future, the time has passed to defer any action while the exact details of climate projections are worked out.

An argument has been made that because the world will continue to grow wealthier, as it has for centuries, reducing greenhouse gas emissions now to avoid climate impacts in the future would essentially be transferring wealth to an even wealthier future generation.[11] There are both economic arguments and ethical arguments that suggest that the costs should be borne by future generations, because they will be wealthier and also bear the brunt of climate change impacts. The costs of trying to avoid climate change by reducing greenhouse gas emissions currently appear to be front-end loaded while the benefits are back-end loaded. Also, waiting to act leaves options open, such as developing a truly revolutionary technology that could reverse greenhouse gas emissions or the effects of climate change. While acknowledging this argument, I do not address it directly. This book begins with the proposition that immediate action is necessary because of the small but significant probability of catastrophic consequences. To the best of our current knowledge, future generations will *probably* be wealthier, but there is a very significant chance that they will not. For one thing, as higher global temperatures increasingly degrade environmental quality, its marginal value increases, making further environmental deteriorations more costly than typically estimated by economic models. But more frighteningly, global climate change is alone among environmental problems in posing the risk of such vast environmental changes that the effects could destabilize entire economies, countries, and regions. The effects of climate change could be so severe that world consumption could be less than 1 percent of current levels, in real (inflation-adjusted) terms; this is not future generations doing without eight-terabyte iPods; this is future generations in developed countries having to queue up for food and drinking water. Although there is something that seems flimsy about the large bands of uncertainty about catastrophic climate outcomes, the potential downsides are serious enough to warrant action analogous to insurance. Billions of people have, in fact, been observed to insure themselves against outcomes less probable and less disastrous than climate change. Moreover, our best current projections suggest that acting sooner is, in addition to being less dangerous, much cheaper than waiting. This book addresses how we must act.

Climate change activists and some politicians may talk about the need for fundamental change to avoid climate change, but the idea of a carbon tax has been oddly left out of the discourse. There is no policy instrument that is more transparent and administratively simple than a carbon tax. Therein lies the political problem: a carbon tax places an explicit *price* on emitting carbon dioxide, and the price is more overt with a carbon tax than it is with other instruments. Voters, politicians, and emitting industries see the price very clearly, and can calculate how much they think it will cost them. The carbon tax thus starts out with a big political strike against it. However, decades of experience with environmental law have taught us this much: environmental measures that purport to be painless are either misleading or are likely to accomplish nothing. If the world is going to act at all, a carbon tax is an essential start.

Chapter 2

Climate Change Policy Alternatives

What are the main policy alternatives for addressing the climate change problem? While the many possibilities for greenhouse gas regulation have been treated extensively elsewhere, a brief review and definition of the regulatory instruments would helpfully frame the discussion. A comprehensive treatment, involving the scores of ideas and many of the variations of the four main climate policy instruments, is beyond the scope of this book.

Several other caveats are in order. The focus of this book is on carbon dioxide emissions from fossil fuel combustion. Carbon dioxide remains the largest contributor by volume and by potential to warm the planet. Carbon dioxide emissions also pose the greatest challenge and represent the most interesting aspect of the climate change problem—they involve the most global actors (since the vast majority of people consume some fossil fuels at some level), are the most ubiquitous of all greenhouse gases, and are a fundamental aspect of economic activity in so much of the world. What has been called the "greatest and widest-ranging market failure ever seen" is most true with respect to carbon dioxide emissions.[1] While this book proposes an expanded carbon tax that includes a small number of non-fossil emissions, it does not purport to cover all greenhouse gas emissions. Indeed, several new greenhouse gases are being discovered that create new concerns for scientists. It could well be that cheaper and more powerful abatement strategies exist for these other greenhouse gases, and that climate policy should prioritize these strategies. For example, in recent years, the emergence of "black carbon"—the sooty particles that are emitted by extremely primitive methods of combustion, used mainly by the ultra-poor in developing countries—has taken on greater prominence, and may even be the most pressing problem to solve *right now*. These dark, sooty emissions are doubly destructive because they not only trap heat like carbon dioxide, but—when they migrate toward the poles, as they often do—they also increase the glacial absorption of solar radiation and the melting the glacial formations. Black carbon is clearly trouble. But without in the least bit doubting that other policies badly need to be adopted to address other greenhouse gases, this book focuses on that which can be accomplished with respect to emissions of carbon dioxide and a few other greenhouse gases. As a simple first step, nothing else is quite as important.

Finally, excluded from consideration in this book are *adaptation* and *geo-engineering* measures. *Adaptation* is the general term for a wide range of things that can be done by a country to prepare for and adjust to life in a climate-changed world, at least as it can best be foreseen. Adaptation could include, for example, relocation of populations away from areas vulnerable to tropical storms, or the genetic modification of seeds to yield more drought-resistant crops, or the construction of sea walls to protect a city from the intruding sea. *Geo-engineering* measures aim to directly reduce the heat-increasing effects of greenhouse gases, by either reducing atmospheric concentration of greenhouse gases or by reducing the amount of solar radiation that is absorbed. Like adaptation, geo-engineering consciously does not address the sources of the greenhouse gases. Proposed geo-engineering measures have included the promotion of ocean algal growth (which would in theory capture carbon dioxide from the atmosphere), the launching of tiny particle-sized mirrors into the upper stratosphere so as to reflect sunlight and prevent it from reaching the Earth, and simply painting roofs white so as to reflect sunlight more effectively and increase the amount of heat that is radiated back out into space. As I have noted in my other work, adaptation and geo-engineering, despite their own significant risks, begin to look like more palatable options as international climate negotiations continue to founder.[2] The problem of international coordination among countries (which I argue in this book is best addressed by a carbon tax) currently seems challenging enough to warrant some diversification of approaches to climate change. While the international legal community balks at the unilateralism inherent in adaptation and geo-engineering as a climate strategy, options that do not require global and crosscultural politicking begin to look attractive. Moreover, the potentially catastrophic effects of climate change are such that a portfolio of policies is likely required.[3] All that said, it is most sensible from the perspective of greenhouse gas mitigation to cabin off these kinds of strategies from the question of how to reduce emissions. It is complicated enough to consider what mitigation policies should be pursued, without complicating the question by adding in analysis of adaptation and geo-engineering measures.

To reduce greenhouse gas emissions, I consider four main options: (1) a carbon tax (2) traditional environmental regulation, sometimes referred to as "command-and-control" regulation, (3) "cap-and-trade" programs in which allowances to emit are allocated and freely traded, and (4) government subsidies targeted at low-carbon technologies and processes. Again, many other ideas and combinations of ideas are a part of the wide climate change discourse, but in order to focus in on the advantages and disadvantages of the carbon tax as a fundamental approach, this book frames the discussion in the context of the main alternative policy approaches.

Carbon Taxes

A carbon tax targets fossil fuels, by far the greatest contributors to carbon dioxide emissions and to global climate change in developed countries—about 80 percent in the United States.[4] The nature of the three primary fossil fuels—coal, natural gas, and oil—is such that the carbon content is generally known or easily ascertainable once it is extracted and placed into the stream of commerce, and so a carbon tax based on carbon content can be easily established. This means that a carbon tax will generally track the actual quantity of carbon dioxide emitted, avoiding economic distortions that occur when there is a mismatch between the tax and the damages from emissions. This will also be true of a cap-and-trade program that assigns allowances based on carbon content.

Regulating or taxing fossil fuels has the advantage of being attachable to a global paper trail, which is initiated whenever a fossil fuel is extracted almost anywhere in the world. A carbon tax can be levied at several points, from the early extraction or processing point (*upstream*) right up to the point immediately preceding combustion before the carbon dioxide is released (*downstream*), or points in between. In the Canadian province of British Columbia, which has pioneered the first significant carbon tax in North America, the tax is generally collected relatively downstream, and every firm or "person" (in the broad legal sense) that sells or imports a fossil fuel is required to collect a carbon tax by a specified amount. The BC carbon tax was first levied in 2008 at the amount of about $10 per ton (Cdn) of carbon dioxide, increasing over five years to $30 per ton (Cdn). The original statute actually listed, in a detailed schedule, each of the twenty fossil fuels, and the carbon tax amount for each of the fossil fuels, as a dollar amount per liter, ton, or cubic meter, depending on the fossil fuel and how it is commonly denominated. The carbon tax was explicitly listed for each fossil fuel for each of the five years in which the carbon tax would be phased in, up to 2012, when the carbon tax actually reaches $30 per ton (Cdn).

In terms of tax collection, the BC carbon tax essentially deputizes every fossil fuel retailer as a tax collector, requiring the collection of the tax at the retail sales level. For example, gasoline retailers—fueling stations—are required to collect the carbon tax at the fuel pump. Of course, gasoline retailers are already required to collect a variety of other provincial and federal taxes at the fuel pump, so the administrative burdens of collecting the carbon tax are trivial. Similarly, the dominant natural gas supplier in British Columbia, Terasen, simply adds the carbon tax onto customers' bills. Of course, carbon taxes can be designed and administered in any number of ways, so the British Columbia experience is not necessarily indicative of how a government would implement a carbon tax. But the British Columbia case is illustrative, demonstrating how a carbon price can be adopted and carried out with relative ease, again, building upon a well-established tax-collecting infrastructure.

Carbon dioxide is emitted in a variety of nonfossil processes, as are a number of other greenhouse gases. According to a study by David Weisbach and Gilbert Metcalf, an expanded carbon tax that covers some nonfossil carbon dioxide emissions and also some of the other greenhouse gases could, at relatively little cost and administrative burden, cover as much as 90 percent of all greenhouse gas emissions in the United States.[5] Weisbach and Metcalf reach this conclusion by finding at a number of industries and processes that emit greenhouse gases for which measurement and monitoring would be relatively easy. For example, cement is usually manufactured by heating "clinker," a collection of lime and other materials, to temperatures high enough to emit carbon dioxide. The amount of carbon dioxide emitted in this process scales with the amount of lime used, so that a carbon tax could easily be broadened to include fugitive emissions from cement manufacturing. Provided that monitoring and enforcement mechanisms are in place or are easily put into place, all of the instruments evaluated in this book can be used to address carbon dioxide alone, or to comprehensively address multiple greenhouse gases. Oftentimes in this book, the stated goals of reducing carbon dioxide emissions and more generally greenhouse gas emissions will be used interchangeably.

To sum up, a carbon tax is for the most part a tax on consumption—mostly consumption of fossil fuels that lead to the emission of carbon dioxide. A slightly expanded carbon tax would also tax emissions of a small number of other sources of emissions, both carbon dioxide emissions from nonfossil sources, and emissions of other greenhouse gases. Apart from these nonfossil emissions, a carbon tax is levied by some governmental authority at some transaction point at which ownership of a fossil fuel changes hands. Thus, superficially, a carbon tax seems to most resemble other consumption taxes, such as a sales tax or a gasoline tax. As will be argued more fully later in this book, this is a mistaken and unfortunate perception.

Command-and-Control Regulation

Command-and-control regulation is considered "traditional" pollution regulation because some of the earliest pollution statutes in the United States were drafted so that enforcement would be feasible for agencies such as the US Environmental Protection Agency, or "EPA." If you asked an environmental lawyer thirty or forty years ago how you could get an air polluter to reduce its emissions, the lawyer would probably suggest that you require the polluter to adopt what would be considered a state-of-the-art or nearly state-of-the-art technology that somehow treated some stage of the industrial process so that less of the targeted pollutant was emitted.

For example, early attempts to limit sulfur dioxide pollution were of a command-and-control type. Coal combustion, particularly at coal-fired power plants, produces sulfur dioxide, an air pollutant.

Sulfur dioxide mixes with moisture in the air to produce sulfuric acid, which falls back down to Earth as acid rain. The well-known process has produced tremendous amounts of acid rain during the last century, acidifying thousands of lakes and rivers, changing entire ecosystems by sometimes reducing the pH so that they are more acidic than Coca Cola.[6] This weak sulfuric acid falling from the sky has also damaged forests and agricultural crops, stained and eroded statutes, buildings, and other manmade structures. In terms of damages to humans and the natural environment, sulfur dioxide pollution has, over the decades of coal-fired power plant pollution, likely caused many trillions of dollars of damages.[7] While many of the harms from sulfur dioxide pollution are only now becoming fully understood,[8] the most obvious harms from sulfur dioxide pollution have been familiar for a long time.[9]

Environmental law's solution to the sulfur dioxide problem was part lawyering and part engineering. "Flue gas desulfurization" units, or "scrubbers," were developed to take the emissions from the coal combustion process and subject them to a chemical reaction that removed much of the sulfur dioxide out of the emissions stream. What emerged from the smokestack was thus an emissions stream, or "flue gas," that was as much as 90 percent free of sulfur dioxide. The command-and-control regulatory answer then, was to require coal-fired power plants to install scrubbers. As long as the scrubbers are installed and operated properly, we could expect large reductions in sulfur dioxide pollution. This mandate was a classic command-and-control regulation.

Command-and-control regulation has evolved considerably since its earliest forms. Regulations are more likely now to be couched in terms of requiring a minimum *level of performance* in pollution abatement. For example, a command-and-control regulation is more likely to mandate that emissions from a specific type of facility emit pollution at a *rate* no greater than some level of performance. How are these levels of performance determined? There are a variety of ways, but some are, ironically, derived from the measured performance of certain *specific* pollution abatement technologies.

Consider the following performance standards for emissions of nitrogen oxides, or NO_x, from coal-fired power plants under the Clean Air Act's Acid Rain Program. Listed below are six types of coal-fired power plants, along with the maximum permitted emissions rate per heat content of coal (mmBtu is millions of Btu)[10]:

Tangentially fired	0.40 lbs. NO_x/mmBtu
Dry-bottom wall-fired	0.46
Wet-bottom wall-fired	0.84
Cyclone	0.86
Cell-burner technology	0.68
Vertically fired	0.80

The seemingly random numbers in this schedule just happen to be the emissions rates that are achievable when each of the above types of coal-fired power plants installs a particular technology called "low-NO_x burner" technology. As long as coal-fired power plants installed this technology, they could be reasonably assured of hitting these emissions rates. If there is any doubt that the goal was to provide electricity generating companies a safe harbor for emissions, section 407(d) of the Clean Air Act provides:

> The permitting authority shall, upon request of an owner or operator of a unit subject to this section, authorize an emission limitation less stringent than [those listed above] upon a determination that—(1) a unit . . . cannot meet the applicable limitation using *low NO_x burner technology.* . . (emphasis added)

Command-and-control regulations are generally no longer so clumsy. There are a wider variety of forms that performance standards could take, making the label "command-and-control" more of a category of instruments rather than a specific one. The Canadian province of Ontario even requires major emitters to download an air quality model and to run the model to simulate the effect of their emissions on local air quality.[11] Clearly, as agencies have become more sophisticated, the extent to which they "command" and "control" has also gotten much more sophisticated.

The distinguishing feature of command-and-control systems, however, is that compliance is largely an administrative matter, one for which there could be an administrative adjudication, and sometimes ensuing litigation over inevitable ambiguities. As noted above, command-and-control regulation can be used to refer to a broad range of administrative actions. For many command-and-control regulations, it is largely a matter of whether an emitter had adopted the right technology or industrial practices. For other, more flexible command-and-control mechanisms, it is a matter of whether, playing within a set of pre-set rules, an emitter is living up to some standards devised by an administrative agency.

Cap-and-Trade

As opposed to this traditional agency-centered command-and-control approach to environmental regulation, cap-and-trade programs have increased in importance during the last two decades. Rather than defining compliance in terms of administratively set standards, cap-and-trade programs involve the issuance of *allowances* to polluters that permit them to emit a quantity of pollution. Compliance is determined solely by whether the emitter has enough allowances to cover its quantity of emissions. Allowances may be traded, and economic theory posits that overall industry costs are minimized as the allowances flow to those for which emissions reduction would be most costly. Cap-and-trade programs thus take emissions reduction decisions out of the domain of government policy and place them almost entirely into the hands of emitters.

The most notable and successful cap-and-trade program to date has been the US sulfur dioxide trading program, which covered nearly all of the fossil fuel–fired electricity-generating plants in the United States.[12] In keeping with the cap-and-trade design, each plant was required to have an allowance for each ton of sulfur dioxide, or "SO_2," emitted. Each of the power plants (which were actually listed by name in the legislation) was allocated a certain number of allowances based an historical baseline—a string of years in the 1980s—and subjected to a considerable amount of subsequent political gerrymandering. In its totality, the cap was lower than the historical baseline so that some overall emissions reduction would be achieved.[13] The program reduced SO_2 emissions nationwide from more than 21 million tons in 1994 to just under 14 million tons in 2006.[14]

So apparently successful was the US SO_2 cap-and-trade program that it is often invoked as an example of how successful cap-and-trade programs can be. In part because of its success, much of the developed world seems to have gravitated toward an acceptance of cap-and-trade as the presumptive way to globally regulate and reduce greenhouse gas emissions. The Kyoto Protocol specifically contemplates a global emissions trading program, with individual nations establishing their own cap-and-trade programs, but set up to participate in a market for emissions allowances that is global rather than merely national. An added advantage of this scheme is that it can be designed, in theory, to cover not just carbon dioxide but other greenhouse gases as well. Since other greenhouse gases trap heat much more powerfully than carbon dioxide, a global greenhouse gas cap-and-trade program could (and Kyoto does) assign different trading values to allowances for different greenhouse gases. An allowance to reduce one ton of emissions of methane, twenty-five times more powerful at trapping heat than carbon dioxide, would be worth twenty-five carbon dioxide allowances. The European Union has already dutifully adopted its own EU-wide cap-and-trade program governing the largest carbon dioxide emitters in Europe, hoping that it will be integrated into a future global cap-and-trade scheme.

In its purest form, cap-and-trade programs involve a relatively hard "cap" on total emissions. Herein lies one crucial difference between the cap-and-trade program contemplated by the Kyoto Protocol and the US SO_2 cap-and-trade program: the potential to raise the cap by means of "offsets," credits that can substitute for allowances, awarded for projects that do not necessarily reduce existing emissions, but reduce or "offset" emissions that *would otherwise* occur. The Kyoto Protocol specifically contemplates the issuance of emissions allowances if an entrepreneur finances some project and it can demonstrate that the project will reduce emissions relative to some baseline course of events. The US SO_2 program had this feature to a very limited extent, allowing for the "opt-in" of power plants not covered by the original program, but the potential scope of opting in was fairly small, limited as it was to power plants. By contrast, these offset programs under the Kyoto Protocol — the Clean Development Mechanism[15] and the Joint Implementation Mechanism[16] — tap into a potentially endless parade of supposedly great ideas to reduce emissions. As will be discussed below, this has been the source of considerable controversy and criticism.

Other variations of cap-and-trade also seek to soften the "hardness" of the cap. One particularly dubious variation has sought to replace the hard cap with a cap that varies by productivity, seeking to reduce not the absolute amount of greenhouse gases but greenhouse gas "intensity." After an initial allocation of allowances, an emitter that produced more cars or electricity, refined more oil, or produced more per unit of emitted carbon would receive some additional allowances. The "cap," as it were, was not a quantitative limit but a *ratio* of carbon emissions to productivity. While this approach would make emitters more efficient with their emissions, there would obviously be no assurances that emissions would actually decrease. In fact, many industries routinely improve their productive efficiency, and an "intensity-based" program would simply reward them with more allowances. Even apart from this fatal environmental flaw, an intensity-based approach acts as a distortionary output subsidy, which creates economic inefficiency by encouraging overproduction. Because the extra allowances created by intensity improvements have value, they create an economy-wide incentive to direct resources into production of these goods. The intensity-based trading idea was a favored approach of the Bush Administration and continues to be in the mix of proposed Canadian federal policies, but recent developments suggest that this idea seems to be making its way into its rightful place in the dustbin.

Other variations of the cap-and-trade idea seek to address the price volatility issue. A cap-and-trade program could include a "safety valve," a price ceiling for allowances. This is easily accomplished by the unlimited issuance of allowances at the safety-valve price. If allowances are trading for a price below the safety-valve price, then the quantity of emissions remains at the cap level; otherwise, the cap increases. In essence, the safety valve acts as a carbon tax if allowances turn out to more valuable than the safety-valve price. A similar variation imposes a price "floor," below which prices will not be allowed to drop. Under a price floor scheme, a number of allowances must be held in reserve for distribution by auction with a minimum purchase price. It is important under these schemes that some number of allowances be auctioned so that the remaining allowances will be scarce enough to command a price above the price floor. Both of these variations, the price ceiling and the price floor, constitute hybrid approaches between the cap-and-trade idea and the carbon tax idea. Both of these variations, however, attempt to mimic a carbon tax by stabilizing the price, raising the question: why not just impose a carbon tax?

Economic theory treats carbon taxes and cap-and-trade programs with roughly equal favor, at least relative to command-and-control programs. Cap-and-trade programs have been proposed much more often and been met with less resistance than carbon taxes, but the reasons for this have little to do with the merits. Certainly, either type of program can be designed to mimic the other, and cap-and-trade programs have in fact begun to look more and more like carbon taxes.

Government Subsidies

Finally, there is never any shortage of proposals that involve, to varying degrees of *chutzpah*, government subsidies for various programs or projects that may or may not lower greenhouse gas emissions, but at least purport to do so. In theory, government subsidies could accomplish the exact same things as carbon taxes or cap-and-trade programs. While carbon taxes and cap-and-trade programs seek to raise the price of all things carbon, subsidies seek to lower the price of things noncarbon or lower-carbon. All of these programs seek to address *externalities*—costs that result from an action that are not fully taken into account. Pollution externalities are thus the costs of pollution that the polluter does not fully consider when deciding how much and how to produce. By raising the price of carbon emissions, carbon taxes and cap-and-trade programs seek to *internalize* the externality of carbon dioxide emissions—the contribution to climate change made by the emitter, be it a large industrial emitter as it makes decisions about production, or by an individual as she decides whether to drive or take the bus to work. A carbon tax or a cap-and-trade program would raise the cost of emitting, inducing the industrial emitter to produce less or emit less, and making driving more costly for the commuter. A subsidy might internalize the externality by rewarding the emitter for emitting less, or rewarding the commuter for taking the bus by reducing her fare. On the blackboard, then, one might see taxes and subsidies as mirror images of the same price-oriented approach. In practice, subsidies raise a number of issues that make them much less effective and much more costly than either carbon taxes or cap-and-trade programs.

It is worth distinguishing between two kinds of government subsidies in the climate change context: price-oriented subsidies and research and development funding. Price-oriented subsidies are commonly awarded to some renewable energy sources. Certain specific renewable energies enjoy the benefit of a payment for every kilowatt-hour of electricity generated.[17] Utilized in this way, subsidies really do internalize an externality generated by greenhouse gas emission. Burning fossil fuels and emitting carbon dioxide is forgoing a marginal benefit in the form of the per-unit subsidy. Two things are worth noticing about this kind of subsidy, however. First, offering a subsidy for renewable energy requires a definition of "renewable energy." In the Internal Revenue Code, the production tax credit applies to *"certain* renewable resources,"* (emphasis added) which includes "refined coal," which must be certified by the emitter as producing a "qualified emission reduction."[18] It excludes many other renewable energy technologies that have not yet been discovered or been recognized by lawmakers as having economic or environmental potential. Second, the subsidy does not necessarily scale with the environmental harm prevented, like a carbon tax does. A renewable energy subsidy helps all renewable energy sources as against any energy source not on the list of recognized "renewable resources." Thus, it provides a comparative advantage as against all fossil fuel sources, without discriminating—carbon-intensive coal and much less carbon-intensive natural gas are disadvantaged equally. In fact, depending on how "refined coal" is treated, an electricity producer could receive a subsidy for burning coal *instead of* natural gas.

A second kind of subsidy in the climate change context is direct government support of research and development, including the funding of pilot projects and prototypes. The subsidized projects are believed, in the long run, to help lower emissions. For example, a great deal of attention and government support is currently offered for development of "carbon capture and sequestration" technology, which seeks to suck out the carbon dioxide from fossil fuel combustion (mostly coal) at some stage, and store it in leakproof containers or underground caverns, where it will not affect the Earth's climate. This type of subsidy seeks to address the public benefits of research and development, boosting activity because it may produce knowledge and discoveries in a market that does not fully reward such pursuits. It also recognizes that research and development with respect to low-carbon technologies is doubly under-supplied since, in the absence of a carbon price, markets do not yet fully reward the development of low-carbon technologies.

An almost uncountable number of other seemingly greenhouse gas-reducing programs, initiatives, projects, and research ideas also vie for public monies. Subsidies take on a very wide variety of forms, and are difficult to define. Even the US federal home mortgage interest deduction is a subsidy. In this book, however, a government subsidy is defined as a policy with two characteristics: an explicit reference to carbon dioxide or another greenhouse gas, and an explicit reference to government funds. In other words, the definition of subsidies is limited to those with relatively direct price tags.

Chapter 3

Ten Arguments for a Carbon Tax

This chapter outlines ten arguments for a carbon tax, breaking out each argument into a separate part. The most salient hypothetical is that a federal carbon tax be adopted in the United States or Canada, but clearly a carbon tax could be adopted by any number of countries or subnational jurisdictions. The arguments and considerations outlined in this book apply equally whether it is proposed as a US federal carbon tax, a Chinese federal carbon tax, a state or provincial law, or potentially even a law adopted by cities and municipalities.

There is no dispute that reducing carbon dioxide emissions requires that there be a *price* established on carbon dioxide emissions. Voluntary initiatives and moral suasion will clearly be insufficient to induce the widespread changes in behavior required of individuals, firms, and governments. This is especially true when almost every individual in the entire world is participating in the buildup of carbon dioxide. In such a situation, in which everyone is to some extent *guilty*, people who voluntarily reduce their own emissions will have to fight a sense that their voluntary actions will be pointless.

In the comparative analysis that follows, a carbon tax is sometimes compared to a cap-and-trade program, sometimes to command-and-control, sometimes to government subsidies, and sometimes to any combination of the three. Some comparisons are obviously worthy of analysis: the economic efficiency of carbon taxes and cap-and-trade versus command-and-control and government subsidies, for example. Others are less compelling. In order to make this chapter as readable as possible, I will avoid undertaking this comparative analysis in a systemically comprehensive fashion, comparing everything with everything and telling the reader that I am doing so, or perhaps not doing so. Rather, the aim of this chapter is to sketch out the policy instrument choice considerations when it comes to reducing carbon dioxide emissions.

One: Economic Efficiency

A common economic prescription for reducing pollution is the imposition of a "Pigouvian" tax, named for the economist Alfred Pigou.[1] A Pigouvian tax is a unitary tax levied to make an emitter pay for the externalities caused by its emissions—no more, no less. A carbon tax could be a Pigouvian tax. In theory, a Pigouvian carbon tax would be set at a level equal to the marginal damages of the emissions of a ton of carbon or carbon dioxide.[2] That is, the tax would be such that it mimicked a payment for the *increment* of damage—the marginal damage—caused by each *individual* ton of carbon dioxide. If this calibration could be achieved, a Pigouvian tax would induce just the *right amount* of carbon dioxide emissions reductions. Further reductions would cost too much (more than would be saved in terms of environmental damages), and lesser reductions would be too environmentally harmful (more costly than further reductions would cost). No value judgments are made in levying Pigouvian taxes; the only goal of a Pigouvian tax is to achieve an economically efficient outcome. Punitive damages and moral judgments are completely outside of the realm of Pigouvian taxation.

Few pollutants are as well suited for Pigouvian taxation as carbon dioxide. Most individuals in the world, even in poor countries, contribute by burning something that produces carbon dioxide. It is thus difficult to demonize emitters as immoral, since the production of carbon dioxide is so widespread. Some toxic pollutants are dangerous enough that allowing polluters to "pay to pollute" is discomforting. Not so with carbon dioxide: while the massive buildup of carbon dioxide poses grave threats to the Earth, no emitter in the world emits enough to pose any immediate threat. Some pollutants are difficult to measure as they are emitted from a smokestack or tailpipe. Not so with carbon dioxide: at least with respect to fossil fuels, measuring the amount of carbon dioxide emitted is trivial, as the carbon content of almost any fossil fuel is known when it is extracted. Finally, some pollutants cause more damages in some places rather than others, and at some times more than others. Not so with carbon dioxide: carbon dioxide emitted anywhere on Earth and at any time makes the exact same marginal contribution to the climate change problem.

The problem with the Pigouvian taxation of carbon dioxide is that there is a great deal of controversy over estimates of the marginal damages of carbon dioxide emissions. Efforts to estimate the marginal

damages of carbon dioxide emissions are complex, varied, and controversial. A plethora of modeling issues and assumptions make huge differences in marginal damages estimates. A 2005 survey of marginal
damages studies by Richard Tol found a range of estimates from zero
to more than one thousand dollars per ton.[3] More recently, a study by
William Nordhaus estimated the marginal social damages at about
$7.50 t/$CO_2$.[4] A much higher estimate was obtained in the UK govern-
ment–commissioned Stern Review, by Nicholas Stern, a former chief
economist of the World Bank, which estimated current marginal damages at about $85/$tCO_2$.[5]

There are a number of differences that account for the wide disparity in estimates. Both Nordhaus and Stern, bookends in the climate
damages debate, include estimates of the costs of catastrophic risks
(unlike many other studies), but Stern assumed higher likelihoods and
greater costs. The Stern Review included estimates of nonmarket impacts, described as "impacts on the environment and human health,"[6]
which would include impacts on wildlife and unpriced effects on human health such as increased spread of disease due to climatic
changes[7]; Nordhaus finds these costs a bit speculative.[8] Most important, Nordhaus and Stern employ vastly differing approaches to discounting—the rate of discount to apply to future damages and costs.
Stern assumed an unconventionally low (though not necessarily unjustifiably low) discount rate of 1.4 percent, and assuming a pure rate
time preference of virtually zero. This was justified by Stern on ethical
grounds, who argued that there is no reason to place any less importance on the welfare of future generations, other than the small probability that the human race might not survive into the future.[9] Stern's
low discount rate produces much higher estimated costs of future
damages and therefore the marginal social damages of emissions.
Nordhaus and Tol scoff at this, arguing that it has no empirical support in real life; if one were to look at how thousands of common financial instruments worldwide discount future costs and benefits,
Nordhaus argues, a more realistic discount rate would be closer to 3
percent.[10] This debate has gotten quite personal at times, Nordhaus
having written that the Stern Review "should be read primarily as a
document that is political in nature and has advocacy as its purpose,"[11]
and Tol telling BBC News that "[i]f a student of mine were to hand in
this report as a Master's thesis, perhaps if I were in a good mood I
would give him a 'D' for diligence; but more likely I would give him
an 'F' for fail."[12]

There is yet a third view that expresses wariness about taking cost-benefit analyses too literally. Economist Martin Weitzman argues for a little humility in estimating marginal damages, given the small but nonzero probabilities of extremely catastrophic and costly outcomes occurring as a result of climate change. If one accepts, as most climate scientists do, that there is a chance of catastrophic occurrences in which world GDP would plummet to a mere 1 percent of current levels, then any probability-weighted estimates of damages are meaningless. The results would be almost completely driven by the assumptions about the "fat-tailed" ends of the probability-weighted distributions of risk. Weitzman has criticized the Stern Review, but concluded that the abundance of precaution prescribed by Lord Stern was correct, only for the "wrong reasons."[13] Along similar lines, Thomas Sterner and Martin Persson, using Nordhaus's own model, find that including estimates of nonmarket impacts, and accounting for the possibility that as environmental goods might become relatively scarce and therefore much more valuable under a climate-changed future, even a high discount rate would yield a damage estimate as high as Stern's.[14]

What to do about such a controversial and complex debate? How do you set the level of a carbon tax if you do not know the marginal damages of carbon dioxide emissions?

The right thing to do is to forge ahead with a carbon tax without resolving this debate. Even a very modest carbon tax, along the lines of what Nordhaus suggests (about $7.50/ton of CO_2), would serve important economic efficiency objectives. The important thing, especially at this early but critical stage of addressing the climate change problem, is to begin to send the right *kind* of price signals, without obsessing over whether the price signal is of exactly the right magnitude or not. Energy and transportation costs have been so low and the effects of carbon emissions so hidden from consumers that we usually have no idea how carbon-intensive products are. The harm from carbon dioxide emissions probably constitutes the most pervasive externality ever created, and the least discernible. Unpriced emissions distort markets at so many points and transactions in our economy, that it is hard to tell exactly what we are doing or consuming that is causing the most harm.

Fundamentally, the most important thing that a carbon tax can do is to *sort* industries by carbon dioxide emissions. This sorting is accomplished by subjecting the most carbon-emitting industries and businesses to a penalty proportional to their carbon emissions. Much is often said about the need to completely restructure economies to be less carbon intensive, to reduce reliance on coal for electricity generation, make more fuel-efficient cars, drive less, make buildings and appliances more energy efficient, and a wide variety of other climate-friendly actions. How do we decide which strategies and what mix of them to pursue?

Consider, for example, how an all-powerful energy policy czar might decide on a mix of energy sources. Coal is abundant and cheap, and in the era of railroad deregulation, relatively cheap to transport to almost every major city in the United States, Canada, and Europe, bringing the energy to where the people and businesses are. Depending on market fluctuations, natural gas is slightly more expensive to much more expensive, and is somewhat constrained by pipeline infrastructure, but can generally also be brought to population centers. Renewable energy sources such as wind and solar are intermittent, making them not ideal for baseload applications. In addition, wind energy is generally abundant where people are not. Geothermal energy is constant and therefore appropriate for baseload supply, but best exploited only in certain areas. Finally, there are strong suspicions that the greatest carbon dioxide savings can be had through energy efficiency and conservation measures. A plethora of ways to increase energy efficiency and conservation potentially provide tremendous opportunities for meeting or managing energy demand in a lower-carbon way. But all of these options involve many market factors, such as the availability of land or ocean space for wind and solar facilities, the market price of materials needed to better insulate homes and reduce heating costs, the availability of transmission lines to transport generated electricity long distances, and above all, the technological uncertainty about which energy technologies will ultimately work the best and under what conditions.

It is not even easy to determine whether many carbon-reducing technologies actually reduce carbon dioxide. Even if some technologies seem to reduce greenhouse gases when compared head-to-head with existing technologies, it is important to bear in mind the emissions that are *embedded in* these technologies and products. A compelling case in point pertains to the current debate over how eagerly we should embrace biofuels as a substitute for gasoline. Biofuels, which are fossil fuel substitutes that are derived from crops, have been hyped as having lower greenhouse gas emissions. Biofuels emit carbon dioxide when burned, but because they are derived from plants, they also sequester carbon dioxide in the plant growth stage. Ethanol, a biofuel that can be derived from corn or sugar cane, seems particularly attractive, especially to farm-state politicians hoping for a further infusion of agricultural subsidies. As a first-order calculation, using corn-based ethanol to power motor vehicles may produce as much as a 30 percent savings in carbon dioxide emissions over conventional gasoline. But this estimate is only of the combustion stage, and an aggressively optimistic one at that. If one considers the *life-cycle emissions*— the total net changes in carbon dioxide emissions attributable to producing ethanol, then its comparative advantages over gasoline become ambiguous or even turn into disadvantages. This is an enormously complicated determination—there are many stages in the production of ethanol and gasoline, and accounting for the emissions of each stage is tricky. Here are some of the considerations in calculating the life-cycle emissions of ethanol:

> *Farming practices*: how much fertilizer is used for an ethanol crop, and how fossil fuel–intensive is the fertilizer used?
>
> *Farm workers*: what is the energy needed to sustain and transport the farm workers, relative to those in various stages of the gasoline production process?
>
> *Harvesting and transportation energy*: what energy is required to harvest and transport the crop, relative to the energy required to transport petroleum?
>
> *Production process*: what energy is required to convert the crop into ethanol, relative to the oil-refining process?
>
> *Plant construction*: what energy is required to construct the conversion plant?

This list does not even include the important question of whether ethanol entrepreneurs would cut down trees to grow corn, destroying important carbon sinks and canceling out some carbon dioxide emissions. But even apart from predicting the land use changes that ethanol production would induce, how would one go about disentangling all of these effects from many other economic effects, to determine the carbon footprint of ethanol? To try to actually quantify the greenhouse impacts, one would have to make many assumptions and educated guesses about energy prices, elasticity, and the contribution fossil fuels make to each element of production. Fertilizer to help grow biofuel crops, for example, is very energy-intensive, but exactly how much so, and how much energy exactly would be required to fertilize crops destined for ethanol production? Just this subcalculation is complicated. The Natural Resources Conservation Service of the US Department of Agriculture has an "Energy Estimator" website that calculates the approximate amount of energy required to fertilize crops.[15] The user is required to input a zip code, check off the fertilizer materials, and for each crop fertilized, the amount of nitrogen applied to each crop per acre, the season of application, the method of application, and whether the fertilizer is an "efficiency-enhanced product." This is a lot of information, much of which would be challenging to collect, apply to a diverse set of situations, and sum up. How are macro models supposed to estimate the amount of fossil fuels used in the production of fertilizers used for biofuel crops?

The EPA commissioned a study to actually do these calculations, in an attempt to answer the question of whether or not we should invest government resources to support the biofuels industry, and if so, which biofuels to support. The 500-page peer-reviewed report, conducted by an outside contractor that screened its own reviewers, concluded that lifecycle emissions of corn ethanol would be better over 100 years, but not over 30 years.[16] This was not good enough for farm state senators, who bitterly attacked the study and its authors with accusations of bias.[17]

Apart from the fact that these kinds of analyses always seem to anger somebody, this kind of an inquiry is going at it backward. If carbon dioxide is the problem, far better to place a price on carbon dioxide emissions rather than trying to have a team of government analysts collect information and figure out the best of a dizzying array of alternatives, often by trying to figure out what the outcome would be *if there were a price*. Not only is the former easier, it can never be known if the best of the alternatives have been identified, or have even yet surfaced.

The simple genius of a carbon tax is that it aggregates disparate pieces of information, transmitting a price signal at every stage in which there is fossil fuel usage, and transmitting it in proportion to the carbon emissions of the production process. No data collection is required, and no model is required. If a fertilizer is applied often and is heavily fossil fuel-based, then the price of the fertilizer will be high, and if ethanol is highly dependent upon such a fertilizer, then it will price itself out of the market for motor vehicle fuels. If not, then biofuel advocates have nothing to worry about. But no agency, or even a combination of agencies, can assemble all of the relevant carbon information. Only the ubiquity of a widespread *price* on carbon dioxide can consolidate such a large amount of information. That is, after all, what markets do: knit together disparate pieces of information in all nooks and crannies of the economy and consolidate them into one price signal.

The instrument choice question is this: is a carbon tax the right policy for generating this price signal? In essence, all of the alternative instruments seek to create a carbon price indirectly. Cap-and-trade programs seek to impose a price in the form of the market price of a tradable emissions allowance. Government subsidies seek to *lower* the price of activities that are deemed to be less greenhouse gas-emitting than current technologies and practices. And even command-and-control programs seek to impose a price on emissions in the form of an administrative penalty, hopefully large enough to make violation of some standard prohibitively expensive. What makes the price signal transmitted by a carbon tax any better? I address each of the alternatives in ascending order of effectiveness.

In the United States, command-and-control regulation of greenhouse gas emissions would fall under the ambit of the Clean Air Act. The EPA, having issued the finding that greenhouse gas emissions "endanger" the "public health and welfare,"[18] is empowered to issue regulations, industry by industry, pertaining to greenhouse gas reduction measures that will be required as a condition of a permit under the Clean Air Act. The Canadian counterpart to EPA, Environment Canada, issued an analogous finding far earlier (in 2005), that greenhouse gases fell within a statutory definition of "toxic substances," in that they, among other effects, "have or may have an immediate or long-term harmful effect on the environment or its biological diversity."[19] Environment Canada is thus also positioned to issue command-and-control-style greenhouse gas regulations, although other forms of regulation are possible under the Canadian statute.

One might think that command-and-control regulation, by potentially imposing the highest price on emitters, would be the most effective in re-ordering economies to be lower-carbon. The mistake is to equate an administrative price with a market price. Under command-and-control regulation, an administrative price is imposed by an agency. This price need not bear any relation to greenhouse gas emissions. Most often, the key consideration in setting standards is the state of technology of pollution abatement. If abatement technology seems "cheap" or "feasible," then it likely factors into the setting of an administrative standard. This is, in very rough measure, an agency's attempt to balance costs and benefits: if requiring abatement technology seems somehow "worth it," by an eyeball estimate of the compliance costs and environmental benefits, then it becomes law.

Over the past several decades, command-and-control regulation has been continuously and successfully attacked on efficiency grounds. The most common arguments are that: (i) command-and-control regulation is clumsy, its uniformity of standards sometimes too stringent and sometimes too lenient, resulting in wasteful over-abatement in some cases and missed opportunities to abate more in other cases, (ii) fails to strike a correct balance between costs and benefits as administrative agencies make poor guesses about compliance costs, (iii) being a fixed administrative price, fails to offer incentives for emitters to find innovative ways of reducing emissions, and (iv) provides fodder for delay and litigation by well-funded and disgruntled industry groups.

These well-rehearsed criticisms are thoroughly treated elsewhere. I argue here that, in addition to these arguments, command-and-control regulation sends an *uneven* price signal to greenhouse gas emitters. While there is controversy over the amount of damages from greenhouse gas emissions, it is still worth making the price *proportional* to greenhouse gas emissions. Command-and-control regulation, because it imposes a different requirement for each industry, imposes a different price for each industry. A price signal that is different from one industry to another is no price signal at all, if the goal is to sort industries by carbon emissions. If the price varies from industry to industry, then the sorting is not accomplished by carbon emissions, but by an administrative agency. Moreover, command-and-control regulation has in the past generated so much litigation, the administrative "price" often does not emerge at all. Because the locus of so much decision making and adjudication is at the administrative agency, and because these decisions and adjudications invariably invite comparisons with those that affect other industries, perceptions of unfairness (accurate or not) run rampant through command-and-control regulation. So not only does an uneven price signal frustrate greenhouse gas reduction objectives, but sometimes litigation or just the threat of litigation erases the price signal completely.

Government subsidies, at least of the price-oriented kind, are another way of sending a price signal, albeit in an indirect fashion: not by pricing carbon, but by lowering the price of things non-carbon or low-carbon. This way of installing a negative price is patently clumsier than directly pricing carbon dioxide emissions, since it is hard to identify those technologies, processes, and products that are most worthy of subsidization. Government subsidization has, however, the advantage of political expediency: the uneven price signal it transmits does disadvantage some industries vis-à-vis others, but it is somehow harder to complain about the government giving away money to a competitor than it is to complain about the government setting standards of uneven burden. Moreover, government subsidies are doled out by Congress, which precludes litigation as an avenue of redress.

Such political economy considerations, however, should not be determinative, else there might be little left to talk about in terms of the instrument choice problem. As it turns out, the general merits of government subsidization as a primary climate policy instrument are generally quite weak. The situations in which government subsidization is superior to the direct pricing through carbon taxes or a cap-and-trade program are narrow.

The case *for* government subsidization is, as a theoretical matter, straightforward. An unpriced externality like carbon dioxide emissions can be remedied by either a positive price imposed by carbon taxes or by a negative price created by subsidization. If we know, for example, that lowering the carbon dioxide emissions from the energy sector will require the development and deployment of renewable energy technologies, then it would seem to make sense to provide government funding for wind, solar, and other renewable energy technologies. This would be true whether the subsidy takes the form of a per-unit production subsidy, or direct funding for research and development: either way, the goal is to lower costs and concomitantly lower prices.

Compare, then, the effects of taxing carbon and of subsidizing renewable energy. At the margins, raising the price of carbon-emitting energy has the same competitive effect of lowering the price (through subsidies) of renewable energy. The net effect of subsidizing renewable energy instead of pricing carbon is a transfer of money from taxpayers to the entire energy industry—to the renewable energy industry through subsidies, and to the carbon-emitting energy industries by not taxing them. Since pricing carbon would raise energy prices, the net effect on the average person, who is both a taxpayer and an energy consumer, would appear to be roughly a wash.

There are three core problems with this argument. First, and most simply, higher energy prices are needed to spur energy conservation. Low energy costs undermine incentives to make industrial processes more energy-efficient, drive less, better insulate homes and construct more energy-efficient buildings, and to develop and sell (and buy) energy-efficient appliances. Energy conservation measures may in fact turn out to be the greatest source of greenhouse gas reductions. A recent report by the consulting firm McKinsey found that some fairly routine and well-known energy conservation measures could produce a whopping $680 billion dollars worth of net energy savings, and reduce projected energy demand by the year 2020 by 23 percent.[20] Many energy conservation measures actually have a negative abatement cost—that is, their energy savings exceeded the amortized cost of the upfront investments. These included insulation retrofits for residential and commercial buildings (especially the latter), switching residential lighting from incandescent bulbs to LEDs (light-emitting diodes), and capturing methane escaping from landfills to generate electricity.[21] As Dieter Helm has observed, a problem with climate policy is that it has by and large focused on reducing greenhouse gases from production, and not consumption.[22] Reducing consumption does not sound like a good thing for love-starved politicians who have no stomach to curb energy consumption through taxation, even as we waste energy in mind-boggling ways. But the simple truth is that efforts to combat climate change will be unsuccessful without steps to reduce consumption. And there is nothing as effective as higher prices if the goal is to reduce consumption.

Second, there is a limit on how low energy prices can be made through subsidization. Lowering the price of renewable energy lowers the demand for fossil fuels. But lowering demand for fossil fuels means that it will lower the price of fossil fuels. A lower price for fossil fuels encourages its use, exactly what we don't want. This "rebound" effect of lowering fossil fuel prices by subsidizing its alternatives dampens the effectiveness of subsidies in altering consumption choices. Rebound effects for various renewable fuel standards policies in the United States are estimated to be on the order of a quarter to a third of reduced emissions.[23] Moreover, at a certain point, energy prices become so low that they become irrelevant. If, hypothetically, you had a choice between buying electricity from a coal-fired plant for 3.7 cents per kilowatt-hour or buying electricity from a wind farm for 3.4 cents per kilowatt-hour, which would you chose? The answer could well be, "who cares?" For many energy consumers, the savings does not justify the time needed to investigate. Such is the pushing-on-a-string effect of trying to lower prices for everyone instead of raising them. So while higher taxes and lower energy costs may *seem* to be a wash, they are not.

Third, the effectiveness of government subsidies assumes without justification—in fact, in the face of a mountain of evidence to the contrary—that it is possible to identify the "best" renewable energy technologies, or in general the "best" ideas to reduce greenhouse gas emissions. Too often, legislators think they catch wind of a great idea—such a revolutionary way of doing something that they can hardly resist the temptation to lend some assistance (all the better if the idea comes from a constituent or potential donor). It requires a bit of gullibility to ignore the failure of these supposedly great ideas to attract sufficient private financing. The danger is not so much in the waste of taxpayer dollars—this is addressed in another part of this chapter—but that emissions reductions will be both smaller and costlier than if a better instrument was used.

It is worth noting a few instances in which subsidization may be the best option. Some greenhouse gas problems are genuinely difficult to address without a carrot (subsidy), rather than a stick (tax). For example, it is hard to imagine a regulatory scheme dealing comprehensively and effectively with the prevention of deforestation, which accounted for 12 percent of greenhouse gas emissions in 2005.[24] How, for example, is anybody to stop the deforestation of the Amazon rainforest by those that either legally or illegally have the ability to cut down trees? Where state enforcement of illegal logging has been poor, the offer of periodic cash payments to private individuals to keep trees standing *may* be more effective. In situations involving poor enforcement mechanisms—most prominently in developing countries—the infusion of money may be required. In some developing countries, there is insufficient economic wealth for markets to actually exist, so that market mechanisms do not create markets at all.

Generally, however, subsidization as a governmental policy on reducing greenhouse gases has not been targeted at developing countries, or other situations in which subsidies genuinely work better. Government subsidization has been mere political grease, an overused salve for the perceived pain from the prospect of economic restructuring. Rather than actually minimize the pain, however, it merely shifts it into onto unwitting taxpayers, current and future. Government subsidization should be viewed with skepticism, rather than being the presumptive first option.

Finally, a carbon tax is in most cases economically superior to a cap-and-trade program. Martin Weitzman's foundational article, *Prices Versus Quantities*, was the first to ask the question of what uncertainty does to the analysis of overall economic efficiency of taxes and cap-and-trade.[25] This work is applied to the climate change problem and is addressed later in this chapter. But this part of the book presents the very different and separate argument that *as a matter of policy design*, carbon taxes are *generally* more comprehensive than cap-and-trade programs, and therefore more efficient.

Comprehensiveness is important to carbon pricing for the same reason that command-and-control regulation is inefficient: an *uneven* carbon price will fail to sort industries by carbon dioxide emissions and cause economic distortions. Subjecting some industries or sectors to a carbon price but not others is obviously unfair, but the unfairness is of only secondary concern. The problem is that the economy will receive an inaccurate signal about which industries, sectors, or products are most valuable, diverting resources to the wrong places. For example, legislative proposals have sometimes included the idea of applying climate legislation only to power plants. Since electricity utilities contribute by far the most to annual carbon dioxide emissions in the United States (more than 38 percent),[26] it would seem to make sense to attack this sector first, if a comprehensive bill could not be achieved. However, this approach would distort the economy by leaving out important sectors. Industrial sectors sometimes generate their own energy, so that a cap-and-trade applied only the energy sector could drive some electricity generation in-house and away from regulation. If a cap-and-trade system is not comprehensive, the cap would not be very tight.

In fact, the cap-and-trade programs implemented to date have not been comprehensive. The Regional Greenhouse Gas Initiative, a program among ten northeastern US states, only requires power plants to participate in its cap-and-trade program. The broader European Union Emissions Trading System, or "EUETS," covers most industrial sources, including cement, steel, glass, and metal manufacturing, pulp and paper processing, and oil refining, but the 11,500 covered sources still represent only about 40 percent of the EU's carbon dioxide-emitting sources. Notably absent from the EUETS are emissions from commercial and residential sources, or from fossil fuel combustion in transportation. It makes no economic or logical sense to only concentrate on these 11,500 sources. Why should costs only be imposed on industry and not consumers? Why emissions from the commercial sector or from transportation not similarly targeted? This would be of particular concern if say, such a program were to be grafted onto a regulatory system in China or India, where exploding populations of middle-class households are buying automobiles.

The most likely answer to the question of why these 11,500 were singled out is that these industrial sources have had to report their carbon dioxide emissions for years now, and the EU therefore has data and monitoring capability for them. Other sectors that emit are not asked to reduce emissions because the EU does not know how much they emit. The EU just states on their website that

> Of course, the Member State can and should also take other measures. Other sectors also generate greenhouse gas emissions: in the EU, transport is responsible for 21% of EU greenhouse gas emissions, households and small businesses for 17% and agriculture for 10%. So, Member States can and should also take measures to reduce emissions in these sectors.[27]

Understanding that EU politics can make for tricky navigation, it makes no sense to concentrate on reducing the emissions from sources that account for less than half of the EU's emissions and *hope* that member states pick up regulation of the rest. *Everything* that has a carbon footprint must be on the same level playing field; a carbon price on one sector but not on another would create a distortion that would channel resources into the unpriced sector. Moreover, this kind of leakage has a way of being exacerbated by the price effects of regulation. Suppose industrial facilities that burn natural gas found ways to conserve because of their obligations under the EUETS. That could make natural gas cheaper, and encourage residential and commercial consumers of natural gas to use more of it. This is the essence of carbon leakage: pricing carbon will reduce usage of fossil fuels, and concomitantly reduce price, which will rebound when unregulated sectors snap up the suddenly abundant and cheap fossil fuel. Imposing a price on carbon emissions for only part of the economy is tantamount to treating only part of a cancerous tumor.

A cap-and-trade program *could* be designed to be as comprehensive as a carbon tax, by imposing the cap-and-trade system *upstream*, at the point of extraction or processing of the fossil fuel. Emissions allowances would then be required of the party that extracts or processes the coal, natural gas, or crude oil. If this is going to be the regulatory point, then many of the advantages of a carbon tax over cap-and-trade fall away. More generally, David Weisbach has argued that there are a number of designs that could render cap-and-trade programs just as efficient as a carbon tax.[28] Some significant differences remain, and are treated in subsequent parts of this chapter. The orientation of this part of the book is to focus on the implementation issues inherent in the instrument choice problem, and to analyze the merits of each instrument in the context of their likely implementations.

To sum up, despite its bad reputation, a carbon tax is almost certainly the cheapest way to reduce carbon dioxide emissions. Government policy can and should correct market failures, but should do so by sending simple price signals, not by trying to simulate an efficient economy through governmental policy and expenditures. Because greenhouse gas emission reduction opportunities are so widespread, it is presumptuous to think that government policy and expenditures can be fashioned to magically achieve the best results without the benefit of prices to signal misallocations of resources. To the extent that a carbon tax most consistently and comprehensively covers carbon dioxide-emitting activity throughout the economy, it best transmits this market signal.

Two: Excessive Formation of Capital

People seem to think that *physical* capital in the form of buildings, facilities, and structures is an unambiguous good. Capital is obviously necessary for wealth creation, and constitutes much of the long-run investments that are necessary for long-term economic growth. People also seem to think it follows that government policy should encourage the formation of capital to foster economic growth. The US Internal Revenue Code, of course, provides favorable tax treatment for capital, in the form of a different schedule of rates for capital gains[29] and its potential for deferring income for "like-kind exchanges."[30] There is even a Washington-based advocacy group that extols the virtues of capital formation for its own sake, the American Council for Capital Formation.[31] This emphasis on long-lived physical capital, however, has at times had harmful environmental consequences. Because it often takes years—and even decades—for the environmental harms of a practice or industry to be discovered, the longevity of physical capital has been a serious environmental problem, making it difficult to change or switch away from technologies that cause environmental harm. And yet, the solution for making these difficult policy changes has typically involved the creation of more if different kinds of capital. This fixation on physical capital is a side effect of government subsidization and command-and-control regulation, and is avoided by a carbon tax.

If anything, the whole problem of climate change, being a long-term problem caused more by coal combustion than anything else, should have sensitized us to the danger of fixating on the formation of capital. A superficially attractive but erroneous line of thinking has saddled the United States with a stock of coal-fired power plants that has cost hundreds of billions of dollars. This line of thinking goes something like this: cheap electricity is an unambiguously good thing, lowering production costs and generally making life better for the general populace. But cheap electricity requires expensive capital, and government assistance to help form this capital must be a good thing, too. Coal for electricity generation has thus always been heavily subsidized, enjoying numerous tax benefits that are often (but not always) enjoyed by other natural resources. The sale of coal itself can be eligible for taxation at a lower rate, at the capital gains rate,[32] or may be deducted from income under a favorable "percentage depletion" method, which allows a deduction that *exceeds* the value of the coal itself.[33] This has all been in the name of cheap electricity, which has been unfortunately conflated with the cause of electricity generation through coal combustion. And this assumption continues to haunt energy policy today, as we dream up even more tax benefits to try and maintain our coal-related physical capital, all the while continuing to discover a widening circle of environmental harms.

Even leaving aside climate change, coal-fired power plants are anachronistic in a world that has begun to understand the massive environmental costs of extracting, transporting, and burning coal to generate electricity.[34] But one of the biggest obstacles to addressing climate change has been the resistance from the industries that have the billions of dollars irretrievably *stuck* in the coal combustion business. Power plants and coal mines represent huge "stranded" costs. The owners of this massive capital have not only fought vigorously to minimize regulation but also to maintain government policies that benefit and protect them.

In hindsight, it is clear that encouraging and subsidizing the formation of this kind of capital was short-sighted in ignoring the possibility that alternative forms of capital could have delivered the electricity powered by coal at a much, much lower environmental cost. Certainly, there are ways of generating electricity that are less greenhouse gas-intensive.[35] Natural gas-fired power plants could have provided the same amount of electricity with far less environmental harm. If it were not for the massive construction of coal-fired power plants, one wonders whether penetration by natural gas plants and low- and no-carbon energy technologies would have emerged earlier and more economically. The problem with capital is that once we have it, its high cost makes it difficult to dispose of.

The trouble with so many plans to reduce greenhouse gas emissions is that they fall into this trap again: that capital is needed to spur growth in some way that is desirable, such as by supporting the development of "clean coal technology." As noted above, "refined coal" even qualifies for the renewable energy production tax credit, giving the phrase "renewable energy" an adventurous interpretation only lawyers could find sensible.[36] Government subsidization of renewable energy technologies may seem more desirable on the grounds that the few environmental costs are more than outweighed by the prospects of reducing carbon dioxide emissions. This, however, is dangerously close to the "cheap electricity" rationale that sustained coal development for such a long time. In Spain, where the government embraced solar energy as an end in and of itself, extremely generous government incentives created not only a national glut, but a worldwide glut for solar panels. The *New York Times* reported that solar panel manufacturing plants in Spain began producing too many solar panels and of poor quality, only to have the Spanish government belatedly learn that it could not afford to sustain this subsidy. Spanish cities, towns, and local economies that sprouted up around the solar panel manufacturing industry dried up overnight, leaving behind new forms of economic dislocation and hardship.[37] And in the rush to boost renewable energy, not much has been said about the potential environmental harms of these technologies. Not very much has been said about the ecological side effects of wind energy, such as its effects on wildlife that may be harmed by turbines, or the effects of solar photovoltaic energy (such as its effects on the desert biota or the toxic materials generated by the semiconductor fabrication process), but these effects should have a fair hearing over the course of time.

The overlooked danger is that by supporting specific renewable energy technologies now, we run the risk of effectively *locking them in* for decades, and perhaps missing the chance to find renewable technologies with even smaller carbon or environmental footprints. Wind turbines have an expected lifespan of twenty to twenty-five years,[38] solar photovoltaic panels about the same.[39] Although these *seem* like environmentally and economically sensible renewable energy technologies, what will be learned in the next twenty or thirty years? Already, concentrated solar power has emerged as a possibly cheaper and simpler alternative to the previously dominant solar technology, photovoltaic solar energy.[40]

Environmental organizations, oriented by their missions to "get things done," have again fallen into the trap of wedding themselves to certain technologies. Today's environmental savior may be tomorrow's environmental pariah, and the problem with mandating an expensive environmental technology is the economic irreversibility of capital expenditures. A recent technological mandate sought by some environmental groups was Integrated Gasification Combined Cycle technology, a technology that gasifies coal so as to be able to separate out the carbon for later capture and sequestration underground. The Natural Resource Defense Council and other organizations sued the EPA to force it to require IGCC as part of any new coal-fired power plant as part of its "New Source Review" program.[41] Failing to learn the past lessons of the New Source Review program, the NRDC seemed to have overlooked the possibility that if coal-fired power plants with

IGCC were actually built, carbon dioxide emissions might be abated but better and environmentally cleaner opportunities to reduce emissions would be lost for generations.

Presuming that somehow we have identified the "best" greenhouse gas reduction ideas is dangerous because we live with these decisions for the next twenty, thirty, or fifty years. It is far less dangerous to spur growth by taxing that which is undesirable, than encouraging capital formation around that which we think, at this time, is desirable. First, as argued above, some measures to reduce greenhouse gases do not involve capital at all, but are simple measures to conserve energy and use it more efficiently. No capital formation is necessary for people to figure out how to drive less by bundling tasks, carpooling, riding the bus, bicycling, or embracing any number of other ways to reduce their transportation emissions. Second, if incentives are required to form capital around a meritorious capital project that reduces greenhouse gas emissions, a carbon tax, if it presents a stable enough of a price signal, provides the economic stimulus for private capital to flow into those supposedly desirable areas. Underlying this argument is the belief that private capital is at least as able to discern the value of investment as government. Admittedly, at recent times private capital has been spectacularly and widely mistaken. But it is hard to believe that government can actually do better than private capital over the long run in picking clean technologies. And finally, as the climate change problem is one that will play itself out over the better part of a century, it is essential to maintain an open economy for innovation and for new technologies. To the greatest extent possible, greenhouse gas policy should not encourage the formation of expensive capital. To the extent that it does, it guarantees some "stickiness" and some longevity that is in part born of the difficulty of changing course.

Regulating greenhouse gas emissions under the command-and-control-oriented US Clean Air Act is thus deeply problematic. EPA cannot avoid issuing regulations to reduce greenhouse gas emissions except by dictating, or at least biasing, certain expensive capital decisions. It would appear that regulating greenhouse gas emissions under the Clean Air Act is better than nothing, given the failure of the US Congress to enact comprehensive climate legislation in 2010. It is very possible that regulating under the Clean Air Act is better than no regulation at all. But the Clean Air Act poses a serious danger that it will induce expensive capital decisions that will be locked in for decades.

Some small, immediate emissions reductions *might* be achieved under the Clean Air Act, but over the long run, this mode of regulation might preclude an entire generation of technologies that could prove vastly superior in reducing greenhouse gas emissions. That is the danger of command-and-control regulation of greenhouse gas emissions.

By contrast, a carbon tax is capital-neutral: it does not encourage the formation of expensive physical capital that would inhibit future changes in production. Private capital will only rush in to fund expensive projects if they make more economic sense than other, smaller measures that could reduce a carbon tax liability, which is how it should be. And which expensive projects move forward should not be determined by political convenience, but by how effectively and cheaply they reduce carbon dioxide emissions, which is how it should be. A carbon tax also avoids, at least as well as other instruments, the creation of political economies that would inhibit future policy changes. Today's political grease is tomorrow's obstacle to change and reform, as the powerful coal lobbies have taught us. To be sure, sticky, long-lived capital *will be* formed, no matter what the policy, given the capital-intensive nature of electricity provision. Climate change is too large of problem and requires too much change in the world's industrial economy to avoid huge, unprecedented expenditures for infrastructure and other physical capital. But a greenhouse gas policy could at least minimize exposure to costly long-lived mistakes by being neutral toward the formation of capital. The only impetus for capital formation should be a sustained carbon price, not other heavy-handed policies that seem to get more tangible results.

Three: Non-Interference with Other Regulatory Instruments or Jurisdictions

The debate over greenhouse gas policy, drawing in some of the most prominent thinkers in the world, has raged for almost two decades, though more raucously in recent years, as the Nordhaus-Tol-Stern disagreements demonstrate. Debates get personal when people believe they have the "right" answer, and this has been a problem with climate change. There has been a tendency to operate from the assumption that there is a single correct way of addressing climate change. For a threat this serious, and a problem involving every nation and every person in the world, it would seem that a variety of responses are required. The politics of climate policy are still such that it is challenging to achieve legislative action, so there is a real and continuing danger of paralysis by analysis. Vital first steps are absolutely necessary, lest the world become so despondent that the pursuit of greenhouse gas reduction is given up altogether.

If one accepts that policy must start somewhere, and perhaps start in several places, a carbon tax would have the advantage, because of its simplicity, of forming the strongest foundation upon which other policies can stand. A carbon tax could coexist with all of the three alternative policy measures considered by this book (though implementing the others may undermine the efficiency benefits of the carbon tax). Although a cap-and-trade program would send one price signal, and a carbon tax another, the two programs could work side-by-side without legal or administrative conflicts. If some emitters wound up facing the sum of two price signals, some adjustment might be appropriate, as long as further distortions were avoided.

The same cannot necessarily be said of some possible combinations of the other policy instruments. For example, a cap-and-trade program would be foiled by a simultaneous command-and-control program that uniformly mandated some technology and essentially deprived emitters of the choice that a cap-and-trade program could offer. Moreover, a command-and-control technology mandate that forces emitters to reduce emissions could produce so many excess allowances so as to depress the price and discourage emissions reductions elsewhere. Or, imagine trying to meld two different cap-and-trade programs, one enacted by a state or regional body, and one by a federal body: how do the respective bodies determine which entities are covered by the cap-and-trade programs?

There is a second compatibility issue, and a more serious one. To what extent does a greenhouse gas policy interfere with programs enacted by other jurisdictions? The problem can arise when different levels of government enact greenhouse gas laws that may produce inconsistent legal obligations. For example, if a federal and state government each enacted a command-and-control law that required different greenhouse gas abatement technologies, emitting firms would be left to wonder which mandate to observe. This is a problem of environmental federalism: whether state and federal governments can concurrently regulate the same environmental problems, and if they do, whether they can effectively draw lines of demarcation between the two. This issue could also arise in the European Union, which dictates to its member states a number of trade and environmental "directives" in an attempt to harmonize trade, environmental, and economic policy. While the EU Emissions Trading System (EUETS) obligates the EU member states to participate in a Europe-wide cap-and-trade program, it is not always clear what other measures may be taken by member states *in addition* to participation in the EUETS.

A carbon tax has the advantage of sidestepping most of the jurisdictional conflicts that would occur as a result of parallel policies being undertaken by multiple jurisdictions. In most countries, the revenue-raising prerogative of both the federal government and state or provincial governments is such that a wide variety of taxation measures are permitted. The jurisdiction over environmental regulation can be unclear; hence the federalism battles over environmental statutes and regulations, most notably in the US Supreme Court.[42] But despite the fact that a carbon tax would have obvious environmental ramifications, courts in most countries (or the EU) would be reluctant to strike down a carbon tax as extrajurisdictional environmental lawmaking. All taxes, after all, have incidental effects other than the raising of revenue. It would be a treacherous path for a court (or the EU) to start trying to evaluate the primary purpose of a carbon tax, and whether it either had the primary effect or intent of raising revenue or reducing carbon dioxide emissions (with the intent of striking it down in the latter cases). It would simply be too difficult to distinguish carbon taxes from other consumption taxes. By contrast, a cap-and-trade program would necessarily involve some direct regulation of an emissions source by an administrative agency; requiring an entity to hold an emissions allowance, without any pretense of revenue-raising, triggers an entirely different, and more problematic set of constitutional considerations.[43]

If a federal government legislated to reduce greenhouse gas emissions, the jurisdictional question would be whether it had infringed upon state or provincial powers. In the United States, the Constitutional power to regulate interstate commerce confers broad regulatory powers on the federal government. The question then becomes whether, in the case of overlapping state and federal legislation, the federal government precludes, or *preempts* the state legislation. The case law in the United States of preemption—whether a federal law preempts state or local law—has become somewhat muddled in the last several decades, but in the area of greenhouse gas regulation, it is likely that any federal legislation will be explicit about what it seeks to preempt. In the absence of an explicit legislative statement, there are general factors that a court would consider if a preemption case were before it, but the stakes involved in greenhouse gas regulation are so great that it is inconceivable that Congress would be able to duck the federalism issue.

The American Clean Energy and Security Act, cosponsored by Congressmen Henry Waxman and Ed Markey, and passed by the House of Representatives in June of 2009, explicitly provided for the preemption of regional cap-and-trade programs, including the Regional Greenhouse Gas Initiative (or RGGI) among ten northeastern states that has been up and running for several years now.[44] Regional programs, such as the RGGI or the developing Western Climate Initiative cap-and-trade program, which includes several US states and Canadian provinces, are not and will not be perfect, but do represent interesting attempts to regulate greenhouse gases.[45] For example, RGGI auctions a certain fraction of its emissions allowances, a method of allocation that has always been politically unpopular for cap-and-trade programs. Perhaps, just perhaps, if RGGI were to provide some pleasant surprises—like unexpectedly low compliance costs, or minimal increases in energy prices (RGGI only applies to power plants)—some of the taboo of allowance auctioning might be diminished. It certainly would be a shame if RGGI were to be preempted by federal legislation so obviously choked with special interest giveaways (discussed in greater detail later in this chapter).

Canadian federalism may be even more of a challenge for would-be climate legislators. Americans proud of their strong federalist tradition are usually surprised to learn that Canadian provinces have much greater autonomy than American states do. In fact, there is some uncertainty as to whether the Canadian federal government even has the power to regulate greenhouse gas emissions. Unlike the United States, the Canadian federal government does not have broad powers to regulate national commerce, which serves as the basis for federal jurisdiction for so much US federal environmental law.

Canada does have a constitutional clause that provides that the federal government has the exclusive authority to legislate for the "Peace, Order and Good Government of Canada," which, depending on the nature of the greenhouse gas legislation, could conceivably be invoked to justify federal action. There are several doctrinal "branches" of the POGG clause, two of which *might* be invoked to support a federal initiative to regulate greenhouse gases. The first, the "national concern" branch, pertains to matters that are necessarily national, those that provinces are somehow unable to address by themselves. The Canadian Supreme Court, however, has expressed reluctance to apply the national concern branch of POGG clause too broadly, since the exclusive nature of this power means that federal assumption of responsibility in an area would preclude provincial authority altogether, something that the court has explicitly rejected in the area of environmental regulation. A much more promising branch is the "national emergency" branch of POGG, which is not, despite its label, limited to emergencies or even necessarily short-term problems. They must, however, be temporary measures, which could be ensured by careful drafting. For most forms of greenhouse gas regulation, the national emergency branch of POGG could probably be invoked to support federal action, especially since, unlike the national concern branch, invocation of the national emergency branch does not preclude action by the provinces.

The Canadian federal government also has the power to enact criminal laws, an exclusively state function in the United States. An important part of federal environmental regulation, part five of the Canadian Environmental Protection Act, provides for the regulation of "toxic substances."[46] This is the statute under which Environment Canada issued its 2005 finding that carbon dioxide and other greenhouse gases are "toxic substances" that warrant federal regulation, and is predicated on the federal government's *criminal law* powers. Violating the provisions of the Canadian Environmental Protection Act is considered a criminal offense, though not necessarily punishable by imprisonment.

Taking the statutory definition of "toxic substance" literally, it would seem defensible to classify carbon dioxide as a toxic substance, as the emission of carbon dioxide "may have an immediate or long-term harmful effect on the environment or its biological diversity,"[47] or "may constitute a danger to the environment on which life depends,"[48] or "may constitute a danger in Canada to human life or health."[49] However, in practical terms, if emitting carbon dioxide could be classified as a criminal act, then what limits are there on the federal exercise of jurisdiction? Aren't all Canadians, to some degree, responsible for carbon dioxide emissions by virtue of their fossil fuel consumption, and therefore potentially criminally liable just by having a nonzero carbon footprint? At the time of writing of this book no federal greenhouse gas regulation had yet been promulgated. If Environment Canada were actually to promulgate federal greenhouse gas regulation (a number of false starts during the past several years give one reason for skepticism) and base it on the provisions of the Canadian Environmental Protection Act, a constitutional challenge would be almost certain, and the outcome uncertain.[50]

Why bother? It is difficult enough to muster the fragile political coalitions necessary to pass climate legislation; the last thing that would-be climate legislators and regulators need is legal uncertainty. If, in the case of the 2009 Waxman-Markey bill, the preemption is made explicit, there is no legal uncertainty. But then there would be a chilling effect on other nonfederal jurisdictions seeking to enact their own climate policies. The RGGI and the incipient Western Climate Initiative (WCI) were bold political moves, undertaken by states and provinces at a time when the federal governments of Canada and the United States were obstinately doing nothing. What if federal legislation ultimately fails to sufficiently reduce greenhouse gas emissions? Will state and provincial governments again undertake to forge legislation to make up for federal failure?

While both of these regional initiatives—RGGI and WCI—fall short of covering the entire economy (though WCI claims it will cover 90 percent of all emissions sources[51]), both should remain free from substantial interference from parallel federal attempts in Canada and the United States to regulate greenhouse gas emissions. And these two regional initiatives are only two of many subnational efforts to step into a vacuum created by federal fecklessness in both Canada and the United States. The US Conference of Mayors Climate Protection Agreement, a network of more than 900 US cities with a total population of more than 80 million Americans, has agreed to attempt to meet the Kyoto Protocol targets of reducing emissions by 7 percent below

1990 levels by the year 2012.[52] Ever in front, California's movement on the California Global Warming Solutions Act contemplates a variety of greenhouse gas-reducing measures in addition to its cap-and-trade program as part of WCI.[53] And, as noted above, the Canadian province of British Columbia has implemented the first significant carbon tax in North America.[54] A federal carbon tax by Canada or the United States would easily mesh with these subnational initiatives. The prospect of federal preemption of WCI, the California Global Warming Solutions Act, and RGGI is disquieting to regulators and to entities regulated under these programs.[55]

It is not just that these are laudable efforts that deserve a chance to be played out. These incomplete efforts are important to the overall emissions reduction effort because it is increasingly clear that reducing greenhouse gas emissions will require *many* governmental efforts. Rather than focusing on "getting it right," the mindset of greenhouse gas regulators and legislators should be to learn about the variety of ways in which emissions might be effectively regulated.

There was a time when environmental regulation was presumed to be best undertaken at the federal level. Only federal governments, it was believed, had the resources and the enforcement capacity to regulate environmental transgressions. Environmental organizations therefore focused much of their resources on influencing federal legislators, particularly in the United States. But even before President George W. Bush embarked upon a deregulatory environmental agenda, there were hints that states and cities might be better environmental regulators, not only because of administrative reasons, but because the political conditions were, in some places, more favorable toward environmental causes. For example, California has always, under Republican and Democratic leadership, been ahead of federal air pollution control efforts. Its leadership on climate change was a product of its Republican governor, Arnold Schwarzenneger. Before her service as US Health and Human Services secretary, then-Kansas governor Kathleen Sibelius stunned Washington pundits when she blocked approval of construction of a coal-fired power plant in her home state. When Kansas, one of the most conservative and reliably Republican states, is ahead of the federal government on environmental regulation, it is time to reexamine traditional assumptions about the inherent superiority of federal intervention. One cannot help but sense that the possibilities at the state level have expanded, and those at the federal level somewhat diminished.

It is clear that state and local governments, and perhaps some private networks, will have to supply some of the efforts to find an effective battery of regulatory instruments to reduce greenhouse gases. And yet the point is not that the federal government should continue to mark time while local, state, and regional authorities take up the climate challenge in earnest; the point is that federal initiatives should interfere as little as possible with ongoing efforts at other levels of government to regulate greenhouse gases. To maximize the chances of successful greenhouse gas regulation, we must multiply our efforts, trying different instruments. A carbon tax, because of its compatibility with other instruments and its insulation from jurisdictional conflicts, should be the centerpiece of greenhouse gas reduction efforts.

Four: Government Is Better at Reducing "Bads" Than Increasing "Goods"

When faced with a problem as large and daunting as climate change, there is a temptation to expect too much from governments. We demand that governments actually *solve* the problem, rather than create the conditions under which a solution is found. In an era of endless political campaigns and promises, voters in democratic countries have gotten accustomed to the idea that government should play the role of fixer. Caution is warranted. There is a saying, the exact attribution of which is difficult to trace, that goes something like this: "governments are bad at picking winners, and losers are good at picking governments."[56] It is not necessary to be so cynical as to believe that governments inevitably tend toward corruption. It is only necessary to see that governmental actors are at least susceptible to being hoodwinked by industries peddling snake oil for the environment.

In his January 28, 2003, State of the Union address, President George W. Bush announced that he would provide $1.2 billion in research and development funding for hydrogen fuel technology, so "America can lead the world in developing clean, hydrogen-powered automobiles."[57] President Bush continued:

> A simple chemical reaction between hydrogen and oxygen generates energy, which can be used to power a car, producing only water, not exhaust fumes. With a new national commitment, our scientists and engineers will overcome obstacles to taking these cars from laboratory to showroom, so that the first car driven by a child born today could be powered by hydrogen and pollution-free.[58]

Hydrogen fuel cell technology already had a long history by the time the Bush Administration discovered it in 2003: Welsh physicist William Grove first combined hydrogen and oxygen to produce electricity and water in 1842. In the 1950s, NASA, taking advantage of the fact that the process produced drinking water as a byproduct, began using hydrogen fuel cell technology for US space missions, continuing its use all the way up to the modern space shuttle. In 1968, General Motors built the first hydrogen fuel cell vehicle, but the fuel cell was so large that the vehicle had no passenger capacity. In the

1980s, a Canadian engineer named Geoffrey Ballard developed a smaller and more powerful hydrogen fuel cell that fit onto a motor vehicle. Ford and Chrysler invested $750 million in Ballard's company, but neither has come close to commercializing the technology for mass automobile use. It was in the wake of these failures that the Big Three—Chrysler, Ford, and General Motors—sought and received assistance from the Bush Administration. Needless to say, the hydrogen fuel cell initiative was almost exclusively for the benefit of these three companies.

Two technical problems have plagued the continued development of hydrogen fuel cell technology for the automobile: the energy required to extract hydrogen from hydrogen-containing substances in the first place, and the distribution and storage of hydrogen onboard a motor vehicle. Despite billions of dollars of taxpayer funding to support the commercialization of hydrogen fuel cell technology for automobiles, these problems have never shown any indication of nearing a solution. A report by the consulting firm McKinsey and Co. concluded that "hydrogen vehicles are a nascent technology that could prove an alternative solution. Based on current knowledge, the abatement cost is extremely high."[59] This is true despite more than a half-century of efforts to develop this technology for commercial applications. The US government seems to have belatedly caught on, as the Bush Administration wound up slashing the 2009 research budget by 69 percent,[60] and the Obama Administration slashed it another 67 percent for 2010.[61]

So why, given the long-standing and long-known problems with fuel cell technology, were the Big Three even interested in hydrogen fuel cell technology? The answer is a matter of speculation, but it is surely worth noticing that President Bush's announcement had several effects: (1) it served as a response to intense political pressure to raise vehicle fuel economy standards by promising an alternative; (2) by putting off an increase in fuel economy standards, it allowed the Big Three to maintain a huge competitive advantage over Japanese automakers it had built up by building bigger, less fuel-efficient but more profitable sport-utility vehicles; (3) it addressed (albeit it did not ultimately alleviate) fierce criticism of President Bush for having walked away from the Kyoto Protocol; and (4) it benefitted the important swing state of Michigan, a year before the presidential election year of 2004. In the vernacular of political economics, this would be considered a case of "rent-seeking," the use of government instruments for private industrial advantage. Pure rent-seeking is never clear-cut, intertwined as it often is with public benefits, so circumstantial evidence is often the best one can do. One can rarely do better than this case.

What was the alternative to hydrogen fuel cell technology, and what were Japanese automakers doing? Toyota and Honda were working on hybrid electric vehicle technology which, with the help of a federal tax credit and spiking gasoline prices in 2005, they would parlay into a huge competitive advantage over the Big Three. Toyota and Honda chose to work with a technology that might not have had quite as bright of an upside, but had far fewer technical problems to solve. The market success of hybrid vehicle technology seem to have vindicated this strategy, while GM and Chrysler averted bankruptcy in 2009 only because of government generosity, yet again. Ironically, when the Ford Escape hybrid finally arrived on market in September 2004, it did so by licensing Toyota's hybrid electric vehicle technology.[62]

How could this outrageous boondoggle happen? Apart from the cynical political economies of the Big Three and the Bush Administration, this misadventure occurred because the Bush Administration offered Americans a solution. It was a poor solution, and one that no government should have offered, but made possible by an understandable desire for a solution to a difficult problem.

Fundamentally, there is a critical difference between government taking action to prevent bad things from happening (like pollution and crime) and government taking action to try and make good things happen (like investing directly in specific technologies). In environmental policy, government agencies have usually been quite competent at identifying environmental "bads," pollution problems that pose threats to human health or the environment. The unfortunate reality that subsequent political interventions sometimes handcuff agencies and render them unable to do anything about these "bads" is beside the point. For all of the criticism leveled at the EPA, its record at identifying pollution problems that threaten the health of the American populace has been quite respectable. While often fighting rearguard actions against politicians with anti-environmental agendas, EPA has done a credible job of regulating numerous air and water pollutants, including lead, mercury, vinyl chloride, nitrogen oxides, sulfur dioxide, particulate matter, fine particulate matter, and has most recently started grappling with the difficult problem of nanotechnology. One may quibble with whether EPA has been, by some accounts, overbearing, or whether, by other accounts, EPA has been stiff enough in its dealings with polluters. But no sustained argument has ever been made that EPA either cries wolf too often, or that EPA is systemically lax about at least identifying environmental threats.

By contrast, governmental agencies and legislatures have a poor record when it comes to identifying and fostering the development of certain types of "goods"—products, processes, or ideas that supposedly improve social welfare. Certain "public goods" such as policing and national defense are obviously government functions, but when some endeavor contains mixed public and private benefits, it becomes tricky to determine the proper extent of government involvement. Basic research, such as that undertaken or funded by research agencies such as the National Science Foundation, still rate high enough in public benefits to warrant governmental intrusion. But trouble often starts when research is more applied, seemingly more practical, and serendipitously inuring to the benefit of some private firm like General Motors. Government resolving to "tackle" a problem usually means spending money, and comes up when a governmental actor thinks it sees a great idea. Subsidizing great ideas always sounds good, except when, as is often the case, it turns out not to have been such a great idea after all. The common mistake is in failing to recognize the other side of the ledger. When governmental officials see a great idea, they often fail to see the downside; when they see something bad, they often fail to see the upside. Fortunately, when somebody in government sees something bad—like the pollution byproducts of a product—*markets* are present to place a countervailing value on the upside—the value of the product itself. The same cannot be said when government gets behind a great idea; there are rarely markets that signal the existence and severity of the downsides of a supposedly great idea.

Both the United States and Canada appear headed down this treacherous path again. Another impending and potentially misguided government initiative is the subsidization of "carbon capture and storage" technology. "Carbon capture" refers to the capture of carbon dioxide emitted as a result of any combustion process, while "storage" refers to the permanent containment of the carbon dioxide, so that it does not enter the atmosphere and contribute to climate change. Carbon dioxide would typically be injected into underground "pore spaces" where it would be stored for, it is hoped, eternity. While the carbon capture and storage concept may be applied to all industrial combustion processes (and even for some noncombustion carbon-emitting processes), most of the discussion and technological development has been for coal-fired power plants.

The technology seems attractive, salvaging trillions of dollars of capital worldwide wrapped up in fuel combustion, and what enthusiastic policy wonks would call a potential "game-changer." Some have likened the urgency of developing carbon capture and storage to the development of the atomic bomb. In a 2009 floor speech, US Senator Lamar Alexander said "we should launch another mini-Manhattan Project and reserve a Nobel Prize for the scientist who can get rid of the carbon from existing coal plants, because coal provides half our energy."[63]

But the lofty rhetoric seems misplaced for a technology that remains prohibitively expensive. As recently as 2008, demonstration costs remained in the range of 60 to 90 Euros per ton of CO_2 stored (approximately 88 to 131 US dollars per ton[64]), but were expected to "come down to" about 30 to 45 Euros per ton by 2030 (approximately $45 to $62 per ton, using a 2010 currency conversion).[65] Even if this bears out, this would still be much more expensive than many dozens of other emissions abatement and reduction strategies, even notoriously expensive nuclear power.[66] Moreover, the physical challenge of capturing and storing even a modest amount of American carbon emissions is staggering. The United States currently emits around 1.5 billion tons per year of carbon from coal-fired power plants,[67] and the world's largest sequestration project, at the Sleipner gas field in the North Sea, is sequestering 1 million tons a year of carbon dioxide, or about 0.06 percent of United States emissions.[68] If carbon capture and storage were to capture all of the carbon dioxide from US coal-fired power plants, the total weight that would need to be transported would equal three times the annual volume of natural gas transported in the United States by pipeline. Dr. Joan Brennecke, director of the Notre Dame Energy Center where researchers have been working on carbon capture and storage technology for years under DOE grants, laments that despite recent advances, economical carbon capture technology is still at least a decade away from commercial application, remarking that "no matter what, it is going to be painful to do CO_2 capture."[69] It is surely telling that an industry consortium formed to pursue and support a pilot carbon capture and storage project, FutureGen, lost two of its biggest industry backers, the two largest electricity providers in the

THE CASE FOR A CARBON TAX

United States: the American Electric Power Company and the Southern Company, in the face of the high costs of development.[70]

Given these challenges and setbacks, it seems slightly overenthusiastic to call for another Manhattan project for such an expensive technique, and one that has been studied for decades with disappointing results. Once again, an expensive idea has emerged from the convergence of politics, rent-seeking, and the convenient illusion that government can provide (i.e., fund) a solution. Not all of the motivation is scandalous: the temptation for such an important problem is to see the greenhouse gas reduction effort as a "war," in which carbon capture and sequestration can be a "game-changer" in much the same way that the atomic bomb was perceived to be *the* game-changer needed to stop the Axis powers. Wishful thinking creates a desire to find "game-changers." Recent technologies labeled as game-changers include: electric vehicle batteries,[71] electricity storage technology generally,[72] shale gas,[73] small nuclear reactors,[74] nuclear reactors that burn spent fuel,[75] underground coal combustion,[76] ocean thermal power,[77] a transmission line linkage,[78] and General Motors' plug-in hybrid vehicle.[79] Some of these could actually be significant breakthroughs. But most often, politicians proposing technology subsidies for speculative technologies seems more like the behavior of the destitute and desperate, sadly spending their last dollars on lottery tickets instead of undertaking the hard work of change.

Nothing insulates a polity from its government's appetite for waste and profligacy, not even carbon taxes. But at least spending money is not the *point* of a carbon tax, as it is with a government subsidy. Indeed, if the goal is to reduce greenhouse gas emissions, then a policy instrument should draw on what government does well—tax—rather than on what it does poorly—make strategic market decisions. With a worrying problem such as climate change, it is too easy and too dangerous to fall into the trap of thinking that governments can "fix" the problem directly, funding a potential "home run" or "game-changer."[80] It is harder to create the markets that will spur development of a solution, harder to trust markets, and hardest still to tell voters that they have to help pay for the solution through higher prices.

Carbon taxes and government subsidies represent opposite ends of a spectrum. In economic theory, they represent opposite approaches to externality pricing. In government policy, they represent opposite philosophies about the role of government. Up to this point, I have argued that when it comes to greenhouse gas policy, the former approach is not only superior, but that government subsidies should generally be presumed to be wasteful and ineffective. Specific technologies often seem appealing, and for those that believe in proactive government, worthy of subsidization. However, it is important that climate policy remain "technology-neutral"—that it not push vast economies and governments toward any particular technology, no matter how attractive. Even our relatively successful experiences with subsidization usually turn out to have unexpected negative consequences.[81] The same arguments apply, albeit to a lesser extent, to command-and-control regulation and to cap-and-trade programs.

Command-and-control regulation does seem to draw upon what government knows best: preventing bad things, rather than promoting good things. But as in the case of subsidization, governmental actors who set pollution standards may not actually know the best way to reduce emissions. While command-and-control regulation is much more sophisticated now, and doesn't strictly "command" nor "control" anymore, it still unjustifiably presumes agency knowledge of technological and economic matters.

In the 1970s, Congress sought to tighten the command-and-control standards applicable to, in particular, coal-fired power plants. As discussed earlier, under the 1977 Clean Air Act Amendments, coal-fired power plants were required to meet certain emissions standards for sulfur dioxide emissions rates. At the time, there was only one way to meet the mandated rate: install "scrubbers," massive end-of-pipe devices that expose the exhaust stream to a chemical reaction that removes the sulfur dioxide out of the stream. Two things were wrong with this mandate: the new standard didn't solve coal's other environmental problems (like carbon dioxide emission) and it did not kick in unless a new plant was being constructed or an existing one subjected to a "major modification." Absent new plant construction or a major modification, plants were *grandfathered* into the old emissions standards. This gap in regulation, between the expensive scrubber requirement and the old, grandfathered standards meant that existing power plants had a huge advantage over new or modified ones. Predictably, coal-fired power plants simply found ways to avoid new plants (which would be cleaner and more efficient), or make any modifications that might be considered "major" (which could potentially make plants cleaner and more efficient). It is quite plausible that the turnover of power plants was slowed so much that the amendment actually increased pollution.[82]

Less obvious are the machinations behind the ill-advised command-and-control mandates. Weren't the responses from the electricity industry expected? Wasn't this an expected outcome?

In their widely cited and praised book, Bruce Ackerman and William Hassler[83] document the political deal that led to the scrubber requirement: it involved an odd coalition of eastern coal interests and environmental groups. For eastern coal interests, the threatening alternative to scrubbing was the import from the Western United States of low-sulfur coal—low enough that substantial sulfur dioxide emissions could be achieved without any capital costs. The higher transportation costs of lugging the coal across the country would be more than paid for by savings from not installing expensive scrubbers. Meanwhile, environmental groups worried that without a scrubber requirement, regions that currently had good air quality might backslide. If the emissions standard at the time—1.2 lbs of sulfur dioxide per million Btus (a measure of the energy content of the coal)—were ratcheted downward but without a scrubber requirement, some new coal-fired power plants might spring up in these clean regions, and might opt to burn the low-sulfur coal rather than scrub. All other things being equal, environmental organizations preferred to make new plants install scrubbers.

Incredibly, what naïve government actors and environmental groups failed to understand is that a scrubbing requirement only applied to new construction projects might as well not apply at all. Environmental organizations that pushed for this solution expected that over the course of time, these power plants would die a natural death and be retired, and their replacements would be cleaner power plants with scrubbers. This "grandfathering" of existing power plants into old regulations had the entirely foreseeable effect of firms taking heroic measures to keep their old power plants up and running, and fighting tooth and nail to prove to regulators that they had not undertaken a "major modification" that would trigger the scrubber requirement. Who indeed would replace an aging plant with a new one if the new one was subjected to an expensive scrubbing requirement whereas the old one wasn't? The environmental organizations, along with the congressional representatives that listened to them, were duped.

So government subsidies and also command-and-control programs often turn out poorly. What about cap-and-trade programs? Surely these types of programs are less vulnerable to rent-seeking.

On the contrary, the most important program design element of a cap-and-trade program is how to allocate emissions allowances. The most efficient way of allocating allowances is to auction them, and allow emitters to bid for the right to emit. The revenues from an auction provide a revenue stream, and can be used to reduce other taxes such as income taxes, which some view as being distortionary and a drag on productivity. Auctioning also provides the potential to alleviate the economic impacts on the poorest energy consumers, by providing funds to compensate them. It is simply the fairest system, since it requires the emitter to bear the initial cost, rather than the taxpayer. While energy providers and other emitters would pass on at least some of these costs to the consumer, at least those costs would be proportionate to consumption, which is the point of pricing carbon.

But the political advantages of not auctioning allowances, and instead writing the distribution into legislation are apparently very powerful. The US sulfur dioxide trading program actually contained a provision that allocated a special clump of "bonus" allowances to utilities in Indiana, Ohio, and Illinois for the years 1995–1999, to be split in proportion to their baseline emissions.[84] The Waxman-Markey bill passed by the US House of Representatives in 2009 was far worse. The free allocation of allowances under Waxman-Markey reads like a Christmas list of people and industries that lawmakers deemed deserving of relief. Some of the would-be lucky recipients of free CO_2 emissions allowances included:

- Electric utility companies, getting 35 percent of the allowances;
- Local natural gas distribution companies: 9 percent;
- States: 10 percent from 2012 to 2015, 7.5 percent from 2016 to 2017, 6.5 percent from 2018 to 2021, and 5 percent thereafter, to invest in renewables and energy efficiency, and also 1.5 percent for programs to benefit users of home heating oil and propane, an issue of primary concern in the Northeast;
- Energy-intensive industries, including pulp, paper, cement, and steel: 15 percent in 2014, but phasing out by about 2 percent per year;
- Oil refiners: 2 percent starting in 2014 and ending in 2016;
- Carbon capture and storage efforts: 2 percent of the allowances from 2014 to 2017 and 5 percent from 2018 and beyond; and
- Automakers get 3 percent through 2017 and 1 percent from 2018 to 2025.[85]

Assuming an average price of $15 per ton over the thirteen-year period of 2012 to 2025, the cumulative value of allowances granted to the electricity generation industry has been estimated at $378 *billion*, far more than the American bailout package for AIG that generated so much hostility.[86] Small wonder that the run-up to the bill's introduction saw an unprecedented amount of lobbying, much of it from coal-state Democrats.[87] It was reported that 1,150 groups lobbied the US Congress in just the twelve weeks leading up to passage of Waxman-Markey.[88] Not surprisingly, Representative Waxman and his fellow Democrats emerged from closed-door meetings with some ideas on how to distribute these billions of dollars of allowances. Yet even still, Washingtonians were dissatisfied with the allocation of allowances in the Waxman bill. Agriculture Secretary Tom Vilsack was quoted as calling for a cap-and-trade allowance allocation that was somehow friendlier to small family farmers. The former Iowa governor actually said "[t]his isn't just about the survival of the planet, but it's also about the survival of rural communities. . . ."[89] It is remarkable that the agriculture secretary should refocus a bill to arrest climate change and turn it into a rural aid bill.

It just seems irresistible for legislators to write a cap-and-trade bill and allocate the allowances by legislative fiat. To the extent that allowances are given away for free, lawmakers are essentially printing money, for distribution to appreciative donors and constituents. Prospective and appreciative donors and constituents know this, and therefore have come to *expect* to be courted. The result is the inevitable but inelegant marriages of rent-seekers and lawmakers.

To be clear, while the cap under the Waxman-Markey bill may be too generous or too stringent, the argument offered here is not that the caps are set at inefficiently high or low levels; it is that the allocation of allowances is vulnerable to rent-seeking. The problem with cap-and-trade programs is that the allocation of valuable allowances is really a vehicle for *government subsidization* of politically favored groups. As such, it is costly for society to adopt these programs for the same reasons as for government to subsidize too many favored technologies.

Is a carbon tax safe from rent-seeking? Obviously not. The encyclopedic Internal Revenue Code provides a great deal of evidence that taxes are subject to exemptions. Moreover, it is true that many exemptions exist with respect to several of the carbon tax programs in effect throughout the world. Competitiveness concerns have prompted some exemptions to protect domestic industries from carbon taxes in Norway, Sweden, Finland, the UK, and Denmark.[90] But it is also true that carbon taxes can be relatively free of special treatments, as in the case of the carbon tax in British Columbia—an export-oriented province with manufacturers exposed to intense trade competition.

A carbon tax is thus not invulnerable to exemptions that protect (or at least purport to protect) domestic industries. But a carbon tax provides a natural and intuitive weighting: carbon content. Special dispensations may be necessary to secure passage of a carbon tax. But provided that these goodies are *decoupled* from the incentives at the margin to emit carbon dioxide, the carbon tax still preserves the incentive to change behavior at the margins. This is also not to deny that many other distortionary tax benefits contribute to a carbon-intensive economy. A carbon tax cannot undo all of these distortions and correct them in one fell swoop. But a carbon tax can represent a counterweight to existing distortions. Above all else, a carbon tax imposes a marginal price on emitting.

Fundamentally, the problem of climate change is one in which government is uniquely poor at making certain kinds of detailed decisions, such as which form of technology to adopt as an alternative to carbon-based energy sources. The more disparate information about a problem becomes, the less able that government, even gargantuan agencies such as the US Department of Energy or the EPA, can harness all of the relevant information. Even if we limited ourselves to reducing emissions from energy (an unwise limitation for the reasons set out earlier this chapter), there are a huge number of economic factors that go into the pricing of each moving part in a power plant, fossil fuel-fired or not, or into the production of motor vehicles. If the job is to figure out new ways to do things that *private* firms typically do— like generate electricity, build cars, and produce the locomotion for cars—then the government is out of its league if it attempts to participate. Climate change could well turn out to be a more important problem than national security, space exploration, or the confrontation of fascism. But it does not necessarily follow that taxpayer dollars must be spent on carbon capture and storage or any other seemingly great idea. The most important thing that governments throughout the world can do—most emphatically not the only thing—is establish the price of emitting carbon to create markets necessary for carbon capture and storage, as well as likely better technologies, to thrive. Rents for climate solutions can be appropriated, and governments must create the conditions for them to be appropriated, most simply by imposing a carbon tax.

Five: Incentives for Innovation—
Price Effects

It is clear that reducing emissions and minimizing climate change will require not only some fairly large-scale behavioral changes, but also innovation in technology and in a myriad of everyday practices and processes. While much can be accomplished with what is already known, new knowledge will be needed. And just developing the human resources and infrastructure required to conduct the research needed to bring about these changes will be challenging. Both private and public spending on energy-related research and development have declined, both in real terms and compared with research and development in other sectors, such as pharmaceuticals and technology.[91] These trends must reverse themselves in order for humankind to have a chance at averting climate change.

It is economic doctrine that both Pigouvian taxes (in our case, carbon taxes) and cap-and-trade programs provide incentives for innovation in emissions reduction technology and practices. Both of these types of programs impose a *marginal* cost on emitting, as opposed to the sunk costs that characterize expensive pollution control investments made under command-and-control regimes. A Pigouvian tax, by imposing a cost on every single ton of pollutant, *constantly* engages the polluter with the task of reducing her pollution tax bill. By contrast, a command-and-control scheme that mandates a one-shot, irrevocable installation of pollution control equipment allows the polluter to stop thinking about pollution reduction. Why, if compliance is achieved by the installation of equipment, should the polluter search for other ways to comply?

It is possible under a command-and-control regime that discoveries could be made that simultaneously make it cheaper to meet a command-and-control standard *and* reduce pollution by improving the emissions rate. Those are the discoveries that both improve the environment and are in the interest of polluters to find. But that is a fundamentally different directive than the general charge of finding ways to save money by reducing overall pollution. It is not that the latter is a more honorable pursuit; it is that the latter directive leaves open a broader array of options, and therefore richer possibilities for discovery. Command-and-control, by requiring that any changes still hew to the mandated emissions *rate*, rules out innovations that might increase the emissions rate but decrease overall pollution somehow.

Take for example, a rate standard for emissions of NO_x which, as introduced in chapter 2, was based on the emissions rates achievable by a specific technology, "low-NO_x burner" technology.[92] Innovation under this regime would be limited to finding cheaper ways to run the low-NO_x burner technology, while still meeting the emissions rate standards. Alternatively, the polluter could find another NO_x control technology altogether that was *both* cheaper and met the rate standards. Under these extreme forms of command-and-control, incentives exist only to find those innovations that serendipitously deliver lower pollution *and* lower costs.

Under a Pigouvian tax system, *anything* the polluter does to reduce overall pollution saves money. A polluter could find a way of running low-NO_x burners more efficiently that costs more, but that improves the emissions rate and reduces pollution. If the pollution savings offset the extra cost, the polluter would pursue it under a Pigouvian tax system, but not under command-and-control. A polluter could find an alternative technology or a new technique that costs more but emits at a lower rate; the polluter might pursue it under a Pigouvian tax system (if the savings offset the extra cost), but not under command-and-control. A polluter could find a way of running low-NO_x burners that emit at a higher rate, but can produce more electricity; if the extra electricity is valuable enough, the polluter might shut down or reduce operation at other times. This option would be pursued under a Pigouvian tax system, but not under command-and-control. Finally, since a Pigouvian tax only pertains to the total quantity of pollution emitted, it leaves open additional possibilities to allocate pollution over different time periods, so as to minimize cost. The most flexible command-and-control regime still requires polluters to emit at a maximum *rate*, so that pollution can never spike, even if overall pollution over a period of time is reduced. The elimination of the time element from Pigouvian taxation is an additional source of flexibility for polluters looking for ways to reduce pollution. Almost all of these advantages of Pigouvian taxation over command-and-control schemes apply equally to cap-and-trade programs, where the cost of an allowance represents the marginal cost of emitting.

The evidence is somewhat mixed, but this bit of economic doctrine—that market-based instruments deliver more innovation than traditional command-and-control regulation—is largely accurate. The few truly market-based pollution programs have by and large borne this out. A Swedish NO_x tax was introduced in 1985 at 40 Swedish kroner per kg of NO_x emitted,[93] or approximately 4.2 Euros or 5 US dollars per kg of NO_x.[94]The Swedish NO_x tax was only imposed on electricity generation firms with outputs of at least 25 GWh per year, covering about 40 percent of NO_x emissions in Sweden at the time. NO_x emissions from facilities covered by the Swedish NO_x tax program declined from about 325 thousand tons in 1990 to just under 250 thousand tons in 2003, a decline of about 23 percent,[95] a striking result when compared with NO_x emissions from electricity-generation plants in the United States, which only moved from 6,663 to 6,232 tons for a comparable eight-year period of command-and-control regulation.[96] One reason NO_x emitters in Sweden emitted less was that firm managers awarded bonuses to employees that discovered ways of reducing NO_x emissions.[97] This is the kind of recruitment of the engagement of employees with firsthand knowledge of ways of reducing NO_x emissions that is accomplished by environmental tax programs. And importantly, the tax does not dictate how NO_x emissions may be reduced, allowing firms to take advantage of the wide range of knowledge of line employees.

The Swedish NO_x tax is particularly noteworthy because it refunded the tax proceeds back to the taxpaying facilities, *in proportion to the amount of electricity generated*. The tax, by rewarding those firms that figure out a way to reduce NO_x emissions *per unit of electricity produced*, almost presents a double incentive to reduce emissions: the charge itself, plus the extra large refund for extra electricity produced per amount of NO_x emissions. The incentive is not strictly double, because even the laggards in innovation would still receive a refund for their electricity produced, just less than the clever firms. But at the margins, there are multiple effects at work in inducing innovation. While this type of refunding scheme may, by this anecdotal evidence, support the argument that it induced innovation, it also has a downside—by providing a net reward to those electricity-generating plants that improve efficiency (in terms of electricity per NO_x emissions), the refunding scheme is in effect an output subsidy, a distortionary channeling of proceeds to the electricity-generating industry.[98] Innovation is thus induced, but at the cost of having an electricity-generating industry that may be less efficient in aspects other than NO_x emissions. Also, this type of program does little to discourage innovation that would reduce consumption.

The other major example—much more widely cited—is the US sulfur dioxide trading program. Under the program, firms found ways to reduce sulfur dioxide emissions at surprisingly low cost, in ways that did not occur under the previous command-and-control regime. Faced for the first time with a *marginal* cost on emitting sulfur dioxide, coal-fired power plants found surprising ways of reducing emissions, and from unexpected sources. For example, the rail industry, newly deregulated and sensing opportunity, found ways to serve electric utilities that were considering the long-distance shipment of low-sulfur coal mined in the western states. Rail firms increased their stock of cars, especially lighter aluminum cars, doubled and tripled up on tracks, and found ways to increase the speed of loading and unloading coal, all the time working closely with the low-sulfur coal mines and the electric utilities.[99] As well, the competitive threat of these alternative strategies (previously unidentified) to scrubbing seemed to light a fire under the scrubbing industry. The scrubber industry, after the advent of the sulfur dioxide trading program, found itself being cajoled by electric utilities (their customers) to become a little more economical and efficient.[100] They responded. Scrubbers became cheaper and removed more sulfur dioxide from the flue stream.[101] And both utilities and the scrubber industry took advantage of the time flexibility offered by cap-and-trade: because coal-fired power plants were no longer governed by a rate standard that required them to constantly maintain a particular emissions rate, scrubber manufacturers and power plants found they could do without the spare, redundant scrubber module that maintained the emissions rate when the main scrubber was shut down for repairs or maintenance. Under the sulfur dioxide trading program, a scrubber could actually be shut down and SO_2 emissions allowed to spike temporarily, with the spike simply paid for by the purchase of extra allowances. Previously, the command-and-control rate standard had forced all scrubbers to build in this costly redundancy.

The lessons from the Swedish NO_x program and the US sulfur dioxide trading program seem to be that a market price on emitting can produce surprising innovations, both in new technologies and in process changes. *Ex post* estimates of the compliance costs under the sulfur dioxide trading programs were considerably lower than expected, ranging from 40 to 140 percent lower than *ex ante* estimates.[102] If designed correctly, a cap-and-trade program does indeed provide incentives for firms to find ways to reduce emissions, in much the same way that a tax would.

Some evidence suggests that the sulfur dioxide cap-and-trade program even changed the corporate *attitude* of regulated entities. In a command-and-control regime, environmental compliance tends to be an unambiguous cost. A dollar spent on compliance in the form of pollution control equipment is a dollar that cannot be spent on productivity. Moreover, compliance under such a regime is often an uncertain legal matter. Remember that some pollution control requirements kick in when a "major modification" is made, an ambiguity that is tantamount to waving a red cape in front of a lawyer. Under these circumstances, emitting firms understandably resist when they feel like legal resistance can either win them relief from regulation or at least buy them some time. What the sulfur dioxide trading program did was change an emitting firm's disposition toward compliance. By imposing a real marginal cost on emissions, the sulfur dioxide program moved environmental compliance matters from the legal counsel's office to the business office, engaging entrepreneurial rather than legal creativity. Hence, electricity generating companies could imagine experimenting with blending high- and low-sulfur coal, a practice previously thought to be risky to the physical plant, but also pointless in light of the command-and-control nature of regulation.[103] For some environmentalists, there was no value in such experimentation; that which does not destroy coal-fired generation is insufficient. What this blinkered viewpoint overlooks is that innovation will help drive emissions reductions, legal bludgeoning less so.

All this evidence, from just these two programs, is anecdotal of course. It is a different matter to try to establish conclusively through analytical methods that market mechanisms such as taxation or cap-and-trade deliver more innovation. This is problematic because there is the question of how one defines and measures "innovation." One way to do this is to use research and development spending as a proxy for innovation. The obvious problem with this is that there is no established correlation between R&D spending and innovation. Another way of measuring innovation is to look at patent filings. This also presents some issues, as patents are classified in ways that do not necessarily comport with the empirical framework of a researcher trying to figure out whether pollution regulation induces innovation. For example, are we interested in innovations that reduce operating costs, or are we interested in innovations that deliver less pollution? In a study of coal-fired power plants in the United States from 1985 to 1997—a period that straddled the introduction of the US sulfur dioxide trading program—David Popp found that before the 1990 introduction of sulfur dioxide trading, there were more innovations leading to cost savings than to sulfur dioxide removal efficiencies; after 1990, there were more innovations leading to greater removal efficiencies.[104] There are a number of such wrinkles that render analytical links between instrument choice and innovation difficult to come by. There is a long and comprehensive review of empirical work on instrument choice and innovation by Popp, Richard Newell, and Adam Jaffe.[105] Of the *empirical* papers that bear most directly on the question of which instruments induce innovation (the theoretical papers have too many conflicting and unverifiable assumptions to tell us much), one could probably guardedly say that pollution abatement costs and expenditures, a common measure of industry compliance costs, may increase spending but does not necessarily drive innovation.[106] This would seem to add weight to the argument that the high compliance costs of command-and-control regulation do not necessarily encourage innovation.

Although the weight of the evidence suggests that carbon taxes and cap-and-trade would be better than command-and-control at encouraging innovation to reduce emissions, the two are not equal in their ability to induce innovation. In general, a carbon tax will encourage innovation in ways that a cap-and-trade program does not. There are at least three reasons for this.

First, a carbon tax introduces a steadier price signal that would generally not be present in a cap-and-trade program. Tax levels and cap levels can both change, but both can be too lenient or too stringent. But all other things being equal, a cap-and-trade program presents one extra source of price volatility: the fact that it is regulating a quantity, and not a price.

Innovation in new alternative technologies will generally require as stable a price as possible on carbon dioxide emissions. At least for risk-*averse* firms thinking of investing in innovations in, say, renewable energy, they will only do so if the payback, or recoupment of the investment from savings from not paying for carbon dioxide emissions (through either carbon taxes or for emission allowances), is sufficiently quick and secure. All other things being equal, the shorter the payback period and the more certain the payback, the more attractive is the investment. Risk-*loving* investors may be willing to invest when the paybacks are volatile, but in general, investment dollars are more abundant for projects that yield a steadier stream of benefits.

Cap-and-trade programs, whatever their merits, have not actually been particularly good at providing a steady stream of savings. Prices for allowances have been volatile. Even the successful sulfur dioxide trading program saw some significant price fluctuations, dropping from a high of $326 in 1992[107] to a low of $65 per ton in 1994.[108] Prices have stabilized since then. It is not as if firms don't invent ways of coping with such volatility. But all other things being equal, riskier investments demand a higher rate of return than safer, steadier ones, and price volatility is one particularly irritating source of investment risk. A fluctuating price of a carbon allowance means that the raison d'être of most carbon-saving investments—the ability to generate energy or manufacture goods at lower levels of carbon emissions—takes on fluctuating levels of importance, and the period at which one can say the investment has "paid for itself" becomes less certain, and perhaps longer.

It is true that a risk-averse *emitter* may find the volatility of cap-and-trade prices discomforting, and may take extra measures to avoid it, including innovating. However, with price volatility in cap-and-trade programs, risk-averse emitters may hedge by purchasing more allowances, which is much easier than innovating. With cap-and-trade programs, "smoothing" strategies such as buying extra allowances and banking them for future use may displace innovation strategies. Price volatility of cap-and-trade is thus generally *not* the friend of innovation.

Europe's EUETS provides a case in point. The EUETS has had much more troubling fluctuations than that of the US sulfur dioxide trading program. In the first year following the opening of the EUETS in 2005, carbon allowance prices fluctuated from as few as 5 Euros to more than 30 Euros, with one drop of 20 Euros occurring over the course of just a few days.[109] While some of the programmatic glitches have been worked out and the carbon price environment has subsequently settled down somewhat, the EUETS still provides a somewhat uncertain price environment for encouraging long-term investment in carbon-saving projects. Similarly, prices for auctioned allowances under RGGI dropped by 30 percent in one three-month period between auctions, from June to September of 2009.[110]

In fact, price volatility may be a particularly thorny problem for cap-and-trade programs for carbon dioxide. One thing that is known about carbon dioxide emissions is that it tracks economic activity quite closely. The worldwide economic slump of 2008 and 2009 has resulted in significantly fewer emissions than would otherwise have been the case. US emissions for 2009 fell 7 percent from 2008.[111] What would have happened to a carbon allowance price after a 7 percent drop in emissions in one year? It is hard to know, without an actual market, without knowing what happens with emissions in other countries, and without any measured price elasticity of global carbon allowances. Emissions from sources covered by the EUETS have fallen 11 percent in 2009, putting them *below* the caps.[112] Allowances may be banked, so these will obviously be carried forward to future years, keeping prices nominally above zero. The ability to bank allowances would surely smooth out price fluctuations, but how much is an open question. This does not happen under a carbon tax regime.

A second reason that a carbon tax stimulates more innovation than a cap-and-trade program is that, over time, innovation will reduce the price of allowances, and if innovation is successful enough it will cheapen the price of allowances so that innovation will no longer be worthwhile. Firms innovate to reduce compliance costs, and they will not do so if the marginal compliance cost savings are too small to pay for the innovation. Since innovation will reduce the cost of emissions allowances, there comes a point eventually at which the marginal compliance cost savings—the cost of allowances—are outweighed by costs of innovation. For carbon taxes, the marginal compliance costs savings does not change unless the tax rate changes. In this way, a steady tax rate produces a steadier price signal than a cap-and-trade program. Of course, both cap-and-trade programs and carbon tax programs contemplate increasing stringency over time. The 2009 Waxman-Markey bill specified a declining cap on emissions. Carbon tax programs would contemplate an increasing price over time, to adjust for inflation and to track marginal damages from carbon dioxide emissions, which are expected to increase over time. While both programs contemplate a price that increases with time, only cap-and-trade programs have to *fight* the price-deflating effects of innovation.

There is a third and final reason, related to the second, that a carbon tax stimulates more innovation than a cap-and-trade program, which is only true if a cap-and-trade program gives away allowances instead of auctioning them. In a cap-and-trade program in which some entities are given allowances—either on the basis of historical emissions, or simply as a product of political horse-trading, as was the case under the Waxman-Markey bill—the incentives to innovate will be diluted because innovation reduces the value of those allowances. The free allocation of allowances creates an asset in the hands of emitters, something that does not happen under a tax regime. The fact that innovation could reduce the value of that asset is a disincentive for cost-saving innovation.[113] It could still be, of course, that few innovations are truly great enough to significantly change the market for compliance. In such cases, the private benefits of innovation—from either technological invention or process changes—are probably still great enough to outweigh whatever diluting effects the innovation might have on the value of allowances. However, some technological innovations could be so monumental that the way that an industry thinks about compliance could fundamentally change, such that allowance prices could plummet. Imagine a breakthrough for carbon emissions: for example, a technological breakthrough in battery technology that could dramatically increase energy storage capabilities, making all kinds of renewable technologies feasible, since location and intermittency would no longer pose logistical obstacles to adoption. It seems safe to say that the coal-fired utilities, which received 35 percent of the initial allocation of allowances (worth about $100 billion) under Waxman-Markey, may not be quite as engaged in the development of such technology as it would be if, under a carbon tax regime, it truly had to pay for every ton of CO_2 it emitted.

Earlier in this chapter, I argued vigorously against government subsidization as a greenhouse gas policy. The stimulation of research and development offers a counterpoint to the case against government subsidies to reduce greenhouse gases. There are two reasons for this, though in my view, neither reason is sufficient to warrant very large governmental investments.

First, there is the general argument in favor of funding research and development: that knowledge is a public good, derived from research and development, and providing the foundation for further research and development. Because knowledge from R&D begets more knowledge, and because there is no reward for this "knock-off" effect of generating knowledge, it widely accepted that R&D is a public good and is therefore undersupplied (doubly so in the case of low-carbon technologies, because of the lack of a carbon price). This is an argument for funding research and development generally, however, not just for renewable energy technologies.

Second, some economists have put forward a theoretical argument for subsidizing certain energy sectors, in particular the renewable energy sector. In fact, a number of recent papers seem to have converged on the following conclusion: a carbon tax with a small amount of highly targeted research and development subsidization represents the optimal mix of policy instruments.[114] The reason for the inclusion of a subsidy component is that at least in the energy sector, fossil fuel-based electricity generators already have a huge head start on renewable electricity generators. In 2009, coal-fired power plants accounted for almost half of electricity generated in the United States, and coal and natural gas together accounted for 68 percent. Renewable energy sources other than hydroelectricity (dams) accounted for less than 4 percent.[115] Since industries typically have a baseline level of innovation and "learning by doing," the amount of baseline innovation in the coal-fired power industry swamps the amount of baseline innovation in renewable industries. Even with a carbon tax or a cap-and-trade program, the amount of research and development in the fossil fuel industries is likely to be much greater than in the renewable industries for a long time. Some economists thus suggest that some "catch-up" research and development subsidization is desirable to have fossil fuel-based and renewable energies at similar levels of market share, and therefore research and development funding. Notice that this argument is independent of the well-known argument that lack of a carbon price doubly punishes renewable energy R&D; it has to do with the *existing* small market share of renewable energy vis-à-vis fossil fuel combustion. Hence, the optimal combination would include both a carbon tax *and* the R&D subsidies.

The trouble with this argument, as discussed above, is that it is unrealistic to expect government to identify worthy targets of research and development funding. Government-sponsored research and development on energy technology have not only failed to reduce greenhouse gas emissions, but have not even produced gains in carbon intensity.[116] In fairness, the goal of energy R&D is more often that of combustion efficiency, but given the interrelatedness of efficiency and emissions, it is surprising that government spending in the energy sector has had so little impact on emissions.

Direct, per-unit production subsidies might be less futile, since at least the taxpayer gets some electricity out of the deal. It is true while the selection of what qualifies as a "renewable energy" is effectively picking winners, but since these technologies already produce energy, there is a *better* chance that at least the subsidy is not selecting an abject loser. The United States has long provided production tax credits for electricity generated from renewable energy sources. The tax credit is awarded as a subsidy per unit of electricity generated—1.5 cents per kilowatt-hour, adjusted for inflation[117] — so it truly works like the mirror image of a Pigouvian tax. This kind of a subsidy *could* play the role of providing some catch-up funding. However, Congressional re-authorizations of the tax credit have sometimes been fraught with uncertainty. The 2009 reauthorization was only accomplished after the previous one had already expired, and is only guaranteed through 2014.[118]

A better approach, if the objective is to provide stability of payback, is to award long-term contracts for electricity generated. The Ontario Power Authority, a key governmental power buyer and provider for Canada's most populous province, has recently begun awarding twenty-year contracts for renewable energy. The OPA has set a schedule of *feed-in-tariffs*, guaranteed premium prices for electricity generated by renewable energy sources[119]:

Solar PV	80.2¢/kWh
Windpower	13.5¢
Waterpower	13.1¢
Biomass	13.8¢
Biogas	16.0¢
Landfill gas	11.1¢

That said, it is not as if these premium prices are market prices; only those awarded a contract will receive these kinds of rates. There is still the uncertainty of whether a renewable energy provider will be awarded such a contract. Second, for those lucky enough to be awarded a contract, these prices represent *huge* premiums over the typical market price of about three and a half cents (Canadian) per kilowatt-hour. Seventy-six of the 184 contracts awarded in April of 2010 involved solar photovoltaic generation, the largest subsidy. Moreover, the discrimination between renewable energies that privilege solar photovoltaic cuts against the efficiency benefits. To return to a theme from earlier in this chapter, why subsidize solar photovoltaic—to the tune of twenty-three times the current market price—and not solar thermal?

What is the solution? Catch-up or not catch-up? Some in the intellectual property field have toyed with the idea of administrative "prizes" as an alternative to the patent and copyright systems of rewarding successful research and development. In the context of innovation to reduce greenhouse gases, however, the prize concept begs

the question of how an agency will define a prizeworthy outcome before it sees it. In effect, the prize concept solves nothing in terms of
finding the best renewable energy technologies, or more generally the
best ways of reducing greenhouse gases. The prize concept, if it can be
operationalized, comes the closest to the economists' ideal of funding
the "right" research and development, but does not truly help in defining what "right" means.

Another alternative would be to have a "super"-carbon tax, one
higher than what would be considered the optimal Pigouvian amount,
in effect granting super-premiums to those finding ways to reduce
greenhouse gases. A greater-than-optimal carbon tax may be just as
bad as a too-low carbon tax, but the idea that research and development is chronically underfunded in the nonfossil fuel sectors may justify in part the wastefulness of having a carbon tax that is too high.
Making an excessive carbon tax temporary—at least long enough for
research in nonfossil fuel sectors to catch up—may alleviate some of
these concerns.

It has been said many times that development of greenhouse gas reduction technologies is a "marathon, not a sprint," and that a stable and
sufficient price differential over a long period of time is required to provide the business certainty needed to attract investment.[120] This must
be true in good economic times and bad, and the volatility brought on
by the recent recession seems to suggest that cap-and-trade programs
could be difficult to manage through economic volatility. Both carbon
taxes and cap-and-trade programs can be designed to create a stable
price, but the design challenges are greater if one is setting out to implement a cap-and-trade program. And a subsidy program can obviously
be designed to provide a stable price, but at the cost of potentially having an inefficiently large amount of activity in the subsidized area. Finally, it is worth bearing in mind that cap-and-trade programs have
some inherent limitations in encouraging innovation. If allowance
prices dip, as they have precipitously in the EUETS, innovation would
have no value for some industries. In the end, there is no perfect solution to this innovation problem, but the carbon tax provides the best
base from which to experiment with ways to reward research and development to reduce greenhouse gas emissions.

Six: Incentives for Innovation—Price Breadth

My employer, the University of British Columbia, or "UBC," one of the largest universities in Canada with about 40,000 students, is a relatively small greenhouse gas emitter. It reports that its energy-related emissions totaled 72,600 tons of CO_2-eq in 2006.[121] UBC would not be one of the "large emitters" that would have been regulated under a twice-proposed Canadian federal emissions trading program. Despite the absence of a federal mandate, a variety of factors compelled UBC to seek to reduce its greenhouse gas emissions. First, as an educational institution, it has sought to gain the moral high ground in terms of its environmental impacts. As an institution with a wealth of faculty expertise on reducing environmental impacts, it would be embarrassing if it had been a laggard. Second, the province of British Columbia has mandated that all of its governmental operations, including its universities, become carbon-neutral by 2010. That is, it must somehow take in as much carbon dioxide as it emits. To the extent that UBC somehow fails to zero out its emissions, it must purchase offsets. Finally, there is the BC carbon tax. In terms of its energy emissions, the carbon tax places an added cost on every joule consumed to heat and power UBC's 500 some-odd buildings.

The carbon neutrality mandate and the carbon tax liability have lit a fire under the right people at UBC. Not only do greenhouse gas reductions on campus become more compelling, but the amortized cost of a carbon tax liability has made it attractive to finance some infrastructure changes. Taking a twenty-five-year time horizon, UBC has calculated a net present value of carbon tax and offset liability of about $50 million, to go along with a fuel cost of about $100 million.[122] With this kind of money to save, it becomes straightforward to undertake certain capital expenditures, like installing heat pumps—standard fare in Europe, unfortunately rare in North America—and ground source geoexchange energy systems. UBC also made lemonade from the unfortunate backlog of maintenance projects and sought provincial funding to renovate existing buildings to, besides modernizing and improve their functionality, improve their energy efficiency.

Significantly, this is not simply a feel-good story about a relatively wealthy academic community being willing absorb some nominal costs. UBC is a small emitter that would have flown under the radar of most cap-and-trade programs, including the twice-failed Canadian federal proposals. UBC is a fairly large business, with its own electricity generation capabilities, but with a carbon footprint that looks small when compared with the large emitters in Canada, which are dominated by heavy smelting, refining, and materials-processing facilities. And while these large emitters account for more than half of Canada's carbon dioxide emissions, it seems myopic to completely ignore the fairly large remainder. There are many small- and medium-sized emitters such as UBC that would have been excluded from proposed cap-and-trade programs that could not only find ways to reduce their own emissions, but may even contribute in finding a way for large emitters to reduce their emissions.

And yet, the Canadian and American approaches have been to focus cap-and-trade programs on large emitters. There is nothing to say that cap-and-trade programs could *not*, as has been suggested,[123] apply upstream—at the point of extraction, import, or processing—so that a comprehensive price signal could be obtained. A price, or a cap, applied upstream would create prices at the upstream end of the distribution chain, which would trickle down to end users. That is not how cap-and-trade programs seem to have developed. Canada's current federal greenhouse gas reporting requirement does not even apply to UBC, as UBC's emissions are too low to warrant inclusion, in the judgment of Environment Canada. The EUETS applies to only 11,500 facilities in Europe. In the 2009 Waxman-Markey bill the threshold below which facilities have no responsibility to hold allowances to emit carbon dioxide was 25,000 tons per year of CO_2-eq. A study commissioned by the Nicholas Institute at Duke University reports that at such a threshold level, only 1.3 percent of all manufacturing facilities would be covered.[124] Granted, these 1.3 percent of all facilities account for more than 80 percent of the greenhouse gases emitted by the manufacturing sector. But the problem, in terms of inducing innovation, is completely exempting the more than 345,000 facilities from command-and-control regulation under the Clean Air Act or cap-and-trade regulation. What is to say that there is nothing that can be learned from these 345,000 facilities?

UBC, for example, despite not being a "large emitter," is experimenting with campus planning to try and reduce greenhouse gases. Densification and transportation mode planning, not traditionally part of the university planning missions, have become part of construction and campus planning at UBC, with potentially useful lessons for universities elsewhere. Building on small lessons, UBC has launched the Centre for Interactive Research on Sustainability, a campus building that will house research groups that will develop green building strategies, using the modular building itself as a laboratory. The building will include a ground-source geoexchange unit in the hopes that this energy can be shared with nearby buildings. And faced with a near-crisis in housing affordability for its staff, faculty, and students, UBC is undertaking a large amount of on-campus housing construction, with the hopefully serendipitous result of reducing emissions from commuting. Obviously, these greenhouse gas-reducing developments overlap greatly with UBC's academic mission. But these developments might have been harder to sell to a Board of Governours that is charged with maintaining fiscal soundness if the economic environment in British Columbia did not price greenhouse gas emissions as it does.

More than 3,000 miles away from the UBC campus, James Peret of Boylston, Massachusetts, appears to be making his own humble contribution. Peret was once interested in building his own "greasecar" that could operate on used cooking oil. This technology is not novel. The general principles of converting cooking oil into automotive fuel are simple and have been applied to a number of commercially available home biodiesel fuel kits. Some home biodiesel fuel kits have the unfortunate property of producing home explosion accidents, but despite the hazards, a number of firms sell them, primarily over the web. Faced with an already saturated market (no pun intended), Peret realized that cooking oil could be used to generate energy much closer to its generation source: restaurants. Peret's "Vegawatt" accepts used cooking grease—which restaurants in Massachusetts routinely pay more than $100 per month to haul away—and converts the grease into electricity which can be used to help power the restaurant. The Vegawatt avoids the chemical conversion of cooking oil that has injured and killed several home biodiesel kit owners, and is instead simply a generator that uses cooking oil, with food bits filtered out. With some electrical panel wiring to allow the restaurant's electrical system to accept an alternative source of power, the Vegawatt can supplement the electricity that the restaurant receives from the grid. As a bonus, the Vegawatt can be used as a back-up generator, something that restaurants that store perishable goods always find useful. Peret estimates that the Vegawatt can save $800 to $1200 per month in electricity bills.

Is it a coincidence that electricity rates in Peret's home state of Massachusetts—14 cents per kilowatt-hour as opposed to a 2009 national average of about 9.5 cents—are some of the highest electricity rates in the United States?[125] It may be, and James Peret could have lived anywhere. But the economic advantages of buying a Vegawatt, which is trumpeted by Peret's company website, would sound less dramatic in a state with lower energy costs, like Washington, which enjoys electricity rates of about 6 cents per kilowatt-hour. It is also worth noticing, for the sake of keeping a carbon tax in perspective, that the difference of four and a half cents between Massachusetts and the United States would not be so far off from what a carbon tax of $45 per ton of CO_2 would cost.[126]

How many James Perets and UBC's are out there? How many colleges and universities other than UBC—ones with even smaller emissions—might, if it faced the economic incentives, be compelled to develop ways to reduce their greenhouse gas emissions? One might consult the American College and University Presidents Climate Commitment, a network of (at the time of writing of this book) 629 colleges and universities in the United States that have filed reports and committed to undertake greenhouse gas emissions reductions.[127] Some of these colleges and universities might have something to learn from the UBC experience. At least one university has found use for James Peret's Vegawatt. American University in Washington, D.C., with a carbon footprint of about 58,000 tons of CO_2,[128] announced its carbon-neutrality plan, which set as its goal campus carbon-neutrality by the year 2020. One of the components of the plan was the employment of James Peret's Vegawatt in its dining halls to reduce electricity usage.[129]

From a government policy point of view, is there a way to incentivize these little inventions that potentially have a huge impact? The ACUPCC is a positive step, but a bottom-line incentive might move even more colleges and university into action, perhaps even beyond the 629 that have signed on to the ACUPCC. These colleges and universities will have to learn from others, but also develop more ways of reducing emissions in addition to purchasing (and perhaps even refining) Vegawatts.

Innovation will not only require a stable and sufficient price signal, but also a comprehensive price signal that ripples throughout an economy, in order to take advantage of as many greenhouse gas reduction opportunities as possible. Earlier in this chapter, I argued that a comprehensive price signal is required to avoid distortions that produce leakage of greenhouse gas emissions and divert resources away from the most efficient ways of reducing emissions. This is a different reason to have a comprehensive price signal, and a different justification for a carbon tax over cap-and-trade.

To further build on a theme developed in this chapter, greenhouse gas reduction opportunities are diverse, disparate, and beyond the comprehension of any single agency, group of agencies, or even any network of governmental entities. We drive, we buy houses with the idea that we will drive for every trip taken out of the house, and we build buildings and communities in which wasteful amounts of driving are built into our lifestyle, our infrastructure, and our economy. We turn up thermostats, we build inefficient homes and buildings, fail to weatherize and insulate our existing homes and buildings, and consume energy in ways that would be stunningly simple to avoid. But because energy savings in individual instances are small, it does not seem worth it on the individual level to undertake the costly and sometimes time-consuming measures to reduce emissions and increase efficiency. As summarized in the McKinsey energy efficiency report that found $680 billion of energy savings in the American economy:

> Efficiency potential is highly fragmented, spread across more than 100 million locations and billions of devices used in residential, commercial and industrial settings. This dispersion ensures that efficiency is the highest priority for virtually no one.[130]

In addition, we buy imported toys and other goods and we buy imported produce so that we can enjoy all kinds of foods in all seasons. We use too much carbon-intensive cement, and burn too much coal for electricity and consume too much electricity. Each of these activities imposes a carbon dioxide emissions externality. There are undoubtedly many solutions for each of these externality-imposing activities, as well as the millions of other such activities and products. The problem with the way that some pundits view "innovation" is that it is too often thought of as highly technological, research-intensive, and expensive inventions carried out in the laboratories of universities. This latter kind of innovation for grand changes could be important, but climate policy has neglected the simpler and potentially more widely applicable innovative changes that can be made.

Integrated assessment models lend theoretical support to this conclusion. Those models that include *endogenous* technological innovation—as opposed to simplistic models that merely assume a fixed rate of exogenous technological innovation—show that with greenhouse gas emissions coming from many sectors of the economy, the breadth of a price signal matters much more than improving any specific technology.[131] Thus, the maintenance of a price signal that is as wide as possible is much more likely to reduce emissions and at the lowest cost than putting massive bets of government spending behind a putative "game-changing" technology. For that reason, government subsidies, as argued above, have the shortcoming of backing only a few horses, and too often the wrong horses, instead of opening up the entire horse race.

There are presently an almost uncountable number of ideas to reduce energy consumption and therefore greenhouse gas emissions. Areas in which greenhouse gas reductions can be achieved at little or even *negative* cost include: residential electronics, residential appliances, HVAC retrofits, insulation retrofits, and switching from incandescent light bulbs to energy-efficient fluorescent bulbs or even light-emitting diodes.[132] A host of other low-cost (but probably not no-cost) ideas are also effective in reducing consumption and are ridiculously simple, like installing programmable thermostats, updating home insulation and weatherization. On the front end, a number of new building construction practices have bubbled up from the concept stage into development, and, where there are incentives, into the construction business. These include a renewed emphasis on natural light and heating, green walls and roofs, passive radiant heating, and ingenious ways of combining water and space heating. It has become commonplace in some jurisdictions for new construction of residential homes to include a high-efficiency furnace to heat water that serves the dual purpose of supplying hot water as well as providing radiant floor heating.

The urgency of climate change has caused a groundswell of ideas to bubble up into public discourse. But more than government support, price signals are needed to sustain their development. These types of measures are essentially market mechanisms, and need healthy markets with carbon prices. At the same time, market forces are needed to filter out losers. Some ideas have risen and fallen somewhat out of favor, such as some corn-based biofuels, hydrogen fuel cell technology, and reforestation as a carbon sequestration technique. Some, such as nuclear power, have enjoyed a resurgence.

It is beyond the capability of any governmental entity, even one aimed at compiling information, to identify all of the opportunities to innovate to reduce greenhouse gases, to evaluate their merits, and to tap into them. The ubiquitous nature of fossil fuel combustion means that the opportunities to reduce greenhouse gas emissions are ubiquitous. Moreover, most *everyone* in the developed world does things and uses things that emit greenhouse gases. A carbon tax maximizes the breadth of the potential to innovate in reducing emissions, tapping into the creativity of almost everyone, by offering a monetary incentive in the form of lower costs.

I argued above that a consistent carbon price across the entire economy is necessary to ensure a fair contest among all of these potential solutions. This separate argument emphasizes the need to ensure a contest among *many* alternatives, and reaching *many* activities. A fundamental market tenet is that the larger the number of market participants, the more robust the market. Along the same lines, a thorough search for the most effective and efficient ways to reduce greenhouse gas emissions will require the ferreting out of ideas from all quarters. As I noted earlier, if a cap-and-trade program is applied *upstream*—at the point of extraction, processing, or import—then the resulting price is as broad as it is for a carbon tax, and many of the advantages of a carbon tax over cap-and-trade fall away. This set of arguments presented here fall into that category. This set of arguments, however, still apply to the cap-and-trade programs that seem most likely to emerge: those that are less comprehensive than a carbon tax. A carbon tax, which gets at the fundamental problem of fossil fuel combustion across all sectors and activities, creates the kind of broad-based incentives that no other instrument does.

Seven: Administrability

A carbon tax has a number of administrability and program design advantages over alternatives, most clearly over command-and-control programs. The administrative demands of command-and-control regulation are well known. Issuing a "command," however flexible, still requires the identification of the regulated entities, some administrative determination of how those entities ought to best reduce pollution, and perhaps most vexing of all, what compliance means. In the United States, all of these decisions and more have proven infinitely reviewable by courts. Perhaps most damning of all is the scheme for regulating NO_x from coal-fired power plants, as reviewed earlier. Recall the complicated set of different NO_x standards for each of six types of coal-fired power plants. Now that EPA has set a standard for six of the main types of coal-fired power plants, what about other sources? With NO_x a necessary byproduct of combustion, how realistic is it to expect EPA to issue a different NO_x standard for every single source of emissions? For every emissions problem, EPA would draw up a huge matrix of all types of emitting facilities along one axis, and all the different pollutants along the other axis, and would have to fill in all the boxes with a performance standard.

One way to try and reduce this burden is to key standards to industry practices and standards. The US Clean Air Act provides that when a new stationary source of air pollution (defined in the statute as certain "criteria air pollutants") is constructed or significantly modified, the facility must achieve the "lowest achievable emission rate" if it is located in a heavily polluted zone,[133] and the "best available control technology" if it is located in a less-polluted zone.[134] Existing stationary pollution sources must install "reasonably available control technology" if they are located in a heavily polluted zone, but need do nothing if they are in a less polluted zone.[135] In terms of stringency, "lowest achievable emissions rate" is the most stringent, and "reasonably available control technology" is the least stringent, with "best available control technology" somewhere in between. Environmental lawyers, however, have found considerable ambiguity and fodder for litigation when working with terms such as "reasonably available control technology," and "best available control technology."

There was a time that command-and-control regulation made a great deal of sense. In the earliest days of environmental law, the reality that a regulatory body could not *monitor* the pollution emitted by a facility meant that it was at an informational disadvantage vis-à-vis the polluting facility. Under those circumstances, there was little that EPA or state permitting agencies could do except make sure that a particular piece of pollution control equipment was installed. This has changed with the development of continuous emissions monitors for sulfur dioxide, which automatically monitor and measure an emissions stream for sulfur dioxide content, and automatically transmit that information to a data collection center. Moreover, with the advent of continuous emissions monitors, the Clean Air Act could require (and did) that emitters not only install continuous emissions monitors[136] but also take responsibility for its accuracy.[137] If for any period of time there is a problem with the data transmitted by the continuous emissions monitors, and the emitter cannot provide adequate substitute information, the EPA is entitled to presume that any pollution control equipment was completely offline for that period of time.[138] The effect of continuous emissions monitors was to enable the EPA to not only have a means of monitoring behavior by polluters, but even shift the burden of reporting to polluters. This ability for a regulatory body to ascertain the *quantity* of pollution emitted provides a powerful alternative means of regulation. Much less frequently now is it required for EPA or state regulators to send field representatives onsite to polluting facilities to check up on pollution control operations, a task that has always proved expensive and labor-intensive for understaffed agencies. Information about the presence of installed pollution control equipment now seems clunky and much less relevant, if the actual amount of pollution can now be ascertained technologically.

A carbon tax has some more subtle advantages over its cousin cap-and-trade program. While both draw on the advantage of working within a global fossil fuel regulatory system that is capable of determining carbon content and tracking the movement of fossil fuels all over the world, cap-and-trade programs will require the development of more regulatory infrastructure. In all developed countries and in many developing countries, a number of federal and subnational taxes are already levied at the gasoline pump, and incorporated into the price that is prominently posted at gas stations. A carbon tax can and has been added into prices as just another tax on gasoline. Enforcement thus draws from existing tax collection procedures and institutional arrangements. So, whereas the collection of taxes on fossil fuels is simple even in developing countries, the establishment and administration of a cap-and-trade system is not. In an era of widespread online thievery, even advanced countries apparently have to undertake significant measures to guard against the theft of allowances, as the EUETS has learned.[139] Even in developing countries, there exists the administrative infrastructure to collect taxes on fossil fuels, but not to administer a system of trading allowances.

In the United States, which has already enjoyed, at least by Washington standards, a fairly smooth set-up and execution of the sulfur dioxide cap-and-trade program, the costs of setting up a greenhouse gas cap-and-trade program would be manageable, but nontrivial. A Congressional Budget Office report estimated that a 2007 cap-and-trade bill that passed the Senate Committee on Environment and Public Works would cost about $1.7 billion from 2009 to 2013 to implement, including the cost of hiring up to 400 new employees.[140] But this is for a wealthy country with an agency with ready experience in conducting cap-and-trade programs. Not only would some countries find 1 billion-dollar-plus price tag less palatable, but it could be considerably more complicated for others. When the smoke had cleared from the sulfur dioxide cap-and-trade program, the consensus was that it represented a vast improvement over the command-and-control predecessors. But the comparison with a carbon tax is less favorable.

If one considers the difficulty of passing legislation as part of the administrability challenge, then carbon taxes outperform cap-and-trade on this score as well. Establishing a carbon tax requires fewer delicate decisions than does setting up a cap-and-trade program. Setting up cap-and-trade programs requires, among other decisions, a decision as to which sources will be covered by a cap and deciding how to allocate emissions allowances have been fraught with contention. During the 2009 greenhouse gas regulation debate in the US Congress, mention was often made of the possibility of taking a more modest step, and only addressing emissions from the electricity generation industry, so-called energy-only bills.[141] The electricity generation industry, of course, appropriately took exception to the idea. But the conversation itself is troubling, pointing to the potential for mischief. Of even greater potential for political shenanigans is the question of how to allocate emissions allowances under a cap-and-trade program. As noted above, the 2009 Waxman-Markey bill, doling out allowances with an estimated net present value of $378 billion, was arrived at only after a brutal lobbying battle to secure as many allowances as possible for favored donors and constituents.[142] If, as has been the case thus far, the auctioning of cap-and-trade allowances is considered politically inferior to awarding allowances for free, then there will inevitably be a unsightly legislative process to establish the cap-and-trade program.

A carbon tax only requires the setting of tax levels and a phase-in schedule. This is not to say that there would not be brutal battles to win tax concessions in a carbon tax regime. But at least the core rule— a carbon tax based on carbon content—can form the base policy while the concessions are hammered out, and hopefully decoupled from the price incentives posed by a carbon tax.

The greatest administrability challenge for cap-and-trade programs comes when they allow for "offsets." Awarding a credit for a project that purports to *avoid* emissions increases rather than actually reducing them is a tricky proposition. Offsets have been a popular feature for cap-and-trade programs, because they provide a price release valve for emitters should allowances become too expensive. Moreover, economic theory would support the inclusion of offsets in a cap-and-trade program: emissions reductions should be accomplished at the lowest possible cost, so if offsets can effectively reduce *net* emissions, there is no economic reason to prefer them to actual emissions reductions.

Offsets also have the advantage of enjoying popularity in developing countries. Economic growth will necessarily entail the expansion of energy, so it would seem sensible to promote the construction of low-carbon energy sources by the use of offsets. This is particularly true in developing countries, in which there is no greenhouse gas regulation, and incentives need to be in place to encourage non-fossil fuel sources. Offsets thus become financing mechanisms, whereby developed countries can pay developing countries to build, say, wind farms instead of coal-fired power plants.

But as one might guess, the stories that are told *ex ante* in support of offsets differ greatly from the stories that emerge after implementation of the program. Offsets now appear to be deeply and inherently problematic, and very possibly not worth the trouble. In a now-famous indictment of the Kyoto Protocol's "Clean Development Mechanism" program, Michael Wara analyzes the meteoric rise of CDM projects in China, and the enormous amount of credits that were generated for the construction of facilities producing HCFC-22 (chlorodifluoromethane), a common refrigerant. A common byproduct of the production process is HFC-23 (trifluoromethane), a powerful greenhouse gas that traps heat 11,700 times more effectively than the equivalent amount of CO_2. In developed countries, the

greenhouse gas byproduct is routinely captured, but in those developing countries that produce HCFC-22, the greenhouse gas byproduct
is released into the atmosphere. A common CDM project has been the
construction in China of HCFC-22 plants, but ones built so that
greenhouse gas byproduct is captured instead of released. For puta-
tively avoiding the emissions of a small amount of HFC-23, the plant
developer receives a tremendous amount of CDM credits, since under
the CDM program, the credits are multiplied by HFC-23's global
warming factor of 11,700. Nineteen approved HCFC-22 CDM projects in China generate an estimated 81 million credits per year. In fact,
these CDM credits *far exceed* the value of the underlying product, the
refrigerant HCFC-22[143]; in light of the sudden increase of nineteen
HCFC-22 plants in China, the inference obvious to everyone is that
the HCFC plants would not have been built but for the CDM program. The only reason that that these HCFC plants were built was to
generate carbon credits. Every year, the "cap" is 81 million tons higher
than it should be.

   Therein lies the problem with the whole offset concept. An entrepreneur wishing to claim credit for reducing greenhouse gas emissions
will argue that a particular project has either avoided emissions that
would have occurred or captured emissions that would have been released but for the offset program. Because there is never an obvious
baseline counterfactual—a "business as usual" course of events that
would have occurred without the project—it is impossible to know
whether the proposed project would actually reduce emissions or
whether it is simply snake oil.

   An inherent information asymmetry exists when an entrepreneur
presents an offset scheme to reduce emissions to a regulatory body.
The CDM Board, the body charged with adjudicating the award of
CDM credits, has a general expertise in greenhouse gas emissions, and
the range of activities that generate, sequester, capture, or avoid greenhouse gas emissions. But CDM developers presenting a proposal
clearly know much more about their particular subject area, since the
proposal itself requires the preparation of a great amount of material.
Although the HCFC episode almost seems comedic in retrospect,
how indeed, do we expect an adjudicatory body of generalists to refute
the economic and technological assertions of an HCFC-22 developer?
The technology and economics of HCFC-22 and HFC-23 are not
straightforward, and attempts have been made by Kyoto institutions
to understand them.[144] Some reforms have been suggested for the

CDM process, but in light of the difficulty of solving the information asymmetry problem and the difficulty of ascertaining the baseline counterfactual, the best option is to seek an alternative institutional arrangement for financing such projects.[145] The incentives created by this institutional structure inevitably invite ingeniously misleading arguments for a particular baseline and how a proposed project creates a downward deviation from that baseline. In these situations, the environment always loses.

Libertarians pout when they lament how easy it is for governments, even those in developing countries, to collect taxes. The ability of government to disgorge money from its citizenry should not be taken lightly. But in a situation where there is consensus about the need to price greenhouse gas emissions, the simplest way to impose that price warrants serious consideration. If we are also concerned with minimizing the governmental involvement with (and therefore taxpayer cost of) pricing greenhouse gas emissions, it would behoove us to tap into that which governments do best. Even libertarians would have to concede that it is better to have government in peoples' wallets rather than dictating to people and businesses how to conduct their business.

Eight: International Coordination

On the problem of climate change, just about everyone can agree on two things: (1) international coordination is absolutely essential to curbing greenhouse gases in the Earth's atmosphere; and (2) international coordination is extremely difficult to achieve. Greenhouse gas policy need not be uniform across all countries, but if there is no policy coordination among countries, no greenhouse gas mitigation policy will be effective. The difference in types of policy instruments is subtle but vitally important.

The overriding need to coordinate among countries stems from the nature of the greenhouse gas problem as a *public good*. Public goods are *nonexcludable* in provision and *nonrival* in consumption, meaning that the benefits of the public good unavoidably accrue to everyone (no one can be excluded), and that one person's enjoyment of the public good does not detract from another's person enjoying it also (non-rival). National defense is often cited as an example of a public good. The knowledge gained from research and development is often cited as a justification for government funding, and *basic* research usually does provide many public benefits.

But reducing greenhouse gases is a *perfect* example of a public good.[146] Before climate change came along, no one could have dreamed up even a hypothetical problem that so perfectly illustrates a public good. Reducing emissions is completely *nonexcludable* in that the reduction of emissions by one emitter or country unavoidably inures to the benefit of everyone in the world (in the form of avoided risk and damages from climate change); and "consumption" of the emissions reduction is, similarly, *nonrival* in that one person or country's avoidance of the risk of climate change detracts not one iota from another's freedom from that risk.

The public good nature of reducing greenhouse gases gives rise to the single most important characteristic of the climate change problem: the overwhelming incentive to *free-ride*. Free-riding may take the form of avoiding costly mitigation while allowing others to undertake it, and it may also take the form of avoiding the costs of research and development of new technologies that reduce greenhouse gas emissions. But the free-riding problem is crueler than it is in other environmental problems. The more that one country or group of countries does to reduce greenhouse gas emissions, the stronger will be the incentive for other countries to free-ride. This is because reducing emissions will almost certainly involve reducing fossil fuel consumption, which would reduce the global price of fossil fuels, which would in turn encourage the nonreducing countries to *increase* their use of fossil fuels. This is not only discouraging to the country or countries that reduce emissions, but to some extent it cancels out their emissions reductions, probably hard won at significant economic and political cost.

The implication of the free-riding problem is that action to reduce emissions may need to be nearly universal. As the Stern Review points out—and even Nordhaus agrees—no country or even large group of countries can solve the climate change problem alone. Coordinated action is absolutely necessary.[147] Since it takes time to rally the better part of 192 countries, some countries find themselves in the position of knowing that their participation in an agreement to mitigate greenhouse gas emissions is a necessary, but far from sufficient condition to the consummation of an effective international agreement to reduce emissions.

International coordination is largely thought to be the domain of international negotiators and institutions (though discouraging developments of late have cast some doubt on this), but some policy instruments are better than others in facilitating that coordination. Some instruments reduce the incentives to free-ride, while others exacerbate them. And secondarily, some instruments do a better job than others of redressing the pervasive domestic concerns with international industrial competitiveness that have fueled opposition worldwide to greenhouse gas policy.

Whatever its other disadvantages, government subsidies do less to encourage free-riding than do carbon taxes and cap-and-trade programs. Government subsidies, although generally inefficient in the context of climate change and potentially competitively harmful to meritorious technologies, nevertheless produce returns directly back to the country that spent it. The technological advantage and intellectual property derived from the research and development endeavor is often lasting enough to outweigh the public goods nature of knowledge. Even if some countries learn, say, from Denmark's large deployment of windmills in nearshore marine waters, or its development of municipal waste incineration facilities, it still enjoys a head-start on other countries. Even if there are positive international spillovers and imperfect capture of benefits from technological development, government subsidies at least do not seem to, as carbon pricing does, *promote* offshore free-riding. The increasingly global market in renewable energy technologies creates conditions that, at least better than the alternatives, simulate a race to the top, rather than a free-riding contest.

In fact, as economist and climate policy expert Scott Barrett has argued, in terms of promoting international coordination, joint government subsidization of research and development, along with international standards of performance or technology—command-and-control regulation—best solve the twin problems of international participation and enforcement. Barrett argues that research and development, under a joint funding arrangement, offers the best chance to lower costs of emissions reductions technologies enough that adoption becomes less costly, and international standards hold out the best hope of creating positive network externalities that would create incentive for countries to both participate and comply.[148] International joint funding arrangements do indeed seem less toxic for domestic politics. Moreover, subsidies that seem cost-ineffective from a domestic point of view begin to make more economic sense if countries cooperate, pool research resources, and share the output of such research. The United States is now working with Canada and China on carbon capture and storage research. What seems like a waste of money if the United States were going it alone may not be if the research costs and outputs are shared with two highly interested partners, both countries having huge coal reserves. However, there is no guarantee that what countries agree to develop together is the most productive way to proceed in terms of emissions reductions; what is wrong with subsidization from the purely domestic point of view is also likely to be problematic in the international arena. The fact that the joint effort pursued by the United States with China and Canada is CCS development would seem to be evidence of that. By contrast, one wonders, in light of the guarded manner in which China has promoted and protected its wind industries, whether China has determined that the real winner in terms of climate technology is wind energy. Small victories are possible with international joint funding agreements, but they are unlikely to carry much of a load in terms of emissions reductions, especially when countries jealously guard and protect their most coveted technologies.

As with other comparisons made in this chapter, the comparison between carbon taxes and cap-and-trade is the most interesting one. Perhaps because they seem so similar in approach, both seeking to impose a marginal price on emissions, one would expect there to be little difference between the two instruments. But as in other cases, when considering international coordination as a policy criterion, carbon taxes again come out slightly ahead of cap-and-trade.

At bottom, the international coordination problem stems from the free-riding problem, and the free-riding problem crops up whenever a price—be it explicit (in the case of a carbon tax), market-determined (in the case of cap-and-trade), or administrative (in the case of command-and-control)—is imposed on domestic parties but not foreign ones. Absent international coordination, it could not be any other way, since governments obviously do not have jurisdiction over foreign emitters.

In terms of international coordination, carbon taxes provide an advantage over cap-and-trade in three subtle ways. First, if a country legislates a cap-and-trade program expecting it to be incorporated into an international cap-and-trade program such as that contemplated by the Kyoto Protocol, it cannot realistically expect developing countries, most notably China and India, to join such an international cap-and-trade program. China and India have thus far signaled an utter refusal to consider quantitative limits on emissions. China and India are likely to be more open to a carbon tax that does not smack of a mandate externally imposed by wealthy countries. Moreover, for a carbon tax, governments get to keep the proceeds.

Second, along similar lines, cap-and-trade programs that have been implemented thus far have included offsets, which have the perverse incentive of discouraging international participation in greenhouse gas reduction. Since offsets provide a means for capital flow from developed countries to developing countries, joining an international accord would carry with it the added disadvantage (in addition to the costs) of giving up this source of foreign capital. Finally, under international trade law, a carbon tax will provide a stronger basis for levying import and export adjustments when a country that reduces carbon dioxide emissions trades with a country that doesn't. I expand on these reasons below.

First, cap-and-trade has simply not been an acceptable concept to developing countries. China, in particular, has been very specific about what it will not agree to. It has agreed to "voluntarily" reduce its greenhouse gas "intensity"—its greenhouse gas emissions per GDP—which will not reduce actual greenhouse gas emissions.[149] But at the time of writing of this book, China had steadfastly refused to accept a binding numerical limit on emissions, or any sort of "cap."[150] For those familiar with Chinese foreign relations, it should come as no surprise that China is reluctant to be part of an accord in which international negotiators come up with a worldwide cap on emissions and dole them out to the different countries. For one thing, any cap-and-trade allocation is likely to be anchored to some degree in historical emissions, even if subconsciously, which would heavily favor developed countries. Developing countries can and should argue that a time dimension should be introduced, and some per capita dimension should be introduced, so that developing countries have a chance to catch up, so to speak, to developed countries that have already emitted so much carbon dioxide (and for the benefit of relatively small populations). While this has an obvious deontological appeal, there is no indication at all that this would be an efficient path of emissions reduction. It is difficult, moreover, to imagine that the huge emissions reduction necessary in developed countries in order to create room for emissions growth in developing countries—on the order of 90 percent in short order—would be possible at any reasonable cost. It follows, parenthetically, that this has little chance of political acceptance among the developed countries. Also, cap-and-trade would have poor optics of having mostly Caucasian bureaucrats from Europe and North America decide how much China should get in terms of its "cap." This is likely to always be an irritant for countries like China and India, even it is left unspoken.

But if one reads between the lines of the steadfast opposition by China, India, and other developing countries, one sees room for a carbon tax. An international accord based on a carbon tax scheme would avoid the unfortunate appearance of China being allocated some cap amount by an external bureaucracy, and most important, would not represent, at least in their eyes, a binding limit to economic growth. Moreover, China and the developing countries that sign on get to keep the carbon tax proceeds. These proceeds could be redistributed in whatever way they deemed fit, even to industries that emit greenhouse gases.

Of course, distributions should be decoupled from consumption, in order to preserve the marginal emissions reduction incentives created by a carbon tax. There is no point in collecting a carbon tax only to have the proceeds given back to emitters in proportion to their payments—that would obviously negate any marginal incentives to reduce emissions. So would distributions be, in fact, decoupled from emissions? There is no reason to believe that, for example, a central government such as that in China would be particularly keen to simply rebate carbon tax proceeds. Carbon tax proceeds represent an opportunity for central governments to use however they wish—redistributing money to poor households, improving health care, or even subsidizing clean energy technologies. With Chinese leadership so concerned about wealth inequalities, it seems unlikely that carbon tax proceeds would be used to undo the marginal incentives to reduce emissions.

A carbon tax, if it could be scaled up to an international accord, represents a better chance of engaging China, India, and developing countries and providing their governments with the incentives to put in place and keep in place policies to reduce emissions. Cap-and-trade programs currently have little chance of accomplishing this on either of these objectives.

A second international coordination advantage of carbon taxes over cap-and-trade relates again to the problem of offsets. Steven Stoft has argued that the architects of the Kyoto Protocol and the Clean Development Mechanism have unwittingly created a system that provides China with a lucrative source of capital inflows, a disincentive to join any international accord involving caps, and a strong interest that developed countries enact tight caps with the possibility of offsets. If developed countries of the world join the European Union in enacting caps, and if they are tight caps that promise high allowance prices, *and* if they allow for the purchase of offsets abroad in lieu of an allowance, then what incentive is there for China, India or any other developing country to commit to anything? Excluding the developing countries from any substantive obligations but providing them with a mechanism for drawing capital inflows (through CDMs) places these countries in an excellent position from which they will not easily be budged. What's more, the tighter the caps in participating countries, the greater the economic pressure for CDM projects, the larger the capital inflows. One can hardly fault China, India, and other developing countries for refusing to participate in an international cap-and-trade scheme, given the current gravy train they enjoy.[151]

Finally, a third reason that carbon taxes will better encourage international coordination has to do with its subtle legal superiority in terms of justifying relief for domestic industries that might suffer a competitive disadvantage from domestic carbon pricing. International competition has remained a widespread and powerful political concern with greenhouse gas regulation. Addressing this concern has sometimes involved relief in the form of import or export adjustments, essentially rebating domestic industries that have to pay a carbon tax or are subjected to other costly greenhouse gas regulation. Even though this competitive disadvantage of paying a carbon tax is probably overblown, the possibility of relief goes a long way toward overcoming opposition to greenhouse gas regulation.[152] The problem is that this kind of relief may be inconsistent with international trade rules.

There is a way, however, to not unilaterally disarm, and a carbon tax offers the best chance to regulate domestically without doing so. If a country regulated greenhouse gas emissions and could, via *border tax adjustments*, equalize the international playing field, then greenhouse gas regulation would not necessarily put domestic industries at a competitive disadvantage. A border tax adjustment could take many forms, but most commonly would be the levy of an import tax on products imported from countries that did not regulate greenhouse gas emissions. So products made in countries that do *not* regulate greenhouse gas emissions would face a tax when they seek to export to countries that have domestic greenhouse gas regulations (with a border tax adjustment) in place, eliminating any cost disparities. Similarly, if a regulating country could subsidize the export of a product to a country that did not regulate greenhouse gases, then its exporters would be on the same footing as domestic manufacturers in that nonregulating country.

Without casting any normative judgments, the countries that clearly fit the roles of this drama are the United States and China. Equal access to the huge markets in the United States for all sorts of products is a big deal, and whether a border tax adjustment could be levied on products from prolific producers such as those in China is a question of enormous importance. In the United States, this has the potential to swing legislators around to supporting regulation of greenhouse gases. Also, rising consumption levels in China suggest that the ability of American exporters to send goods to Chinese markets could be of great importance as well. The stakes of the legality of border tax adjustments at least *appear* to be large.

The possibility that a border tax adjustment could legally be levied also has significance beyond just its effect of US-China relations. For better or for worse, the possibility that a border tax adjustment is GATT-legal introduces a potentially very important factor into domestic and international politics. All of a sudden, a new tool is available, and new combinations of policies are possible for any country considering greenhouse gas regulation and negotiating with other countries thinking about the same thing. Combinations of international coalitions to reduce emissions become possible if they know they have a way of protecting industries within the coalition countries.

Would border tax adjustments based on greenhouse gas regulation, say, in the United States be legal under international trade law?[153] Article II.2(a) of the General Agreement on Tariffs and Trade (GATT) provides that GATT's prohibitions on tariffs do not prevent a country "from imposing at any time on the importation of any product . . . a charge equivalent to an *internal tax* . . . in respect of the like domestic product or in respect of an article from which the imported product has been manufactured or produced in whole or in part."[154] Under Article II.2(a), internal taxes that can be recouped by the imposition of import taxes include "indirect" taxes such as sales taxes, excise taxes, or value-added taxes. "Direct" taxes such as corporate income taxes and social security taxes are generally not susceptible of border tax adjustment. In other words, there must be "some connection, even if indirect, between the respective taxes or other internal charges, on the one hand, and the taxed product, on the other."[155]

Would a carbon tax or the cost of an allowance be considered an "indirect" tax that is allowable under Article II.2(a)? It is currently unclear whether a country imposing a carbon tax could seek to equalize competitiveness burdens by imposing the same carbon tax on products imported from countries that do not impose a carbon tax, thereby protecting domestic industries from foreign competition that does not suffer a tax. The same question for cap-and-trade is also unresolved.

It *does* seem certain, however, that a country that imposes a carbon tax stands a *better* chance of being able to impose a border tax without running afoul of GATT than one that enacts a cap-and-trade program. Apart from the live question of whether a carbon tax falls within the Article II.2(a) definition, for a country adopting a cap-and-trade program to reduce greenhouse gas emissions, it must address the additional question of whether the price of an emissions allowance can be considered an "internal tax" that can be used as the basis of a border tax. The answer to this question is far from clear, and as neither carbon taxes nor cap-and-trade programs have thus far been embroiled in international trade litigation, so there is little guidance.

There is some modest guidance offered by existing international trade law. In *United States—Taxes on Petroleum and Certain Imported Substances*,[156] a GATT panel found that the imposition by the United

States of import taxes on certain petroleum and chemical products were "internal taxes" allowable under Article II.2(a). The taxes were levied to equalize the tax burden faced by domestic manufacturers that paid a chemical feedstock tax under the US "Superfund" law. While the feedstock tax was levied on chemicals that were used to produce the finished-product chemicals, the panel did not specify whether the import tax had to be levied on something physically embodied in the finished product, holding only that the tax "on the chemicals used as materials in the manufacture *or production* of the imported substance" was allowable (emphasis added).[157] The United States has also levied, without challenge, border tax adjustments on imports of ozone-depleting chemicals, "or items manufactured with [ozone-depleting chemicals],"[158] although it has specifically exempted the import of chemicals that are "entirely consumed in the manufacture of another chemical."[159]

So the question remains live—a carbon tax with a border tax adjustment may or may not survive a WTO challenge. But the question is far more interesting than if a cap-and-trade program with a border tax adjustment were challenged. Particularly if allowances under a cap-and-trade program were distributed for free to emitters (as is likely to be the case politically), it would be difficult to make the argument that the border tax adjustment was meant to "equalize" a burden. Moreover, it seems that intuitively, a border tax must be easier to justify if there exists a clear price—the carbon tax—than if the price is one derived from trading, especially, as has been the case in the EUETS, the market price has fluctuated greatly. What price does one use to levy a border tax adjustment if the price has been fluctuating? Or, alternatively, does a regulating country with a cap-and-trade program require importers to obtain allowances as a condition of import? If that is the case, that would seem to rule out the free allocation of allowances to trade-exposed industries.

A border tax would not fix the problem of competing with say, Chinese products in export markets (as Canadian cement manufacturers fret about competing with Chinese cement being exported to the United States). But the availability of a border tax would embolden other importing and exporting countries in considering the imposition of a carbon tax, and the importance of alleviating this international coordination problem is extremely important. Minimizing opposition from domestic industries fearful of competition from imports will at least make feasible unilateral action in pricing carbon. And on this score, a carbon tax stands a better chance of surviving WTO scrutiny than a cap-and-trade program.

It is possible to take the analysis one step further, and to assume that a trade challenge would be levied for any domestic greenhouse gas legislation that provided some relief for industries that are perceived to be vulnerable to foreign competition. What would be the outcome? Would it lead to an international system of greenhouse gas reduction, or descend into a lawyers' cornucopia of global legal chaos, likely without any attendant greenhouse gas reductions to show for it?

Assume that domestic legislation is in place that offers relief to such industries. A challenge brought to the WTO would seek a declaration that the relief to vulnerable domestic industries was inconsistent with the GATT. A carbon tax may stand a greater chance than cap-and-trade of surviving such a WTO challenge, but what happens afterward?

If, say, a WTO panel were to rule that a cap-and-trade program with a border tax adjustment (or some other form of relief to vulnerable domestic industries) were consistent with the GATT, what would other countries do? The multiple design features of cap-and-trade are potential sources of disharmony. Countries considering greenhouse gas regulation—especially those that are the targets of border tax adjustments, those trading with countries that have regulated greenhouse gases and protected their domestic industries with a border tax adjustment—would naturally consider greenhouse gas regulation of their own, and would naturally gravitate toward cap-and-trade, having in hand the WTO sanction. But what would the cap-and-trade program exactly look like? Would there be a price ceiling, or a price floor, or both (a price "collar")? Which industries would be covered? What would be the threshold level of emissions for participation in the program? Would it be part of a broader international system? Would offsets be a part of the system? Would banking and borrowing be permitted? There are, as discussed above, many design questions for cap-and-trade programs. The problem, from an international harmonization point of view, is that if the WTO upheld a border tax adjustment for a cap-and-trade program, countries will seek to replicate the cap-and-trade program, but with their own country-specific idiosyncrasies. The result would be a hopelessly complicated patchwork of trading schemes, impossible to coordinate internationally, let alone knit together into one sensible and cohesive market.[160]

Would a carbon tax lead to the same greenhouse gas anarchy? It is certainly possible, since it is meant to work in the same way as a cap-and-trade program. But fundamentally, a carbon tax has fewer working parts that could go wrong. Of course, tax codes all over the world are ridden with exemptions and other giveaways. But for purposes of coordinating international action on greenhouse gas reduction, a carbon tax poses less difficulty in crafting an international compact that, in its essentials, is acceptably uniform across different countries with different legal systems. It is true that even under an international carbon tax scheme, some countries would seek to provide relief to domestic industries to give them an advantage over foreign competitors. But this, at least, is nothing new to the WTO. And the subsidization of domestic industries is at least nothing new to the world of international economics and diplomacy. By contrast, the difficulty with cap-and-trade is that these details need to be part of the international coordination, and settling disagreements about these details is very much a new exercise for international negotiators.

Again, it is worth bearing in mind that the most important thing from a climate change point of view is that any such relief be *decoupled* from the carbon tax so that it preserves the incentives at the margins to reduce greenhouse gases. Wealth transfers, whether within or across borders, may be undesirable but are orthogonal to the question of greenhouse gas reduction. The advantage of carbon taxes is that all of these questions get answered outside of the climate arena, however ugly that process gets. The problem with cap-and-trade is that they are inevitably tied up with the setup of the program, paralyzing efforts to reach consensus.

To sum up, while a carbon tax and cap-and-trade have many similarities, the subtle differences add up to a significant advantage for carbon taxes in terms of how global action to reduce greenhouse gases is coordinated across countries, including the problem of engaging China and India. Conceptually, a carbon tax is a simpler core idea than cap-and-trade. It is not as if a global carbon tax would be free of machinations to prop up domestic industries and erode a global carbon price. But it is true that disputes over these machinations can take place outside of the greenhouse gas reduction arena, improving chances that the marginal incentives for emissions reduction would be preserved.

Nine: Revenue Raising

A carbon tax will raise revenues, as would a cap-and-trade program that auctions its allowances, should that come to pass. To the extent that other instruments do not raise revenues, however, or if cap-and-trade programs do not auction allowances, a carbon tax has a distinct advantage of providing a government revenue source. In jurisdictions with fiscal or budgetary problems (including problems with high budget deficits), and in countries experiencing economic problems, declining tax receipts in the near future are a serious concern. Of all the different ideas that have been floated to increase government receipts, a carbon tax or a cap-and-trade program with auctioned allowances may turn out to be less offensive than the alternatives. It almost certainly imposes less economic cost than the alternatives, even if it does not appear that way.

The revenue raising advantage of carbon taxation should not be overstated, however. First, revenues raised by carbon taxes may need to be refunded to help build political support. Because Pigouvian taxes have been so unpopular in the past and carbon taxes remain unpopular, recent carbon tax programs have been put forth as being "revenue neutral." British Columbia's revenue-neutral carbon tax goes so far as to require the Minister of Finance to forfeit 15 percent of her salary if the carbon tax proceeds exceed the amount distributed through the various revenue recycling mechanisms.[161] Concerns over the regressiveness of carbon taxes may force a substantial redistribution of carbon tax revenues (this is addressed in the next chapter).

Second, while the concept of revenue recycling would appear to be helpful in dividing and conquering opposition to carbon taxes, closer inspection reveals some limitations to this strategy. It is not necessarily clear that voters *believe* that carbon tax proceeds would truly be recycled. There is a lingering suspicion, particularly in North America, that a carbon tax would just be a revenue grab, and that creative accounting could somehow shift government spending on other programs into the "revenue recycling" category, thereby freeing carbon tax proceeds for other nefarious governmental purposes. Countering these kinds of anti-government suspicions is clearly the goal of the British Columbia government in installing the 15 percent penalty on the provincial finance minister for failing to recycle carbon tax revenues. Even with this provision in place, provincial voters have remained highly skeptical, even as every resident of BC received a check for $100 as a "climate dividend." In a study in Vancouver of willingness to pay increased gasoline taxes, almost two-thirds of survey respondents expressed suspicion that the government, even if promising to return gasoline tax revenues to taxpayers, would actually do so.[162]

Third, it is not clear that voters even *want* the money back. People sometimes react in disdain when receiving some small rebate from the government, or being told that their taxes are slightly lower than they otherwise would be in the absence of the fiscal probity of the government. Awash in cash from oil revenues after the conclusion of fiscal year 2006, the government of Alberta issued every Alberta resident a "prosperity cheque" for $400. This was met with surprising scorn and even ridicule, as the traditionally conservative Albertans expressed a preference for funding public school infrastructure and health care delivery. Even the traditionally Conservative-friendly press lambasted the Alberta premier for being fiscally irresponsible.[163] Along the same lines, in a study in liberal Vancouver of willingness to pay increased gasoline taxes, respondents were moderately more enthusiastic about higher gasoline taxes if the revenues were recycled back in the form of lower income taxes. However, respondents were only slightly more interested in receiving the money back in tax refunds than they were in having the proceeds "fund research projects to reduce pollution from motor vehicles, such as developing hybrid electric vehicle technology, hydrogen fuel cell technology, or alternative fuel sources."[164] Of course, this book has generally argued against government subsidies; this finding does not suggest otherwise, only that revenue recycling, even if believed, may play a limited role in mollifying public opposition. Similarly, the literature previous to this study found statistically significant but tepid support for revenue-recycling schemes.[165]

Finally, the purpose of a carbon tax is to reduce greenhouse gases by changing behavior. If it does change behavior, then the revenue stream, in real (inflation-adjusted) terms, becomes smaller. A carbon tax will either be effective and only raise large revenues for a short period of time, or raise revenues for a long period of time but be ineffectual. Assuming that the more important goal is to achieve the former, the prospect of a sustained revenue stream is misleading.

Despite these caveats, raising revenues cannot be a bad thing. Even cranky libertarians would have to concede that if revenues were truly returned to taxpayers, taxing carbon dioxide emissions is better than taxing labor, for example. And with global markets worried about the fiscal soundness of countries, implementing a carbon tax program could play a part in shoring up the finances of some governments and ameliorating concerns about fiscal stability. Moreover, given the massive changes in behavior and infrastructure required to reduce greenhouse gases, a little temporary revenue could be very useful. In the short run revenue could fund the kinds of structural changes that might be needed to help people and communities cope with change. Finally, because climate changes are widely believed to be already occurring and already causing some environmental dislocation, funding adaptation to climate change is now widely accepted as necessary. Sources of funding, however, will continue to be elusive. As a strictly economic matter, while carbon tax revenues *should* be viewed as being like every other dollar collected by the government, in reality, linking carbon tax revenues to adaptation funding would be much more politically palatable if packaged together rather than separately.

Ten: Economic Efficiency Revisited: Prices versus Quantities under Uncertainty

This chapter, in laying out the case for a carbon tax, began with an argument based on economic efficiency, but not one that was based *explicitly* on considerations of social welfare. Most of this book, and most of the arguments made in favor of a carbon tax, are couched in efficiency terms, but has thus far avoided invoking overall *social welfare* as a basis for choosing one instrument over another. In welfare economics, policy choices are judged by whether they increase the overall well-being—usually approximated in terms of wealth—of a society as a whole. To some extent, any argument that one policy instrument "works better" or is "more effective" than another, is either assuming or arguing implicitly that social welfare would be higher under the former instrument. But on a more practical level, many such arguments can be made without necessarily taking on all of the ideological baggage that comes with welfare economics. That has been the approach of this chapter in laying out the case for a carbon tax up to this point. Climate policy has always been sensitive to many, many types of concerns from many quarters, not all of them economic in nature. The sometimes visceral reaction against welfare economics, as popularly misunderstood, is one reason to couch the arguments in a variety of ways, in part to illustrate how economic efficiency really does address a multiplicity of ways that people worry about climate change. The efficiency properties of command-and-control and government subsidization have been addressed earlier in this chapter; these considerations extrapolate to the welfare effects dealt with in this chapter, and so will not be repeated. This part of the chapter only compares carbon taxes to cap-and-trade.

This chapter comes full circle in closing out the argument by building upon an economic efficiency argument made in a seminal 1974 paper on the effect of uncertainty on the choice between price and quantity regulations. It also comes full circle by returning to the work of one of climate policy's most important thinkers, Martin Weitzman, who authored the 1974 paper, but more recently has also made the important argument, alluded to earlier, for undertaking mitigation: the avoidance of the risk of catastrophe. It was Weitzman's somewhat stingy praise for the Stern Review that has rung most true in a way that both economists and environmentalists might accept:

that the conclusions of the Stern Review, calling for a very high carbon price, were "right for the wrong reasons," because of the unbounded downside potential for catastrophe.[166] This argument, from an economist, may mark the beginning of a *post-cost-benefit* era of climate thinking. It is fitting then, that an argument for carbon taxes, which Weitzman supported in his review of the Stern Review, would return to his enduring 1974 work. As opposed to the first part of this chapter, this part *does* evaluate the relative economic efficiencies of each instrument in an explicit welfare economics framework. It is also fitting to return to Weitzman's 1974 work on uncertainty, since the problem of climate change is riddled with uncertainties, with respect to both greenhouse gas abatement costs and the marginal environmental benefits.

Weitzman's 1974 paper, *Prices Versus Quantities*, showed how uncertainty about the marginal cost of pollution abatement affected the relative efficiency advantages of price regulation (taxes) versus quantity regulation (cap-and-trade).[167] The point of *Prices Versus Quantities* was that uncertainty meant that regulators could make mistakes about either taxes or quantities, and that choosing between a tax or a quantity control was all about minimizing the economic efficiency loss in case of such a mistake. Uncertainty or incomplete information about costs are likely to lead to setting a carbon tax too high or too low, or setting a cap too high or too low. These mistakes lead to a loss of economic efficiency in that either *more* emissions reductions are undertaken than are desirable—the environmental benefits of emissions reductions are *smaller* than the costs of reducing them—or that *fewer* emissions reductions are undertaken than is desirable—that opportunities are missed to further reduce emissions and obtain environmental benefits that are *greater* than the costs of reducing emissions. The magnitude of this economic loss is known in economic parlance as "deadweight loss." At bottom, deadweight loss is the cost of making a mistake in regulating too much or too little.

Weitzman's insight was that uncertainty or incomplete information tended to create deadweight loss in different ways depending on whether a price control (a tax) or a quantity control (cap-and-trade) was used. Imagine that a regulator (either an agency like EPA or a legislative body writing the legislation) could either set a tax or a cap based upon its best knowledge of the marginal abatement cost (i.e., monetary cost of reducing emissions) and marginal abatement benefit (i.e., avoiding environmental harm) curves. The regulator would either set a tax or set the cap at the level or restricting quantity to the level at which the marginal abatement benefit is equal to the marginal abatement cost. Marginal abatement cost and marginal abatement benefit curves are shown in figures 3-1a and 3-1b; the horizontal axis is abatement, so that moving to the right means the amount of abatement increases (*not* emissions). Marginal abatement *cost* curves slope upward because we can reasonably assume that emitters take advantage of the cheapest opportunities to reduce emissions first; as the lowest-hanging fruit is picked, it becomes more expensive to reduce emissions. Marginal abatement *benefit* curves slope downward because we assume that the first steps to reduce emissions yield the greatest environmental benefit, while the most extreme steps yield the least benefit. This notion of a declining marginal environmental benefit curve may be more intuitive when one applies it to other environmental pollutants, such as toxins, in which small difference in quantities could matter a great deal. It still likely applies to greenhouse gases, as well.

Now imagine that the marginal cost curve is higher or lower than expected. Weitzman shows that when the marginal cost curve is "flat"—that is, if all of the abatement opportunities are similar in cost—then a quantity restriction (cap-and-trade) is preferable because the deadweight loss from the regulator's mistake is much larger when she sets the tax level incorrectly than when she sets the quantity incorrectly. The intuition is that if the tax is set incorrectly, there could be a very large over-abatement or under-abatement, because of the ready substitutability of abatement opportunities. That would lead to a large accumulation of over-compliance costs or, in the case of under-abatement, many missed opportunities to improve the environment at low cost. Put another way, if the marginal cost curve is "flat" relative to the marginal benefit curve, that means that the marginal environmental harm is increasing rapidly, so that allowing another increment of pollution could be very harmful; under those circumstances controlling quantity could be more important. This is illustrated in figure 3-1a, in which the marginal abatement costs are lower than expected. In figure 3-1a, the two possible mistakes shown are (i) a tax that is set too high, and (ii) a cap that is too loose; the corresponding deadweight loss triangles represent, respectively, monetary over-abatement costs and environmental under-abatement costs. If marginal abatement costs are actually higher than expected, the graph would look slightly different—the "actual" curve would be above the "expected" curve, but the sizes of the triangles would still be the same, and the conclusions the same, but the deadweight loss triangles would repre-

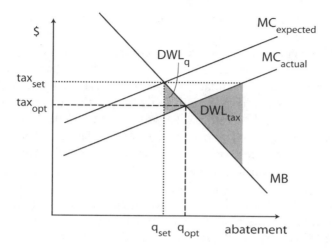

FIGURE 3-1A. MC too low, flat marginal cost, steep marginal benefit.

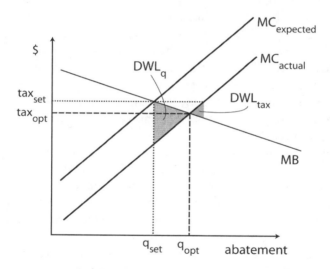

FIGURE 3-1B. MC too low, steep marginal cost, flat marginal benefit.

sent the opposite costs—too low of a tax and under-abatement in the case of a tax, and too tight of a cap and over-abatement in the case of cap-and-trade.

On the other hand, if the marginal cost curve is "steep"—that is, if abatement opportunities are fairly heterogeneous in cost—then a price regulation (tax) is preferable. The intuition for this is that when the abatement level is set too high (i.e., a cap is too tight), the resulting over-abatement will be very costly, requiring polluters to undertake some unduly expensive abatement measures; if the abatement level is set too low, some very valuable opportunities are missed in which the marginal abatement cost would be far below the marginal environmental benefit, and therefore well worth it. Put another way, with a marginal abatement cost curve that is steep relative to the marginal benefit curve, it is less risky to set the tax incorrectly because missing with the tax amount would not cause a very large over- or under-abatement. This is shown in figure 3-1b, again with the marginal abatement costs lower than expected. Again, the marginal abatement costs could be higher than expected, in which case the deadweight loss triangles flip but retain the same magnitude, so that the conclusion remains the same.

Interestingly enough, only mistakes with respect to the marginal abatement cost have implications for instrument choice. In case of a mistake about the marginal abatement benefit (i.e., avoiding environmental harm) it does not matter whether a tax or cap-and-trade was used; the deadweight loss would be the same under both. If a regulator underestimated the amount of environmental harm avoided from further abatement, then the tax would be set too low and the cap would be too loose. Either way, the deadweight loss is due to missed opportunities to obtain environmental benefits at low cost. This is shown in figure 3-2.

These economic subtleties have not actually held much sway in the public debate over instrument choice for climate change. Among those advocating for greenhouse gas regulation, some environmental organizations have supported the idea of a cap-and-trade system, on the grounds that it is more important to achieve a certain amount of greenhouse gas reduction each year, than it is to ensure cost-minimization of emissions reductions. Eileen Claussen, the President of the Pew Center on Climate Change, was an important backer of cap-and-trade early on, saying she was for "environmental certainty."[168] Obama administration adviser Nathaniel Keohane, an economist for the Environmental Defense Fund and a former Yale business school professor, has also advocated for cap-and-trade over a carbon tax on the same grounds.[169] For environmentalists, it is certainly easier to focus on that which is, from an environmental perspective, measurable. How can

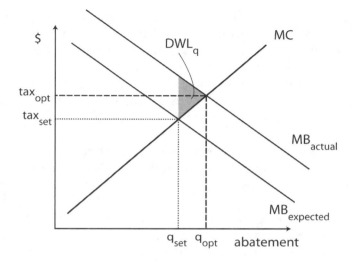

Figure 3-2. MB too low.

you tell whether or not something is working unless there is a measurable standard of compliance?

The climate policy world has also gravitated toward cap-and-trade because scientists seem to offer more direction than economists have about desired targets. In contrast to the wide disparity between Nordhaus and Stern about the desired level of taxation—$7.50 per ton of CO_2 as opposed to $85—climate scientists seem to be at least moving in relative unison on targets, if not converging on a specific level of desired greenhouse gas concentrations. For a time, scientists were willing to say that a doubling of the concentration of carbon dioxide in the Earth's atmosphere to 550 parts per million would yield a temperature increase of 3 degrees Celsius, at once considered an acceptable temperature increase.[170] The projection is still considered reasonably accurate, but the risk from such a temperature increase is no longer considered acceptable. More recently, scientists seem to be arguing for a stabilization of the concentration of carbon dioxide at 450 ppm, as the level at which a 2-degree Celsius warming can be expected, and one beyond which some dramatic and potentially catastrophic changes may occur, such as the melting of the Greenland ice sheet, leading to large rises in sea level, changes in ocean temperature and acidity, and a host of as-yet unknown effects.[171]

So the 450 ppm target, if it persists among scientists, would at least offer the world a goal, and one that would seem tailored to annual quantitative targets. But this focus on quantity, and this illusion of "environmental certainty," is a chimera. Because carbon dioxide is resident in the Earth's atmosphere for 100 years, what happens in any given year is nearly irrelevant. What is important is that the atmospheric *stock* of carbon dioxide be drawn down as soon and as quickly as possible.

A cap-and-trade system *seems* like a reasonable way to set goals to reduce the stock of carbon dioxide in the Earth's atmosphere. Annual emissions reductions seem analogous perhaps to a dieter resolving to eat a little better each day (in this case, a low-carbon diet). But as anybody who has been on a diet knows, it is the long-term resolve that is more important. And as dieters know, some days are better than others, but the long term habits are more important. In economic downtimes, carbon dioxide emissions fall; in those years having a "loose" cap is a missed opportunity to reduce emissions even more, and perhaps develop some lower-carbon "habits." As noted above, carbon dioxide emissions in Europe and in the United States dropped precipitously in 2009. If a carbon tax were in effect in these places, these years could have been years in which structural or process changes were made to reduce carbon dioxide emissions. For example, figuring out process changes to decrease the use of fuel could have been a sensible step for any organization, governmental or private (or households, for that matter), facing tighter financial constraints. It could have been a year in which slack electricity demand could have created the capacity to try new demand management strategies. At the Dogfish Head Craft brewery in Milton, Delaware, forward-thinking plant engineer Greg Christmas, *anticipating* higher energy costs from federal climate legislation (perhaps optimistically) found a number of cheap and extensive savings in the energy-intensive brewing process, one that involves both boilers and coolers. Economic sluggishness in the United States made it cheaper for Dogfish to purchase an energy-efficient cooling system that runs at multiple speeds, to economize when cooling needs were lower. Along with mechanical efficiencies, Dogfish has cut its energy consumption by 15 percent.[172]

These are the kinds of opportunities that are more economical in some years and not others. Dogfish has acted even though there is currently no carbon price in the United States. If there were a carbon price, the economic downturn could have made 2009 a banner year for businesses large and small to find ways to reduce carbon emissions. The basic insight of Dogfish is that it was more affordable to take this action in a down year rather than in a year of robust economic activity. The intuition behind the superior efficiency of a carbon tax is that these kinds of decisions are timing-sensitive, and a cap-and-trade program does not take this into account. They could take this partially into account by banking or borrowing, which involves the delayed or forward consumption of emissions allowances under a cap-and-trade program (discussed below). But these are just tweaks to make a cap-and-trade program work more like a carbon tax program.

There are going to be years in which emissions reduction opportunities make more sense than they do in other years. Capital costs can vary greatly from year to year, and buying expensive equipment when the economy is slow and prices low is one of the fundamental purposes of capital planning. Timing of abatement decisions is thus important for emitters, and very hard to foresee. As argued earlier in this chapter, a steady carbon price is needed to keep up the incentives for innovation in good economic times and bad. This separate argument is that while a cap-and-trade program may produce high carbon prices in good economic years, a carbon tax encourages more innovation in economic down years, and on balance and over time, it is more important to capture the larger opportunities to reduce emissions when economic times are bad. This is the intuition behind a number of studies that have applied Weitzman's analysis to the climate change problem.[173]

On the other side of the equation, the long residency of carbon dioxide is like having a very "flat" marginal abatement benefit curve: the incremental abatement at any given time is not very important. Most of the carbon dioxide that is emitted becomes part of a global carbon cycle in which many parts of the Earth's biota store it, process it, and consume it for photosynthesis. At any given time, there are about 3,000 gigatons of carbon dioxide resident in the Earth's atmosphere,[174] with oceans, plants, and soils removing slightly more than half of all emissions.[175] Within this massive system, even the annual global emissions of about 30 gigatons of carbon dioxide is relatively small. Over 100 years, something on the order of 3,000 gigatons will be emitted. So even if we do not have a very good sense of the marginal abatement benefit curve, or the marginal environmental damage function—the harm from emitting a ton of carbon dioxide—we do know that by sheer numbers alone, the emission of even a fairly large amount of carbon dioxide is unlikely to make a big difference. It is remotely possible that, at any given time, the emissions of an extra megaton of carbon dioxide could increase the atmospheric concentration past a "tipping point"—beyond which some massive and catastrophic climate changes would be triggered. But given the enormous existing carbon stock and the immense size of the carbon cycle, the odds of this being true for any identifiable quantity of carbon dioxide are statistically infinitesimal.

So for purposes of applying the Weitzman analysis to carbon dioxide, the marginal benefit curve would seem to be relatively "flat." Do we have any reason to believe that the marginal abatement cost curve is "steep"? The consulting firm McKinsey compiled an analysis of common greenhouse gas reduction strategies, from big, expensive measures, such as retrofitting coal-fired power plants for carbon capture and storage, to small measures such as switching from incandescent light bulbs to efficient light-emitting diodes. The abatement costs, projected out to 2030, ranged from negative 100 Euros per ton of carbon dioxide to about fifty Euros.[176] Putting aside for the moment that a tremendous amount of abatement can be accomplished at *negative* cost (meaning these measures would more than pay for themselves even without a carbon price), is this schedule of marginal abatement costs "steep"? This is still hard to say, since we could only say it is "steep" relative to the marginal benefit curve. There is still much uncertainty with respect to both the marginal cost and marginal (environmental) benefit curves. There may be many other abatement options out there that have as yet undiscovered, or may progress much more quickly than models of technological change currently allow. But given what we know now, the most reasonable conclusion would seem to be, given the extraordinary flatness of the marginal benefit curve, that this bit of heterogeneity in abatement cost—a range of 150 Euros or 200 some-odd dollars—would seem to suggest that a carbon tax would produce a smaller deadweight loss if there is uncertainty about the marginal abatement costs.

Since Weitzman's analysis only applies when there is uncertainty about marginal abatement costs—that is, when we expect the regulator to make mistakes about the costs of reducing greenhouse gases—it might be fair to ask whether there actually is uncertainty. There is abundant uncertainty with respect to the climate change harms resulting from emissions, but again, mistakes made in estimating the climate change harms will produce the same kind and same amount of dead-weight loss whether a carbon tax or a cap-and-trade program is employed. So is there uncertainty with respect to marginal abatement costs?

Past experience with estimates of compliance costs would suggest that even if we think we know a lot about marginal abatement costs, it is likely that we do not. When the United States passed the Clean Air Act Amendments of 1990 which contained the sulfur dioxide cap-and-trade program, the best government estimates of the total compliance cost were substantially off the mark. The last of a series of estimates made in connection with the 1990 Clean Air Act Amendments projected annual long-run compliance cost of about $4.6 billion.[177] By 1994, EPA had already revised that forecast downward to $2 billion.[178] In 1999, a Resources for the Future report estimated 2010 costs would be just over $1 billion. Incidentally, industry estimates had self-servingly placed the estimate at $7.4 billion.[179]

But the problem of projecting marginal abatement costs is whether *anybody* can accurately project future marginal abatement costs, especially over the long time horizons involved with climate change. It is worth noting how the "best guess" of compliance costs of the sulfur dioxide cap-and-trade program changed so dramatically—an 80 percent drop—in such a short time—nine years. Returning to a theme established earlier, many unanticipated things happen when a broad market price is placed on pollution, such as the unforeseen (and previously unimaginable) opportunism of a deregulated rail industry, taking advantage of chances to move coal across the country more efficiently than other modes. Markets find opportunities that cannot be foreseen, and market prices for pollution create compliance cost-reducing opportunities that cannot be foreseen. Indeed, as a Resources for the Future report has noted, *ex ante* cost estimates of environmental regulation tend to be systematically overstated for regulations such as cap-and-trade that utilize market prices for pollution.[180] Part of the systemic problem would not apply to greenhouse gas abatement, as agencies performing cost estimates tend to err on the expensive side, to avoid being criticized by industry groups for being too optimistic; this is not what is happening with estimates of greenhouse gas abatement. But part of the systemic problem does in fact bias cost estimates of greenhouse gas abatement strategies upward: the part that consistently underestimates the cost-reducing effects of technological innovation. And this is bound to hold truer in the climate context, which poses much, much, broader and greater opportunities and sectors in which to innovate. How many more Dogfish Head Craft breweries are out there?

In the end, is there really a difference between cap-and-trade and carbon taxes when it comes to welfare effects? The differences here are subtle, but most indications are that carbon taxes are likely to be more efficient. If we take the long view, as we must for reducing greenhouse gases, a carbon tax is likely to yield smaller deadweight losses, in large part because the steadier price offered by a carbon price will direct innovation into years in which it is more efficient. But regulators also have to stand ready to change carbon taxes (or caps) when new information emerges. As David Weisbach argues, if either carbon taxes or caps are adjusted quickly to incorporate new information, then there is no difference between the two instruments. Whether regulators or legislators would be willing and able to do so, however, is an open question.

Weisbach also argues that there are design features that could be incorporated into a cap-and-trade that create the same flexibility as a carbon tax. For example, allowing the banking and borrowing of emissions allowances serves to extend the time frame for emissions, so that emitters have some flexibility with respect to the timing of abatement measures. But this is just mimicking what a carbon tax does—allow emitters an infinite (subject to changes in the level of the carbon tax) time horizon in which to make emissions reductions. Why not just have a carbon tax? Would that not be simpler? Another proposal, adopted in the American Power Act, or the Kerry-Lieberman Senate proposal, is to control the price volatility of carbon allowance trading. Price floors and price ceilings (when implemented together, they are called "price collars") could keep trading within a range of costs, and preclude the dramatic dives in price brought on by the recent global economic downturn. But actually implementing this could get complicated. For example, implementing a price floor in a cap-and-trade program would require that some allowances each year be withheld, and if necessary, auctioned at or above the floor price. How many allowances would need to be withheld? This is not an easy question to answer. And again, returning to the fundamental question, why bother? Why take such pains to build in the features of a carbon tax instead of just implementing the carbon tax?

Conclusion

Not all the arguments for a carbon tax apply in all respects when compared to other instruments to reduce greenhouse gases. Indeed, the ten arguments listed above leave room for some reservations. The purpose of this chapter has not been to lay waste to any residue of a doubt that a carbon tax is the best way forward in all respects and all circumstances. Rather, the purpose has been to explore various policy considerations and articulate how a carbon tax enjoys advantages over the alternatives.

Fundamentally, the most important thing is to establish a price on carbon dioxide as soon as possible, and as broadly as possible. Alternatives attempt to achieve this indirectly. The carbon tax does it directly. Taking all considerations into account, a carbon tax exhibits the best combination of characteristics for pricing and reducing emissions. In the complicated world of domestic climate policy and international relations, a carbon tax, because of its breadth, its simplicity, and its ability to piggyback on existing regulatory infrastructure, offers the greatest chance to reduce greenhouse gas emissions immediately.

Chapter 4

Arguments against a Carbon Tax

The fact that carbon tax proposals have failed to advance in North America suggests that alternatives are more currently more popular. At least cap-and-trade proposals have passed the US House of Representatives, seen the light of day in the US Senate, and been the topic of discussion in various Canadian federal and provincial governments. Most outside of the carbon tax tent (but inside the camp favoring action on climate change) favor cap-and-trade, most of the remainder favor government subsidies (without necessarily using that term), and a few, mostly environmental advocates, still favor the use of command-and-control regulation (also without specifically calling it that). In the United States, some environmental organizations still call for regulation of greenhouse gas emissions through the existing command-and-control-oriented Clean Air Act. Whether emanating from a sincere belief in the efficacy of command-and-control, or from a strategic desire to use command-and-control as leverage for obtaining passage of cap-and-trade legislation, this has become a distinctly minority view.

Putting aside for the moment the question of public acceptance of the need for greenhouse gas legislation, to the extent that policy is moving toward greenhouse gas reductions, it does not seem poised to arrive via a carbon tax. Clearly, objections to a carbon tax go beyond those mentioned in passing in the previous chapter. Here, the book turns to the case against carbon taxes. This chapter describes counterarguments to the ten arguments made in chapter 3, as well as responses to these counterarguments.

Political Economy Considerations

Very generally speaking, the study of political economy is the application of economic theory to the behavior of actors in political and administrative contexts. Political economy is the combination of economics and political science. Perhaps most prominently, it is the application of the assumption of self-interested rationality to individuals, groups, agencies, and other actors in the public realm. As such, political economy has come to mean a wide variety of things, so a unifying definition is elusive. The venerable and highly respected *Journal of Political Economy* has branched out such that its boundaries are even broader than that of economics or political science, grabbing onto certain phenomena and areas of study that pure economists and political scientists might not. Because understanding and modeling political actors is such a central aspect of policy research, it is perhaps inevitable that political economy would come to encompass so many things having to do with law and public policy.

With political economy taking on such a variety of law and public policy problems, political economy considerations in environmental law and policy have also taken many forms. Political economy theory has been implicitly or explicitly used to explain: why carbon taxes will never pass a legislature; why cap-and-trade programs *can* pass a legislature; why cap-and-trade programs will be politically sustainable over the long run; why government subsidization remains an important climate policy; why a global agreement *must* take the form of a cap-and-trade program; and why a global agreement *could not possibly* take the form of a cap-and-trade program. There is an old joke about an economist retained by the king for advice, who is asked a simple mathematical question, to which the economist replies, "what do you want the answer to be?" Political economy has much of the same normative malleability as economics.

The political economy of a carbon tax, though, *seems* quite poor. The most common objection to a carbon tax is that it has much political baggage, and a low probability of political passage. This is what people mean when they say carbon taxes are politically "infeasible." It is of little comfort to know that British Columbia, Sweden, Norway, Finland,

Denmark, and the United Kingdom have instituted carbon taxes. The latter four countries have carved out significant exemptions for many industries, especially those exposed to international competition.[1] Sweden and British Columbia are small jurisdictions—British Columbia's population is under 5 million and Sweden's is under 10 million— and it seems a stretch to use these countries as counter-examples of how large, politically complex countries such as the United States might find the political will to institute a similar carbon tax. Even environmentally conscious France, after making noises about carbon taxes in 2009, abandoned efforts to institute a carbon tax in the midst of continuing financial and economic problems in Europe.[2]

At the root of these sometimes too-quick dismissals are some very intricate political economy models. One simple explanation is just that there are not enough constituencies that see the advantages of a carbon tax clearly enough and support the idea of a carbon tax strongly enough, vis-à-vis the alternatives. The natural supporters of carbon taxes—renewable energy providers, manufacturers of renewable energy equipment, and others that could provide a competitive alternative to fossil fuel combustion—would support a carbon tax, but these groups see more realistic prospects of obtaining other kinds of support in legislation. Government subsidies, of course, top that list of potential legislative benefits. Subsidies are not quite as effective as a long-term carbon price, but for the renewable energy industries, they seem easier to obtain. Getting government subsidies would allow the renewable energy industries to move forward without picking a fight with the powerful coal industries, which would of course result in defeat.

There is even some empirical evidence that the political economics of carbon taxes are challenging. A paper on gasoline prices that has been largely overlooked produced a stunning finding: not only do low gasoline prices lead to high consumption (an easily verifiable economic finding), but the converse is actually true: high consumption leads to low gasoline prices! Henrik Hammar, Asa Lofgren, and Thomas Sterner examine the inflation-adjusted gasoline prices for 21 rich OECD countries from 1978 to 2000. They demonstrate that the causality indeed runs both ways: that not only do low gasoline prices lead to high consumption, but that high consumption begets low gasoline prices. The offered reason for this surprising conclusion is that when high consumption of gasoline makes up a larger part of the populace's household budget, that populace is more likely to express its concern over gasoline prices through their political preferences.[3] Because their data set examines variations not only across countries but over time, their conclusions are more robust than the casual observation that Americans and Canadians hate gasoline taxes precisely because they drive so much, and pressure their politicians to keep it that way.

So the political economy of carbon taxes is demonstrably difficult. By contrast, cap-and-trade offers all kinds of interesting political deal-making possibilities. Most obviously, if a cap-and-trade program allocates allowances for free, then it is essentially creating a new source of wealth (along with costs). Giving away allowances is effectively printing money and giving it away, albeit with uncertain denominations. This kind of legislatively created wealth can be effective in lining up political support. The political power of the coal industry and the electricity-generating firms that primarily burn coal are such that they seem to exercise a veto power over climate legislation. They have therefore become central to the crafting of legislation in the United States to reduce greenhouse gas emissions. While coal-heavy states such as West Virginia have exerted pressure through their elected representatives, electricity-generating firms have worked through one of the most powerful trade associations in the world, the Edison Electric Institute, or "EEI," the trade association of investor-owned electric utilities.

Both the Waxman-Markey and the Kerry-Lieberman proposals in 2009 and 2010 provided the disadvantaged coal industries and the utilities that burn coal with enormous payoffs in the form of free allowances. Waxman-Markey, which awarded electricity generating firms more than a third of the total allowances, was written with the EEI virtually as a partner. Energy & Environment News reported that "[s]urprising many longtime observers, liberal Reps. Henry Waxman (D-Calif.) and Ed Markey (D-Mass.) incorporated a proposal from the Edison Electric Institute that helped determine how to slice up emission allocations potentially worth billions of dollars between power companies with a wide variety of fuel mixes."[4] Dutifully, EEI president Thomas Kuhn made a number of post-passage efforts to support a Senate bill that would be compatible with the Waxman-Markey bill that he helped craft.[5]

Such is the price of political support in a representative democracy. In the meantime, those in the renewable energy industries could not object to the introduction of a carbon price. But the political economy point is that unlike a carbon tax, cap-and-trade offers legislators the opportunity to create winners and losers. Even if the losers under cap-and-trade are incompletely compensated, cap-and-trade in all likelihood offers enough in the way of potential political grease to move legislation forward.

But all this is not the same as an argument on the merits. Instrument choice decisions should not simply be about what people think what politicians will and will not do. Putting aside for the moment the potential for misjudgments about what is politically feasible, at some point the instrument choice debate needs to be framed in normative terms, and decisions made with respect what is best for society as a whole. If political economy considerations ruled the day, every country should simply subsidize lower-carbon technologies as a greenhouse gas reduction strategy. Given that public opinion polls seem to show that the American public strongly favors subsidy programs to reduce greenhouse gases but strongly opposes carbon taxes or gasoline taxes, this would be the most politically expedient instrument choice.[6] But few honestly believe this is the right way to address climate change. No reputable economist believes that, even in theory, subsidization can play any more than a supplementary role in reducing greenhouse gases. And not even the love-starved, benefit-distributing US Congress would take the extreme position of relying *only* on subsidization as a climate policy. At some level and to some degree, the merits of instrument choice have to matter, in theory and in reality.

Moreover, what seems "politically infeasible" at one time, over time, can change. For decades, economists argued that cap-and-trade programs represented a paradigm-shifting approach to environmental law, one that could vastly improve not only the efficiency of pollution abatement, but also produce better environmental outcomes. For decades, this instrument languished, as did the economists that advocated it. For decades, cap-and-trade faced seemingly insurmountable political economies that favored the status-quo command-and-control style of regulation. Industries were comfortable with having certainty in their compliance—buy a piece of equipment, and be confident of compliance. Regulators were comfortable with regulating that which they could actually see and confirm: the installation of a piece of equipment. Environmental lawyers and environmental organizations were comfortable and very much invested in a tangled legal system with the ambiguities that command-and-control produces, and with the possibilities for litigation that these ambiguities produce. There was a time in which this iron triangle of vested interests would have seemed difficult to dislodge. And it was not as if command-and-control regulation accomplished nothing; on the contrary, a cost-benefit analysis of the first twenty years of the Clean Air Act—a command-and-control-only era—found that the benefits outweighed the costs by an order of magnitude.[7] But cap-and-trade could promise more.

Over time, the constant haranguing of economists and other academics found more and more audiences, and over time, new political actors emerged, and others began to pick up on the benefits of cap-and-trade as representing a substantial improvement over command-and-control. Some environmental organizations, infused with economic literacy for the first time, came to appreciate the benefits of cap-and-trade. Some conservative politicians, traditionally hostile to government regulation, came to appreciate the libertarian streak in cap-and-trade. It was President George H. W. Bush, and his combatively conservative chief counsel, C. Boyden Gray, who helped push the sulfur dioxide emissions trading program through Congress in 1990. And with the growth of environmental economics as an academic field of study, a new breed of policy analysts were produced from colleges and universities that began to populate government agencies and think tanks and gradually transform the conventional wisdom of environmental regulation. The coalitions that formed to support the sulfur dioxide cap-and-trade—small government advocates and environmental advocates—seemed like strange bedfellows at first but, over time, became viewed as being, if not normal, at least unsuspicious.

Political economy considerations have also featured prominently on the international front, and perhaps with even weightier implications. China and India are absolutely essential to obtaining meaningful global agreement to abate emissions. Like the coal industries in the United States, they, too, essentially have veto power. No effective international agreement could exclude China and India, the largest and fourth-largest greenhouse gas emitting countries in the world, and two of the fastest-growing economies in the world. How to engage them?

I argued earlier in this book that a carbon tax would be more palatable, to two countries with unfortunate colonial pasts, than would a global cap-and-trade program in which others get to decide what their allowances allocations would be. There is a political economy counterargument: as in the domestic case, cap-and-trade creates wealth, which could be used to buy cooperation from holdouts such as China and India. Money can buy cooperation and some forgiveness for past wrongs. But we have seen this attempted bribery at work before in the cap-and-trade context: offsets, specifically CDMs. It has not turned out well. It is not so much that money has flowed from developed countries to developing countries—that is part of the plan—but that offsets have created an indeterminacy on the cap level that raises serious doubts as to whether emissions are reduced at all. Awarding credits for make-work projects just because less offensive than they could possibly be unnecessarily raises the cap.

Alternatively, if offsets are not worth the trouble, and if the wealth transfer takes the form of something other than an offset-type program, how exactly would the allowances be allocated? The low likelihood of developed countries and developing countries agreeing on an allowance allocation scheme is the fly in the ointment for political economy theories about how cap-and-trade is more politically palatable internationally than other instruments. Moreover, we have already seen one of the responses to this political economy counterargument: Steven Stoft's observation that the current situation, with China and India not subject to any emissions limitations, and enjoying the benefits of CDMs, are in an extremely advantageous negotiating position vis-à-vis the developed countries. It will take something else to move China and India at least, into an international agreement.

In short, political economy considerations are of great practical importance. Some political disadvantages of carbon taxes vis-à-vis other instruments might be difficult to overcome. The ability for legislators to create wealth through allowance allocation is a powerful political tool for would-be cap-and-trade architects. But they cannot substitute for robust debate on the merits of instrument choice. Part of the purpose of this book is to get behind political economy considerations and analyze the true costs and benefits of the instrument choices, toward the ultimate goal of more clearly communicating these to an electorate. Carbon taxes are sometimes dismissed out of hand for their poor political economics. Is it not possible to argue that the value of allowances should belong to the taxpayer, rather than powerful industrial interests? In the hands of a skillful populist, this does not seem like a hard pitch to make. Indeed, a bipartisan alternative to the 2010 American Power Act (Kerry-Lieberman) was introduced by Senators Collins and Cantwell: a "cap-and-dividend" bill, which contemplated the auctioning of most emissions allowances.[8]

While the Collins-Cantwell bill fared no better than the Kerry-Lieberman, it did attract attention and support from some notable interest groups, not the least of which was the powerful AARP.[9]

So although carbon taxes would appear to be in the same impossible situation as cap-and-trade was in two decades earlier, one should not be too quick to dismiss carbon taxes. Again, there is reason to be optimistic that carbon taxes can gain traction. In the end, it may simply take some time for the political economics of carbon taxes to start to look at least as good as the alternatives.

Regressiveness

A second class of objections to carbon taxes has to do with its perceived regressiveness. A carbon tax is considered a form of a consumption tax, and without some adjustments or exemptions, consumption taxes tend to disproportionately hurt poorer individuals and households. A familiar consumption tax is the sales tax, usually a percentage add-on to the purchase price of goods. While richer households certainly buy more goods and therefore pay more sales taxes in absolute amounts, sales taxes paid out would ordinarily make up a larger *fraction* of a poorer household's budget. Most sales taxes, however, exempt some basic goods such as food and clothing. These exemptions alleviate, if not largely solve, the regressiveness problem, since expenditures beyond food and clothing are much, much greater for richer households, and not only would they pay more in sales tax but it would make up a larger share of a rich household's budget. Those advocates concerned with economic inequalities could continue to argue that sales taxes, even with exemptions, are more regressive than income taxes, so that revenue increases should come from raising income taxes rather than sales taxes; income tax increases would quite likely leave poor taxpayers untouched. This appears to be a winning argument, as income taxes see much more movement than sales taxes.

A carbon tax would seem to be a particularly regressive type of consumption tax because it is most conspicuously a tax on energy. And with a carbon tax, it is difficult to exempt the purchase of basic goods such as food and water. How would a taxing government go about exempting food and clothing from a carbon tax? It would have to, for example, forgo taxing the gasoline consumed in transporting oranges from Florida, bananas from Chile, or clothes from China. Shipments of these goods would arrive with all kinds of other goods, some of which would be food and clothing and some of which would not. Teasing out the "basic good" part of a shipment by truck, plane, or ship would be impossible. Moreover, it is not necessarily accurate to characterize all "basic goods" such as food and clothing as those that need to be exempted because they are necessary for poorer households. Is it really advancing income equalization to exempt from carbon taxes the catch, refrigeration, and transport of wild British Columbia salmon to New York City?

Part of the problem of taxing energy through a carbon tax is that energy is needed to produce and transport everything, so low energy prices are deeply embedded in everything that modern societies consume. This is *especially* true with regard to food and clothing, which are those staples that we are (and should be) the most sensitive to when we think about regressiveness. The regressiveness problem comes from the fact that low energy prices have redounded to the benefit of everyone, including and possibly *most prominently*, low-income individuals and households.

One significant component of this unnaturally low global energy price is its effect on international trade. International trade in goods has been especially robust in low-cost goods such as food and clothing. This is what economists would expect, and probably would generally support. The development of some lower-income countries has come about by means of offering cheap labor and cheap land to grow and produce low-cost food and clothing. But this robust international trade, which has made the Wal-Marts of the developed world possible, has been predicated on low energy prices. Carbon pricing would, if it could be implemented on international transport, raise prices on a wide variety of internationally traded goods.

Unraveling the wide benefits of cheap energy without compensating poor individuals and households is thus far from straightforward. Moreover, it is not clear the extent to which consumers, especially poor ones, could or would substitute away from goods that become pricier because of carbon pricing. Much of the prediction of the effects of carbon pricing is the product of economic modeling, and in some quarters, mere conjecture.

There is a perception, for example, that energy usage is inelastic, and that therefore poor individuals and households would suffer much more than rich ones, since energy usage comprises a larger fraction of a poor household's budget than a rich one. Without ways to substitute, poor households would just be stuck. Jack Layton, the leader of the New Democratic Party in Canada, in announcing opposition to a carbon tax proposed by a rival party (despite Layton's supposedly strong support for reducing greenhouse gas emissions), said that a carbon tax "would place an unfair burden on low-income Canadians." Layton said that "[t]hose advocating a carbon tax suggest that by making the costs for certain things more expensive, people will make different choices . . . [b]ut Canada is a cold place and heating your home really isn't a choice."[10] Mirroring the federal NDP's position, then leader of the British Columbia NDP, Carole James, campaigned vigorously in 2008 against the British Columbia carbon tax with her "axe the tax" campaign, arguing that the "fuel tax will hit consumers where it hurts," and that "[w]hile big oil companies are raking in record profits, ordinary British Columbians are paying through the nose — whether it's taxi fares, ferry fares, home heating or airplane tickets."[11]

But this populists' objection to carbon taxes is based upon a simplistic and crude conception of energy consumption and of regressiveness. There are a number of economic effects that go well beyond the first-order impression that poor individuals and households are just stuck. I discuss three. First, these types of arguments seem to assume that regulatory costs simply stay where they are imposed. If a tax were imposed on corporations, they would just eat it, and if the cost of a carbon tax were imposed on individuals and households, they would simply suffer. In actual fact, corporations will pass along the price of inputs like energy to consumer in varying degrees, so the dichotomy between regulating, say, "big oil companies" and charging consumers is a false one. Second, it is not true that poor individuals and households are completely bereft of the ability to substitute. As callous as it seems to try and imagine, poor individuals and households *do* find ways to substitute. These substitutions are not always wrenching and painful. Third, many important changes do not involve home heating or electricity or transportation, and many important greenhouse gas-reducing changes need not affect poor households at all. Finally, the problem of regressiveness ought to focus us on the question of exactly what regressiveness means. Is a carbon tax regressive if the lowest quartile of households is hurt more than the second-lowest quartile, but the lower half is better off than the richer half? Should we think about regressiveness in terms of a present snapshot in time, or do we think about the lifetime income or consumption of individuals? I expand upon these points below.

First, there is the misguided notion that for pollution problems including greenhouse gas emissions, the right thing to do is to stick it to the corporations, because they are at fault for spoiling the environment, not individuals and households. Of course, responsibility for the greenhouse gas problem is spread much more widely than just big emitters and big corporations, and it is nothing short of demagoguery for politicians to enable people to evade responsibility for the problem and pin it, along with liability, on big emitters and big corporations. But perhaps even more to the point, it is a mistake to think that imposing a regulatory burden on big emitters and big corporations will penalize only these evil barons. As any undergraduate student in economics would be able to explain, the cost of inputs to a product, such as energy, labor, or raw or processed materials, *may* get passed on down the supply chain to consumers of that product. Whether and how much of an energy price increase from a carbon tax would get passed down to consumers would depend on a variety of *elasticities*— the amount of substitution or adjustment that is made in response to a change in price (price-elasticity) or a change in income (income-elasticity). It is a fallacy that if a tax is imposed on "big corporations," they will simply eat the tax. They might, they might not. A tax imposed on low-elasticity goods such as insulin (virtually no amount of price increase would get insulin users to drop it) would get completely passed down to consumers, since they have no choice. A luxury tax on high-elasticity goods like yachts and sportscars, probably not.

In actual fact, *any* attempt to reduce greenhouse gas emissions will increase costs of not only home heating, electricity, and gasoline, but many other goods as well. The old-fashioned command-and-control regulation was often quite regressive. Requiring scrubbers to be installed at coal-fired power plants, if it were successful (it was not), could be quite regressive, since under the traditional system of regulated utilities, electricity-generating plants could ask their regulatory commissions for rate increases to pay for capital costs like pollution control equipment. While the electricity generation industry has been moving away from the regulated utility model, the lessons from that era still hold. Attempts to focus the costs of greenhouse gas emissions toward large emitting industries are not likely to be successful. More recently, carbon tax opponents that advocate for say, cap-and-trade only on large emitters of greenhouse gases (as the federal and provincial NDP in Canada have), base their advocacy on an implicit assumption that the burden of holding allowances in a cap-and-trade program would stay where they are imposed. This is false.

The second problem with the populist regressiveness argument is the flipside of this first mistake: the notion that poor individuals and households are unable to make adjustments to the increased costs brought on by a carbon tax. Just as a tax on big corporations is unlikely to leave consumers unscathed, so too, taxes on consumers are unlikely to leave big corporations unscathed. Because it is easy to translate—however errantly—a carbon tax into an increase in home heating costs or filling up at the gasoline pump, the focus is misdirected toward these effects and detracts from the myriad of other effects.

Take the example of the effect of a carbon tax on gasoline prices. The story told a little too often is that increased gasoline prices would hurt poor commuters and commuters that have poor access to transit services. This is no doubt true for many poor commuters, especially in rural areas. But it neglects the capacity of *some* of these poor commuters to make adjustments. In fact, the poorest quintile of households in the United States make the most substitutions to increases in gasoline prices.[12] Driving to and from work is *often*—not always—a nondiscretionary expenditure, but a variety of other measures are available that economize on gasoline expenditures, such as trip bundling (running several errands at a time, saving on individual trips), carpooling, and undertaking the sometimes very inconvenient step of relying on transit. No one should trivialize these measures—they can be quite difficult—but adjustments are possible. In terms of energy expenditures, the regressiveness of a carbon tax is usually overestimated. And it would be a mistake to think that a carbon tax imposed on consumers would be unnoticed by gasoline suppliers: the profit margin on a typical gallon of gasoline is on the order of 50 percent for the refiner, 5 percent for the gas station.[13] Widespread adjustments to consumption would likely be met with price adjustments.

Third, many of the substitutions that would take place that would blunt the effect on poor individuals and households may not be undertaken by these individuals and households themselves. A carbon tax increases energy costs, but energy costs are so much more than just home heating, electricity, and filling up at the gas pump. Inordinately low energy costs are deeply embedded in everything that modern societies consume, so that there are uncountable opportunities for substitution of many other products and processes that would lower greenhouse gas emissions. Within the long and complex supply chains for all of the parts and components of everything that we consume, many producers might find it profitable to substitute away from greenhouse gas-intensive products and processes. For example, agriculture could be substantially less greenhouse gas-intensive, and would not necessarily lead to a huge run-up in food prices. Highly mechanized agriculture and highly fossil fuel-intensive fertilizer lead to lower food prices, but not *that much* lower. A switch to more organic farming practices would be disruptive to some agriculture industries, but not to overall food supply or affordability.

Changes in processes that are invisible to consumers may account for some substitution, and may raise prices, but not the one-for-one increase that is feared by champions of the poor. Turning down the thermostat is thus not the only way, and is likely a relatively painful way, for households to economize. Substituting away from cheaper imported toys might be less agonizing. The popular focus on home heating, electricity, and gasoline detracts from the ubiquity of low carbon prices throughout the economy, and creates a mistaken impression that poor individuals and households are limited to these substitutions. This is not to make light of the effects on poor households. Over the short term, most of a carbon tax would indeed likely fall on consumers.[14] Below, I address ways of limiting those effects on the poorest consumers. But bad policy results when the harm to poor households is emotionally overstated for political purposes.

Finally, the discussion of regressiveness has not yet grappled with the question of what "regressiveness" means. Regressiveness could be measured by different delineations of income, and using a large variety of different assumptions about how consumers respond. If we broke the population down into ten deciles, would we require that progressive greenhouse gas policy have a successively greater effect on each successively richer decile? If we think that condition too strict, would we require successive progressivity if we broke the population down into quartiles? A study of the projected incidence of an increase in gasoline prices in the United States was done by Sarah West and Roberton Williams, who estimated separate demand models for each of five income quintiles, one- and two-adult households, and found that under the most severe and simplistic assumptions—that gasoline is perfectly inelastic and people make no adjustments whatsoever to changes in the price of gasoline—the incidence on the poorest quintiles is not substantially different from that of the next two higher quintiles.[15] Is that good enough? That may not be a question that can be answered by economics, but it is a question that does not appear to be addressed by anyone, not even champions of the poor.

Second, there are time and space dimensions to regressiveness that should not be ignored. Defining the affluence of an individual or a household as a present snapshot in time may not accurately capture how "rich" an individual or household may actually be. For example, graduate students or students in professional schools may have very low or even negative incomes as students, but they are often in a far different situation than those that are working and adding nothing to their human capital and nothing to their future prospects for employment. Or, at the other end of a lifetime, retirees with substantial wealth often have very little income, yet could not be considered "poor" by any reasonable judgment. Given these wrinkles, it may be more accurate to use *consumption* as a measure of affluence rather than income.[16] This derives from something called the "permanent income hypothesis," which posits that people smooth their consumption out over a lifetime, such that they consume only slightly less when their income is low than when it is high.[17] Although as an empirical matter the support for using consumption as a proxy for lifetime income is mixed, there is no real controversy that it is problematic to use income at one point in time as a measure of the affluence of an individual or household.[18] A study by Kevin Hassett, Aparna Mathur, and Gilbert Metcalf showed that when estimating lifetime expenditures on energy and a basket of other goods, a carbon tax in the United States is less regressive than widely believed.[19]

There are also regional variations that overlap with temporal variations. It requires little thought to appreciate that an income of $30,000 per year means very different things in the New York City borough of Manhattan and the town of Manhattan, Kansas. This would seem to be a very big problem, especially given the concerns about a carbon tax affecting rural areas (which have fewer or no transit services) more than urban areas. However, as in the case of looking at income over a lifetime, Hassett, Mathur, and Metcalf found that because of this regional variation, most studies overstate the regressiveness of a carbon tax.[20]

The intuition behind these findings is that many people move up and down various stations in life, and into and out of various geographic places in life, at least in the United States and most likely in other developed countries as well. It is true that there are populations that are mired in poverty without the prospects for climbing enjoyed by business, medical, or law students. It would be insensitive, politically foolish, and morally objectionable to dismiss the burden on these populations. But it is also unwise and misleading to define the regressiveness of carbon taxes solely in terms of snapshot effects on these populations, as the reality of regressiveness is considerably more complicated and nuanced than some would have us believe. There are also many, many others in society who deserve to be counted in policy considerations.

All that said, calls for redistributions as part of greenhouse gas policy should not be ignored. Even most advocates for a carbon tax would concede that if the revenues from a carbon tax were simply absorbed into the governmental treasury, then the carbon tax would indeed be regressive, as several studies seem to indicate.[21] The question is, however, how to address these effects. In part this is such a compelling question because the revenues from a carbon tax *can* be used to address the regressiveness. This problem is solvable.

The key to addressing the regressiveness problem of carbon taxes is to return, or "recycle," at least a large portion of the carbon tax revenues. A number of schemes have been proposed or implemented to recycle the tax revenues back to taxpayers in a way that blunts or even reverses the economic pain suffered by poor households. Provided that the recycling or return of revenues to taxpayers is decoupled from consumption decisions, the revenue "recycling" schemes can preserve the incentive for people to consume less while serving as a wealth redistributive scheme.

Revenue recycling has a very limited history, with only a few examples. Sweden instituted a per-kilogram tax on NO_x emissions which, as noted above, has been highly successful, which refunded the proceeds back to the taxpaying NO_x emitters. This revenue recycling scheme, covering only electricity generating plants with more than 25 GWh of production per year, refunded the proceeds back *in proportion to energy production*. The Swedish NO_x charge thus provides a reward in the form of a net subsidy to those electricity-generation plants that are able to produce electricity more efficiently—those that produce more electricity per unit of emitted NO_x. It is an interesting experiment, and one that may have a tangential effect on regressiveness, by keeping electricity rates down while offering a positive incentive to innovate. But it does not substantially address concerns with regressiveness, since ratepayers of the firms that lose out under such a scheme—the electricity generating firms that are less clever and do *not* find a way to emit less NO_x—could themselves be paying more for electricity.

The British Columbia carbon tax is thus the most prominent experiment to date with revenue recycling to reduce regressiveness. Political economy considerations played prominently in the design and implementation of the BC carbon tax. Because the only serious rival in British Columbia to the governing Liberal Party was the politically more liberal New Democratic Party, it was important for the carbon tax to address concerns with regressiveness. It was, in fact, a very interesting political move to split the NDP's traditional base of environmentalists and those concerned with economic inequality. This was done by a promise to recycle revenues. So seriously did the governing British Columbia Liberal Party take this bit of political strategizing that, as noted above, the carbon tax legislation includes a provision that penalizes the minister of finance personally to the tune of a 15 percent salary cut if somehow the proceeds from the carbon tax were not fully returned in the form of revenue give-backs to taxpayers.[22]

Included in the revenue give-backs are: (i) a low-income refundable tax credit (the "Climate Action Tax Credit") of $100 per adult and $30 per child, (ii) a reduction in personal income taxes by 5 percent on the first $70,000 of income, and (iii) reductions for corporate income taxes.[23] In addition, along with the rollout of the provincial budget that detailed the carbon tax and the revenue recycling schemes, the province issued a one-time Climate Action Dividend of $100 per person for every resident of British Columbia as of December 31, 2007.[24]

It is easy to *claim* that the revenue recycling solves the regressiveness problem of the BC carbon tax—as the governing Liberal Party emphatically did—but it is not entirely clear that it was successful, nor what exactly what that would mean. It is an almost impossible claim to falsify, as it impossible to know exactly how much each household paid in carbon taxes. Clearly, it would be impossible to make determinations on a household-by-household basis, but besides that, there are direct carbon emissions—driving a car and burning gasoline—and indirect emissions—buying goods that were made from greenhouse gas-emitting processes, those *embedded* emissions of products consumed by each household. Determining direct emissions in disaggregated income classes would be challenging, and determining indirect emissions impossible. Even gasoline has an uncertain carbon footprint, some of it being produced by traditional methods, and some of it being produced in Canada's oil sands region by extremely energy-intensive refining methods. And aside from fossil fuel consumption, what about the carbon footprint of produce (locally grown producers paying the carbon tax, importers not), or a myriad of electronic components in a myriad of consumer products? Almost every single good consumed has a carbon footprint, and few of them are measurable. Finally, there is adjustment and substitution: even poor households are apt to be willing and able to change some things to economize if there is a price on carbon dioxide. But as the West and Williams study illustrates, it requires some econometric estimations.

Economic estimation is our best bet at determining how different classes of British Columbians have been affected by the carbon tax. The only analysis undertaken on the BC carbon tax was undertaken by the Canadian Centre for Policy Alternatives, a liberal think tank. CCPA analysts Marc Lee and Toby Sanger concluded in 2008 that as the Liberal government had mapped out the carbon tax over five years, only the first year of the carbon tax would be progressive—in their study, meaning that generally, lower quintiles of British Columbia households fare better than richer ones. In the first year, the lowest quintile of households experiences (in their 2008 projections) a net gain of 0.25 percent of income, while the fourth quintile (second-richest) experiences a net loss of 0.15 percent of income.[25] After the first year, the carbon tax, with its revenue recycling measures, becomes regressive as the Climate Action Tax Credit and the income tax reductions start to pale in comparison with the carbon taxes paid; the natural regressivity of the carbon tax starts to take over, with the result that higher-income households are hurt less than lower-income ones. Moreover, the corporate income tax cuts tend to favor richer households that hold investments in these corporations.

There are at least two significant flaws in the CCPA analysis, however. First, as the CCPA report explains, "household size increases with income."[26] This is an acknowledgment that individuals and households move up income strata over time. Over time, single-person households marry and have children, and over time, incomes tend to increase. There is thus an ignored time dimension to the CCPA analysis that was studied by Hassett and his coauthors. Making sure that poorest British Columbians benefit more than others is in part helping people at a certain stage of their lives. It is thus an over-simplification to characterize the British Columbia tax as choosing the rich over the poor, as if *everyone* in the poor category were chronically poor. This also undermines the notion that individuals in higher-income households have larger carbon footprints. Larger *households* do, but because there are more members of larger households.

The second flaw in the CCPA analysis is its admission that it does not take into account any substitution effects.[27] It asserts that a "dynamic analysis would not change the results in a meaningful way in the short term. Because of the small size of the tax, it will have little impact on consumer behaviour."[28] Knowing from the West and Williams study that the lowest quintiles often make the most substitutions, this is a significant leap. Because the carbon tax is quite small, the differences in incidence of the carbon tax are quite small, so even a little bit of substitution has the potential to change the results. It could be that after substitution, CCPA's conclusions do not hold. The West and Williams study used consumer expenditure data to calculate price elasticities of households broken down into five quintiles by income.[29] Incorporating this extra important step would seem to be a reasonable refinement of the CCPA study.

More detailed economic analysis can and has been done on the effects of carbon taxes and cap-and-trade programs on various demographic groups. As noted above, the West and Williams study found that lower-income households tend to substitute to minimize the effects of gasoline price increases. West and Williams found that a straight gasoline tax increase without any revenue recycling is regressive, but under several revenue recycling scenarios, the poorest households can be made to suffer less, and in some scenarios can even be made better off under the carbon tax scheme than without it. The policy that tends to go the furthest in addressing regressiveness problems is the lump sum distribution of money on a per-person basis.[30]

A good number of other studies have also been done on the distributional impacts of carbon pricing. Dallas Burtraw, Richard Sweeney, and Margaret Walls undertake a similarly careful and even more ambitious study of different ways of implementing a cap-and-trade program.[31] They propose ten different ways of allocating the costs of the emissions allowances. One proposal allocates allowances to the carbon dioxide emitters on a "grandfathered" basis, or keyed to some historical level of emissions. The entitlement to emit carbon dioxide thus essentially rests with the emitters. The other nine proposals all involved some method of returning the revenues to households.[32] The study also broke down US households into income deciles, and into eleven regions, capturing important regional differences in heating and electricity costs; the Pacific Northwest, for example, derives most of its electricity from hydroelectric power, insulating it from most increases in coal or natural gas process, while the southeastern United States has high electricity costs but low heating costs. A study by Burtraw and colleagues underscored dramatically what West and Williams and a number of other studies already found: that it makes a tremendous difference whether and how tax revenues (or similarly, the costs of emissions allowances) are distributed. "Grandfathering" them, or essentially giving emitters the entitlement to emit because they had historically done so, is *clearly the most regressive policy*. Again, one intuition for this is that much of the wealth and savings occurs at the corporate end of the energy industries, and much of the benefit of allowance allocation accrues to shareholders of these corporations. But to underscore the political economy point, this point has not been emphatically made in the run-ups to climate legislation in Washington and Ottawa.

In another important modeling project, Sebastian Rauch, Gilbert Metcalf, John Reilly, and Sergey Paltsev model the distributional effects of three prominent bills—the Waxman-Markey bill, the Kerry-Lieberman bill, and the Cantwell-Collins bill, a cap-and-trade bill that largely recycled revenues back to households by way of a lump sum distribution. Interestingly, this study found that *even without revenue recycling*, carbon pricing is not necessarily regressive.[33] The intuition behind this surprising result is that carbon pricing tends to reduce the returns to expensive forms of capital—expensive machinery and assets—which affect wealthy investors more than poor people. So while people can more easily envision the costs of a carbon tax at the gasoline pump, the effects of a carbon tax on a wealthy household's investment returns may be much greater. A second reason for this result is that in the United States, the lowest income groups derive more of their income from government transfers, some of which are indexed to inflation, and are therefore insulated to some extent from the price increases brought on by carbon pricing. Indexing for inflation will have the effect of incorporating the price increases caused by carbon pricing. So while the incidence of a carbon price created by a carbon tax or a cap-and-trade scheme may appear to affect lower-income households more, their inflation-indexed government income will more or less keep pace with the price increases. In a subsequent related project, researchers (including Metcalf) considered individual US government transfer programs, and incorporated specific indexing policies for each program into their model. They found that while indexed programs tend to make the lowest income groups better off, a number of households in the lowest group would be worse off.[34] More research is in the offing in this important area, as perceptions of regressiveness are, as we now understand, based on incomplete conceptions of how people are affected by carbon pricing.

These *ex ante* studies and models are all we draw upon in terms of determining how carbon taxes or cap-and-trade programs are or can be made to be progressive. Since the BC carbon tax is the only program thus far that aims to recycle revenues to address regressiveness, it serves as the only potential data point. But nothing has been done *ex post* to evaluate the BC carbon tax.

Overall, however, some conclusions can probably be drawn from the BC carbon tax and the CCPA report. First, the CCPA is surely in the right in criticizing the reduction in corporate income tax rates as part of the revenue recycling scheme. Addressing competitiveness concerns would seem to be a reasonable part of a carbon tax, and quite understandable from a political economy perspective. But it comes at a large cost in terms of subtracting from the progressiveness of the carbon tax. It would seem that recycling revenues back to households would do much more to solve regressiveness problems than recycling revenues back to corporations would accomplish in terms of addressing competitiveness concerns. Besides, money distributed to the poorest households, generally speaking, is money that gets spent and pumped back into the provincial economy.

Second, while revenue recycling may be useful, the concept of revenue *neutrality* may not actually be enough of a political benefit to be worth the trouble. In most North American jurisdictions, there is always some suspicion that taxing governments find ways to play the shell game with voters that reduce the credibility of promises to recycle revenues. Despite the 15 percent salary penalty that is part of the BC Carbon Tax, BC voters still express some suspicion that the revenues are not fully recycled.[35] In a study, survey respondents in BC were asked about their willingness to pay an increased gasoline tax if its revenues were recycled. Many did, but a whopping two-thirds of all respondents expressed at least some mistrust that even if a BC government promised to recycle such proceeds, that it would actually do so.[36] Given such skepticism, it may be better to use carbon tax proceeds to *actually* reduce poverty, instead of promising to do so. As the CCPA argues in its report, the idea of revenue recycling is not really such a sacred principle that it needs to drive climate policy. Nor is it easily verifiable, given the uncertain carbon tax expenditures of the many demographics.

Third, even if regressiveness is a verifiable notion, these modeling results seem to confirm what we already intuitively understand: that carbon tax revenues (or auctioned allowance proceeds under cap-and-trade) can be a powerful tool to reduce the regressive effects of carbon pricing and, perhaps more ambitiously, reduce income inequality. Based as they are on actual data and on actual economic observations on how people behave—most prominently how people substitute in the face of changing energy prices—these models are fairly good projections on the actual effects, post-adjustment, of how people will fare under carbon pricing policies. While emotional appeals to our sense of economic justice can be a handy politically tool, at the end of the day what we really care about is the economic welfare of those on lower economic strata. Economic models, even if only forward-looking projections, probably tell us a lot more about how the poor will fare than emotional appeals do. And by all accounts, while the BC government did not do all it could to address regressiveness in its carbon tax, it did seem to have the financial wherewithal to make the carbon tax painless for the poorest British Columbians.

Finally, the real-world contexts of the British Columbia carbon tax and other carbon pricing proposals serve to remind us of the relatively small effects of carbon taxation (or more generally, carbon prices) on overall income inequality. For one thing, the wildly fluctuating prices of gasoline have reminded us is how small of an effect that taxing governments actually have on prices. Of all of the ways that government policies either ignore or aggravate income inequalities—including preferential tax treatments for income derived from investments (capital gains tax rates in the United States)—carbon pricing would be one of the most trifling ones.

Regressiveness is an important consideration when weighing changes to tax policy, but the obstacles to designing a progressive carbon tax seem to be solvable. Because economic expenditures are uncertain and because regressiveness itself is susceptible to many definitions, it is probably impossible to *prove* that revenue recycling reverses the regressive effects of carbon pricing. But it is simple enough to formulate a package of tax policies that utilize carbon tax proceeds (or auctioned allowance proceeds under cap-and-trade) to subsidize low-income households and lessen, if not entirely eliminate, any regressive impacts. Those who oppose carbon taxes on grounds of regressiveness often ignore these possibilities, relying on emotion rather than economic facts. At the same time, policy makers have been incredibly timid in shying away from carbon pricing, and allowing the shrill to steer the debate away from carbon taxation. So, we are left with the self-reinforcing notion that even mentioning carbon taxes is political suicide.

Moreover, of all of the types of government policies that are held hostage to income inequality issues, carbon pricing is quite possibly the most important policy, and the one with the smallest regressive effect. In the past several years, the US government has spent tens of billions of dollars saving from bankruptcy two of the most stubbornly inefficient firms in the history of human industry: automakers General Motors and Chrysler. In addition, the United States government has spent billions more on bailouts of financial firms that made unwise strategic investments that they did not even understand. Acknowledging that there were macroeconomic benefits to these bailouts, most of the net winners of this generosity have been shareholders, which are by and large the affluent half of the US population (and of foreign shareholders of these corporations, which are likely to be even more affluent). The effects of spending these billions of dollars will not be obvious to most Americans for a long time, but cannot portend well for taxpayers of modest means. For all of the great many reasons for the unacceptable present and future levels of economic inequality in the developed countries of the world, especially in North America, carbon pricing leading to higher energy prices would be a long, long way from being the most egregious one.

Ineffectiveness

There are those who oppose a carbon tax because they fear it will crimp economic growth. On the other end of the spectrum, there are those who oppose a carbon tax because it will not actually work quickly or strongly enough to reduce emissions. By many accounts, even a high carbon tax on the order of that prescribed by Nicholas Stern may not necessarily bring about the changes that some people feel are needed to avert climate disaster. Smaller carbon taxes, such as the one in British Columbia, seem even less likely to make a difference.

There is some evidence to the contrary: Sweden's carbon tax, instituted in 1990, is quite high—the base rate is typically about 950 Swedish Krona per ton of carbon dioxide, or about 100 Euros per ton.[37] As is true of carbon taxes in Europe, it is less transparent that one would expect or hope. But having been introduced on top of a variety of other long-standing excise taxes on fossil fuels, and in the context of European Union rules on energy taxation and trade, Sweden (like other Scandinavian countries) has a schedule of carbon taxation for different industries and different fossil fuels.[38] Although this is not as straightforward and uniform a carbon tax as British Columbia's, it seems to have reduced carbon dioxide emissions: emissions in Sweden decreased by 7 percent between 1990 and 2005, a period in which the Swedish economy grew by 36 percent.[39] It is difficult to prove that this decrease is attributable to the Swedish carbon tax, in light of the different rates on top of different taxes for different industries and sectors. But the carbon tax makes up the bulk of the tax on fossil fuel emissions in Sweden, and so plays the most important role in pricing emissions.[40] In any case, the long-term decoupling of carbon dioxide emissions and economic growth is striking. Sweden is one of very few countries to have accomplished this decoupling.

While curmudgeons may grudgingly concede that a high carbon tax like that in Sweden would reduce emissions, a smaller one like the British Columbia carbon tax is a different matter. When the British Columbia government introduced its carbon tax in 2008, it admitted that its modest price effects would not have a substantial effect on carbon dioxide emissions in the province.[41] More action was needed, and was in fact contemplated as the British Columbia government also enacted a companion program laying the foundation for a cap-and-trade program as part of British Columbia's participation in the California-led Western Climate Initiative. But the carbon tax is indeed so small that one wonders if it really was meant to accomplish anything. The BC carbon tax was designed to ramp up from about $9 per ton of CO_2 in 2008 to about $30 in 2012. This translates into about 2.4 cents per litre of gasoline, up to about 7.2 cents per liter in 2012. Gasoline prices fluctuate a great deal more than that, spiking in 2005 in the aftermath of Hurricane Katrina to more than $1.12 per liter, only to see a higher spike in the summer of 2008 to nearly $1.50, followed by a dip just a few months later to below 80 cents.[42] In Vancouver, gas stations even commonly lower the price by three and a half cents at nighttime. Does an extra 2.4 cents—or even 7 cents—per liter really change behavior very much?

It is a fair question. The standard economic answer is that a price increase will lead to a decline in consumption. It could take a while, but higher prices always lead to lower consumption, all other things being equal. So for the household wondering if it will drive less because of a small increase in the price of gasoline, the answer could well be no, but there are many, many other consumers that *could* be right at the margins of making a consumption decision. Price *elasticity* is the term that economists use to denote how much of an adjustment consumers, in the aggregate, can be expected to make in response to a price change. Consumption of commodities respond not only to changes in the price of the commodity itself—measured by the *own-price elasticity*—but also changes in the prices of other goods that may be substitutes or affect the economic environment some other way—measured by the *cross-price elasticities*. Finally, consumption of commodities can change to varying degrees as income changes—measured by the *income elasticity*. Bread and milk have low income elasticities. Sports cars and cosmetic surgery have high income elasticities.

Most energy analysis is conducted on own-price elasticities, although income also figures very prominently in energy consumption. There are short-term and long-term elasticities—adjustments that are made in the relatively short term—on the order of a few months—and those that are made for the longer term. Long-term elasticities are invariably greater, since at any given time, the timing may or many not be right for any individual household to make an adjustment. Over a longer period of time, there arise more and more times during which an adjustment—some decision that might be affected by a price—seems appropriate. For example, a family that has just purchased a new sport-utility vehicle would not contemplate replacing it even if gasoline prices rose sharply. One would expect very few adjustments of that sort. However, over a five- or ten-year period, as the sport-utility vehicle starts to age and incur more maintenance costs, and as it nears the end of its useful life, a replacement decision is more likely to take into account gasoline prices. As the same family contemplates what they will buy to replace that sport-utility vehicle, the family has a wider array of options available than it does when it has a brand-new shiny SUV. And in the *aggregate*, over a longer period, more and more households are likely to arrive at that decision point at which they contemplate replacing an aging vehicle, and more adjustments are likely to be made. As long-term elasticity takes into account this greater number of adjustments, it would naturally be larger than short-term elasticities.

Among commodities, fossil fuel usage is one of the more studied phenomena, and the likelihood that people adjust to even small price changes in fossil fuel price is so well-established that it almost rises to the level of an economic maxim. While one might ask oneself whether a family might change their mind about anything if the carbon price is as small as $9 per ton of CO_2 (translating into 2.4 cents per liter at the gas pump), there are a myriad of other decision makers that could well change their behavior. As argued above, the University of British Columbia is just such an entity. Facing a tax liability that would be considered small by industrial standards, but significant to an academic institution or a medium-sized business or industry, it set about finding ways to reduce its reliance on fossil fuels for powering the campus.

For decades, economists have been studying the aggregate responses to change in energy prices. The range of estimates can be quite large, as some studies are limited to certain regions or countries, and some are limited in time, so the economic environment in which price changes are studied can be quite varied. As an empirical matter, it is safe to say that long-term elasticities are indeed greater than short-term elasticities. It is also likely that industrial and commercial consumers have larger long-term elasticities than residential consumers.[43] So it might be misleading for individuals to examine their own personal situation and ask themselves, "would I turn down my thermostat if the price of natural gas went up by 5 percent?" The point is how much, in the aggregate, all consumers of energy change their behavior, and on this score, industrial and commercial consumers, which accounted for half of all energy consumption in the United States in 2008 (with residential accounting for 22 percent),[44] would provide a different answer.

That said, there are certain instances in which the kinds of adjustments predicted by economists have not been made. Homeowners considering the purchase of new appliances have been surprisingly reluctant to consider energy-efficient models and undertake home renovations that would improve energy efficiency and have very short payback periods. In some cases, all that was needed was some information that showed prospective buyers how much money they could save with energy-efficient appliances.[45] In other cases, the homeowner is a landlord that does not actually pay the electricity bills, and thus has little incentive to improve energy efficiency, if she even knows about it; only sporadically do high energy bills get capitalized into rents.[46] Similarly, large organizations and government bureaucracies, at least in the past, have had budgeting procedures and practices that discouraged long-term thrift. Purchasing an expensive piece of equipment has, at least at times, been difficult to justify even if it led to long-term savings.[47] And finally, sometimes liquidity comes into play, as households, firms, or agencies are truly limited in their short-term ability to buy more expensive equipment, albeit less expensive in the long term.[48]

All of these obstacles to the purchase of energy-efficient equipment call for different policy responses. Product labeling requirements were effective in bringing information on the long-term savings of energy-efficient appliances to the attention of prospective buyers.[49] Institutional reforms and enlightened budgeting practices have helped alleviate the fiscal disconnect for many large organizations and government agencies. Government-provided financial incentives have helped buyers get over the hurdles posed by high initial capital costs.[50] It depends on the problem. Policy solutions are plentiful.

But none of this is an argument *against* carbon taxes. It may be true that there are barriers to energy efficiency that carbon pricing cannot solve by itself. That does not mean that there should be no carbon price at all. To return to a theme in this book, a carbon tax could well complement other policies designed to bring about behavioral and structural change to reduce energy usage and carbon dioxide emissions.

The mistake with arguing that a carbon tax is ineffective is that it confuses individual instances of ineffectiveness with predictions about behavior in the aggregate. For small carbon taxes, there is indeed no guarantee that even a significant portion of energy consumers would change their behavior at all, let alone turn down their thermostats. A carbon tax would have to be significant, and would have to increase over time to keep pace with inflation, and with what economists believe is an increasing urgency over time to reduce emissions. If a reasonably large carbon tax can be implemented, there would be a myriad of opportunities to reduce emissions that, in the aggregate, could make a difference. From the Dogfish Head Craft Brewery in Delaware to the University of British Columbia to restaurants and universities buying James Peret's Vegawatt generator, changes large and small are made to reduce carbon dioxide emissions. It could even be unimpor-

tant if the vast majority of households in British Columbia simply ignored the BC carbon tax. The BC carbon tax would serve a valuable
purpose if, in aggregate, other carbon dioxide-reducing changes
throughout the provincial economy add up to something substantial.
The vast amounts of economic research on energy usage strongly suggests that this will be the case.

Crowding Out

A central argument of this book is that a carbon tax is an important
first step, after which many other important steps must be taken, including subsequent increases in the carbon tax itself. What if, as some
people suspect, levying the carbon tax would harm the prospects for
these other important subsequent steps? That would undermine the
argument that the carbon tax is a good "first step."

There is reasonable cause to worry about the possibility that a carbon tax would "crowd out" support for subsequent policies. A line of
"crowding out" experiments have been conducted that seem to support the notion that once people pay some amount of money that is
fixed and announced in advance—something like a tax—they become
reluctant to either pay any more or support any public policies that
would require more costs. Once people have the idea that they have
been "taxed," they are apt to feel that they have done their part—and if
given a choice in the matter, they would just as soon their sacrifice stop
there.

In fact, there is some evidence that once people feel that they have
been taxed for some costly behavior, they become more likely to engage in that behavior. A famous study of an Israeli child care facility
sought to measure the effect of late fees imposed when parents are late
picking up their children. Since late pickups result in staff staying late
just for one or a few children, this is clearly inefficient behavior, not to
mention inconsiderate of the caregiving staff. What economists Uri
Gneezy and Aldo Rustichini found was that imposing a fine for late
pickups *increased* the occurrence of late pickups, a discouraging result
not only for day care centers, but also economists that preach the effectiveness of price signals.[51] Their explanation was that certain social
norms, constituting a more complete "social contract," may play a
stronger role than financial incentives. Similarly, another study found
that charitable contributions were crowded out by a reduction in

wealth when that reduction was explicitly identified as tax.[52] Finally, most significantly for purposes of this book, Timo Goeschl and Grischa Perino found that, in a comparison of policy instruments, willingness to pay for reductions in greenhouse gas controls were lower after the imposition of a tax than for a command-and-control regulation.[53]

The idea that a tax somehow commodifies prosocial behavior, diluting incentives to undertake it, is not new. In fact, it implicitly motivates some of the long-standing opposition to market-based regulation, which would include Pigouvian taxes and cap-and-trade, as well as the variants. Some environmental advocates have never given up a belief that pollution is morally objectionable, and that market-based mechanisms dilute or entirely remove the stigma associated with polluting. If public opinion polls are any indication, a significant portion of the general public also holds this view to some extent.

There are two responses to the objection that greenhouse gas regulation must be stringent enough to meet the moral imperative of averting climate change. The first is that it is deeply misguided to stigmatize the emission of greenhouse gases when emissions are so widespread and have so many different sources. In affluent Western societies every individual, rich or poor, benefits from an economy that is very greenhouse gas–intensive and enjoys unnaturally low fossil fuel prices. At what point along the spectrum, from a struggling lower middle-class family that drives everywhere and shops at Wal-Mart, to the American Electric Power Company (the largest carbon dioxide emitter in the United States) does the conscious emission of carbon dioxide become morally wrong? The answer is that it there is no principled way to distinguish from among the vast majority of greenhouse gas emitters. There is no stigma to dilute or remove. The extent to which people have the desire to reduce their cognitive dissonance by blaming someone else and directing regulation at someone else should be the subject of effective communications policy, not climate policy.

There is a second set of responses to a second, more powerful objection to pricing carbon: that, judging from the Goeschl-Perino study, it might be a very good idea to get the carbon price right the first time or else people will not support any subsequent measures to reduce greenhouse gases. But this objection (which is not what Goeschl and Perino argue) seems to demand too much from carbon pricing. As argued earlier, no single policy currently known can serve as the comprehensive response to the problem of climate change. The alternatives to a carbon tax are generally less effective and more costly.

Building upon flawed climate policies to develop further policies is likely to carry with it the unhappy news that past policies were ineffective, which would itself damage prospects for further rounds of climate policies. So if a carbon tax that is too small winds up being the only policy that can be implemented, then it stands a good chance of being the best policy anyway.

Another response to the serial-policy problem is simply that climate policy cannot be a one-and-done proposition. This unhappy truth is typical of the difficult things that need to be effectively communicated about climate change to a general public still lagging in understanding of the climate problem and the feasible solutions. That a general public would like some finality to climate policy and carbon prices has not stopped economists from prescribing a carbon tax that rises over time, matching the increasing marginal social damages of carbon dioxide emissions. Nor should it. Emitting greenhouse gases will become more costly as the world approaches a likely future with increasingly severe climatic changes. Abating greenhouse gases too much at any given time detracts from efforts to abate at other times. Along similar lines, while people may balk at taking a costly first step that will not necessarily provide a complete solution, the iterative nature of climate science and climate policy is such that this is likely inevitable. This disquieting indeterminacy is fodder for climate skeptics, who have tapped into the uncertainty to sow doubt about the risk of climate change. But honest, forthright policy is not playing into the hands of climate skeptics. Attempting to evade or obfuscate the inconveniences and costs of climate policy *is* playing into the hands of climate skeptics. Further, it has to be courageously said there is uncertainty about climate science, and that a current policy may be too much or may be too little. Again, policy making under extreme uncertainty is not really new; it is just that the analogies to familiar policies need to be made. Very little is known about when the next major earthquake will strike California or the Pacific Northwest. That does not render the policy of seismic upgrading of public schools and nuclear reactors irrational.

Conclusion

A carbon tax does appear to have political economy problems. And a carbon tax could be regressive, but probably not more so than other instruments. In fact, recent findings suggest that the recycling of revenues to favor lower-income groups might be desirable but not even necessary to make a carbon tax progressive. And while a carbon tax may not be fully effective at all times, this would never be a realistic requirement for any greenhouse gas policy. Finally, while a carbon tax *may* set up a political environment in which further action may be difficult, the reality of climate policy is such that this environment is unavoidable, given the shortfalls of alternative instruments.

All that said, if political popularity were any indication of the actual merits of climate instruments, we should forget about carbon taxes. Even though carbon taxes are not often debated openly, the arguments for and against (mostly against) seem to weigh heavily in the background, narrowing the options before influential people invest the time to think about them. If political discussion is at all a functional "marketplace of ideas," then carbon taxation would seem to be an idea with a fairly limited market value.[54]

And yet, if you distill the various arguments for carbon taxes, you find a consistent theme: faith in markets to produce the right results. That faith might be questioned after a memorable series of burst bubbles—the dot.com bubble, as well as more recent market mishaps leading to one of the most horrendous crises in the history of global finance. Markets have failed spectacularly to appreciate risks. And it is true that markets frequently fail: climate change is itself, as Nicholas Stern has pronounced, the "greatest and widest-ranging market failure ever seen."[55] But it is telling that *this* is not among the arguments against carbon taxes. Nobody is arguing that carbon taxes won't work because markets are stupid.

Nobody would contend that a carbon tax is bulletproof or a magic salve to stop climate change. But if carbon taxes are faulted for failing to provide a singular solution, the same criticism can be made of every other greenhouse policy. It is not realistic to think that any one policy instrument can solve such a complex problem. Rather, the point of a carbon tax is to reorient economies by creating the right price signals. All that I argue is that a carbon tax is a crucial first step, and should be a central part of a greenhouse gas policy platform—a platform upon which other policies might be built.

Chapter 5

Carbon Tax Psychology

So why does the idea of a carbon tax remain in political purgatory? Even detractors of carbon taxes would generally concede, in candid conversation, that a carbon tax is at least as effective or nearly as effective in reducing carbon dioxide emissions as other options, especially since most countries already collect taxes on fossil fuels. Most would also have to acknowledge that carbon taxes could address regressiveness concerns, and perhaps, given recent findings, perhaps even do so without revenue recycling.

Some very prominent economists with a variety of political orientations have written in support of carbon taxes. Almost simultaneously in 2006, Nobel laureate Joseph Stiglitz, once President Bill Clinton's chief economic adviser, and Harvard economics professor Gregory Mankiw, once President George W. Bush's chief economic adviser, wrote in favor of carbon taxes.[1] Most economists would likely agree with much of what Stiglitz and Mankiw say, regardless of political beliefs. Economics textbooks usually prescribe Pigouvian taxes to internalize environmental externalities, and few emissions taxes would work as neatly and efficiently as a carbon tax in this regard.

And yet, carbon taxes still have an almost magical repugnance. Political campaigns against proposed cap-and-trade legislation in the United States have often made the argument (not altogether incorrectly) that cap-and-trade is actually a stealth carbon *tax*. This is a very effective means of generating political opposition to cap-and-trade. But why? Why is a carbon tax considered so vile that it serves as the political bogeyman for climate legislation?

There are two interrelated reasons for the persistent opposition to carbon taxes, and to some extent they reinforce each other. Neither has been broadly discussed in policy circles. First, subtle psychological effects have biased people against certain types of public policies. By their nature, people are reluctant to make changes in their lives without full information, and their preferences on public policy reflect this. People also are hesitant to do things that hurt or injure other people, and the more cognizant they are of the negative consequences of certain policy choices, the less popular those choices become. Politicians are keenly aware of these human proclivities, and indeed harbor the same impulses themselves. The reality is, however, that tradeoffs are everywhere, and every policy has a variety of hidden costs and hidden victims. But these disadvantages are not made explicit when policies are packaged and spun out from a Capital Hill or Parliament Hill office. In fact, there is no incentive for politicians to emphasize or even acknowledge the downsides; hence only feel-good, sound-nice policies emerge. There is thus little incentive for politicians to try and package carbon taxes in a more politically attractive manner. So, political motivations lead to a lack of transparency about policies, which distorts public perception of carbon taxes, which in turn further disincentivizes politicians from being forthcoming. Politicians and pundits, citing skewed opinion polls, have created a conventional wisdom based upon profoundly wrong assumptions and errant heuristics. Working around an instrument choice bias is likely to be inefficient, but more importantly, ineffective. The bias must be addressed head-on.

This first reason feeds into the second reason that carbon taxes have remained unpopular. Much of the conventional wisdom that carbon taxes are noxious comes from public opinion polls, which seem to have consistently shown a broad and deep opposition to carbon taxes. But these public opinion polls have usually described climate policies in the same loaded terms used by legislators and others in the policy world, and these descriptions are biased. To be sure, polling organizations have no intent of asking loaded questions. Their questions generally reflect the information that they are given from legislators and others in the policy world. But the information available is often incomplete in a way that skews perception. As a result, policies are inadvertently framed so as to create a bias in favor of instruments that can hide their costs—such as command-and-control, government subsidies, and cap-and-trade—and against instruments that are transparent with their costs—such as carbon taxes. For example, a typical recent study asked respondents if they would favor the federal government "[g]iv[ing] companies tax breaks to produce more electricity from water, wind, and solar power." Eighty-four percent favored such a proposal. Immediately preceding this question, respondents were asked if they would favor the federal government "[i]ncreas[ing] taxes on gasoline so that people either drive less, or buy cars that use less gas," and if they favored the federal government [i]ncreas[ing] taxes on electricity so that people use less of it." 71 percent and 78 percent, respectively, *opposed* these measures.[2] In retrospect, it is remarkable that we could have failed to recognize how leading these kinds of questions had become. One might as well ask, "are you in favor of having the government do something good for the environment?" and "are you in favor of the government making things more expensive?" The answers to questions like these are not meaningful. And yet, these results seem to reinforce the perceived infeasibility of carbon taxes or gasoline taxes. With varying levels of intent, politicians reinforce the notion in voters' minds that carbon taxes hurt them, and other policies are miraculously cost-free.

Debiasing climate instrument choice should begin with public opinion polls, which need to be drafted more carefully in terms of presenting public policy options to the general public. Presenting some options with costs and others without costs is skewing results. Precise comparisons of costs and benefits may be difficult to come by, but polls can certainly do better than to simply omit them. As far as government agencies and political bodies are concerned, standard practice and normal discourse should always include consideration of costs and benefits when weighing competing policy options.

Addressing the psychological part of the bias is more complicated. It is not enough to simply have better information about the costs and effectiveness of different policies. Even when presented with relatively balanced information, people still harbor systemic biases against certain types of public policy. For example, one survey found that only 34 percent of respondents favored "[a]bolishing the payroll tax for all Americans and replacing it with a tax on carbon emissions."[3] This is a proposal that is revenue-neutral on its face; *and* yet it was unpopular despite the fact that respondents in this survey were generally in favor of action to address climate change. Similarly, another study asked respondents if they favored an increased gasoline tax of 25 cents per gallon, with the revenues would be returned to taxpayers by reducing the federal income tax—again, a proposal that is revenue-neutral on its face and again, strongly opposed.[4]

So why is it that people dislike carbon taxes? It is certainly unhelpful that a carbon tax contains the word "tax," but that is unlikely to be the sole cause, as the survey question above pits one tax (carbon) against another (payroll). There is something deeper.

Enter social psychologists and "behavioral economists." There are psychological effects at work, affecting how people view public finance issues generally, that make carbon taxes appear worse than they actually are. Social psychology and the field of "behavioral economics" have generated some insights into how people view the world and make decisions that diverge from what could be considered rational. It is not just irrationality in a dismal economic sense, but a demonstrable inconsistency in the way monetary matters are viewed. People widely rely on over-simplistic *heuristics* to make decisions, which in many cases can leave them worse off than if they had listened to their inner economist more carefully. The widespread opposition to carbon taxes is such a case.

Behavioral economics, more a branch of psychology than economics, began exploding in intellectual popularity even before several massive market failures, or "bubbles," cast a pall over the field of economics. Behavioral economics, by finding regular and systemic deviations from rationality, poses a robust challenge to the fundamental economic assumption of rationality. It is a tribute to the researchers in this field that economists have co-opted it by labeling it "behavioral economics," and usurping "social psychology." The recent economic mishaps—the dot.com bubble, the worldwide recession brought on by the housing crisis, and the doubts over the fiscal soundness of European countries—have only made it fashionable to write about how neoclassical economists have it all wrong. But the intellectual roots of this behavioral challenge to economics are much older and go much deeper.

The purpose of exploring behavioral economics in this book is not to join in the burning of economics texts, but rather to explain how economists actually have it *right* when they advocate for carbon taxes. There are some reasonable grounds on which to oppose a carbon tax, but the most common reasons, stated explicitly or not, are not rational. This chapter delves into why and how these mistaken reasons—these *biases*—have come to be, and how they work against carbon taxes. How do these kinds of biases form? Can it be demonstrated that in *other instances* that these kinds of biases work to the detriment of people that hold them? (The answer is yes.)

Psychological research has shown that given a choice among taxing mechanisms, people seem to prefer *hidden taxes* to transparent ones.[5] Even if the costs of other instruments are comparable, people are likely to balk at carbon taxes. Confronting this bias will require more than just a "labeling" requirement to provide cost and effectiveness indicators. Instead, policy prescriptions will have to address our cognitive anomalies.

Here I propose some behavioral explanations of why people are biased against carbon taxes. Without claiming comprehensiveness, this chapter surveys those behavioral effects that seem most likely to induce bias. There is no particular hierarchy, classification system, or organizational principles to describe these effects. While these behavioral effects have been co-opted as part of economic theory, they do not currently constitute a unified or an internally coherent field of thought. Indeed, there is overlap among some of these effects. Nevertheless, exploring how they might affect the climate change policy debate is critical to understanding why we make certain choices, and how we can make better ones.

Note that there is another set of psychological effects that could shed light on why people believe or disbelieve in climate change. This chapter only addresses how behavioral effects might affect carbon taxation vis-à-vis other climate policy instruments, and not the separate, much larger question of whether people believe that climate change is "real" or not. That is a different, and potentially much larger research agenda.

To be clear, this chapter does not purport to provide *evidence* of psychological biases against carbon taxes. Not only do I lack formal training in psychology, it would be overselling to claim that opposition to carbon taxes is entirely explainable in psychological terms. A burgeoning literature on the psychology of taxation is only now emerging, and being pursued in the rigorous psychological tradition, offering only bits of empirical evidence of some predispositions when people confront taxes. The case for psychological biases against carbon taxation requires careful experimentation that creates robust and replicable results, ones that can provide core insights into the way that people think, and the way that this thinking maps onto consumption taxes such as carbon taxes. That is left to much future research.

People in democratic societies generally say they place a value on governmental and legal transparency; but here is a transparent policy instrument with nothing but political enemies. Despite the fact that carbon taxes are likely to infringe *less* on consumption habits than many other climate policies, people remain opposed to them, and politicians have been extremely sensitive to this opposition. All of this hostility flies in the face of some fairly simple policy considerations and economics. This chapter proposes some psychological explanations for why economists have been unsuccessful in persuading everybody else of the value of carbon taxes.

The "Do No Harm" effect

The following problem has been posed to generations of students: you see a train steaming down the tracks, headed toward five workers on the train tracks. The workers cannot see the train approaching and the train conductor cannot see the workers, and will not stop. You have no time to run down and warn the workers and you cannot yell loudly enough for them to hear you. The train will run over the workers and kill them if you do nothing. You can, however, reach a switch that would send the train onto another track, on which there is only one oblivious worker who would be killed. If you flip the switch, you also have no way to rescue that single worker. Do you flip the switch? A surprisingly large number of people would not. It is apparently so offensive to *affirmatively* cause anyone's death, that many would rather *allow* the death of five than kill one.

This exercise and a number of other experiments have shown a persistent propensity of humans to favor harmful inaction over harmful action.[6] The "Do No Harm" effect, or "omission bias," is an aversion to causing harm, to the point that people would prefer a greater harm to occur by omission. That is, it is a way of thinking that pays more attention to the *nature* of actions than it does to the outcomes. It suggests people often care more about their personal responsibility than the ultimate outcome of their actions. Experimental simulations thus typically pose to research subjects two or more outcomes, one being demonstrably better than the other, and test whether the subjects are willing to take an affirmative action that harms someone in order to achieve the better outcome. Usually, many variations are hypothesized in order to isolate the different factors that come in to play in these sorts of difficult decisions. But the findings have been robust: some people will consciously opt for an inferior outcome by inaction, if their action would unavoidably harm some. Most experiments find that only a minority of subjects will choose an inferior outcome to avoid doing affirmative harm. But it is often a very significant minority, and one that has been present in just about every sample of research subjects in which this type of study has been conducted. Significantly, the Do No Harm effect has been extended to groups, so that people find it as uncomfortable to affirmatively cause harm to certain groups as they do to cause harm to individuals. The Do No Harm effect would prevent some people from imposing increased risks on one group in order to reduce risks in another group.[7]

The pioneer researcher in this area is psychology professor Jonathan Baron of the University of Pennsylvania, who has carried out or taken part in the vast majority of Do No Harm experiments. Baron argues that this way of thinking, which he describes as "non-consequentialist," can not only be misguided, but unethical.[8] Certainly a maxim to "Do No Harm" has deep and practical origins. In many situations, the losses that would be imposed upon one group by an affirmative action could well be more painful and greater than the gains that could be produced for the benefit of another group. If that is the case, then Doing No Harm is clearly the correct course, and poses no conflicts with consequentialist decision-making strategies. But if harm is inevitable and is *clearly minimized* by acting, failure to do so becomes difficult to justify as a matter of public policy.

Given that *some* people have this proclivity *some* of the time, what are the implications for public policy? Baron cites examples from both tort and criminal law as evidence that the Do No Harm effect manifests itself in law and policy. For example, euthanasia is generally illegal in the United States, but "do not resuscitate" orders are legal and common. Similarly, US environmental law regulates air pollution, but is completely silent on the mitigation of naturally occurring radon gas. Radon is responsible for an estimated 15,000 to 22,000 lung cancer deaths in the United States—according to current knowledge, more than are caused by air pollution[9] and only second to the number caused by smoking.[10] Although most legal rules are complex and are affected by many factors other than a Do No Harm effect, sound public lawmaking and policy requires consciousness of the effect, and corrective considerations when it indefensibly and obviously biases decisions.

But is there any evidence that people's reactions in experimental settings translate to the real world? Even if psychologists can measure a Do No Harm effect, could it predict public opinion about policies? Could it explain why politicians take certain positions? Secondly, since public policy problems are so complex, how sure can we be that the Do No Harm effect is actually influencing decisions?

To address these questions, many of Baron's experiments consciously pose salient public policy or legal issues, and attempt to demonstrate that when people are asked to opine on matters of public policy, they are likely to employ a Do No Harm bias. One of Baron's experiments, undertaken with Ilana Ritov, involved a hypothetical question about vaccination. Research subjects were told that a flu epidemic would kill 10 children out of 10,000. A vaccine exists that could prevent the flu, but its side effects would also kill some children. Survey respondents were asked what the maximum tolerable death rate for the vaccine should be. If the Do No Harm bias was not present, subjects should say that the maximum tolerable death rate should be nine or ten. To make the public policy connection, subjects were asked what their maximum tolerable vaccine death rate would be if they were considering: (i) whether to vaccinate their own child, and (ii) whether to support a law making the vaccination compulsory. The results were very similar: in both cases the mean responses were well below nine. In this simplest scenario, the mean response for maximum death rate was 5.4 for the child vaccination and 5.75 for the public policy. While a majority of subjects do in fact choose to both vaccinate their children and support compulsory administration, a very significant minority of people would not. For some, it would appear preferable to assume the risk of letting children die of the flu than the risk of causing them to die from administration of the vaccine. Ritov and Baron employ a number of variations to demonstrate the different group circumstances under which the Do No Harm bias manifests itself. And notice that the Ritov and Baron experiments did two important things: they presented the same problem as a private vaccination problem (your own child) *and* also as a public policy decision; that way, these experiments provide some evidence that phenomena observed at the individual level *can* scale up to affect public policy problems. Second, these experiments isolate as much as can be imagined the Do No Harm effect by making everything else about the two options equivalent. It is entirely plausible that death rates from both the flu and a vaccine can be estimated with reasonable precision and credibility. Because the consequences of omission (not acting) can be well known, this clever scenario truly puts to the decision maker the fundamental question of whether she would be willing to harm some in order to help others. The original sets of experiments, published in 1990, involved somewhat small samples, but the results have been replicated in follow-on studies.[11]

Although the original survey was meant to explore attitudes toward a diphtheria-pertussis-tuberculosis vaccine, ethical debates over vaccination keep coming up over and over again, most recently in the run-up to administration of the hurriedly-developed H1N1 (or swine flu) vaccine. Given these recent world events, and the persistent voices of dissent that oppose vaccination, it would be an interesting experiment to run again. Most important, these and other studies that pose realistic public policy problems put the research subject in the position of a policy maker. Responses to these types of questions really do shed light on public opinion and other influences on law and policymaking. As Edward McCaffrey, an expert on tax psychology, has remarked, "[i]f cognitive errors affect people, then such errors affect tax systems."[12]

Given the prevalence of the "Do No Harm" effect, what are the implications for climate policy? I contend that carbon taxes suffer from the Do No Harm effect. More visibly than any other instrument, carbon taxes *cost* people money. This is a policy that appears to hurt people. People are commonly capable of the simple (if sometimes oversimplistic) economic reasoning that if things cost more, people buy less and producers are hurt by selling less. All of these economic harms are clear first-order effects of imposing a carbon tax. Meanwhile, the harm that would be avoided by reducing greenhouse gases falls under the category of harm by omission, especially since there are so many contributors, and hence diffused blame. This is, however, a problem shared by all climate policy instruments. The Do No Harm effect may be a very powerful explanation for why people still oppose greenhouse gas reduction policy. But our inquiry is about instrument choice, and the question is whether the harm side of the ledger appears different depending on the instrument. Because people are already so accustomed to paying, calculating, and understanding the personal cost of sales taxes, I contend that it does. People are more skeptical of carbon taxes because they comprehend the costs more clearly.

Does it matter that carbon taxes only impose *economic* harms, and not necessarily physical ones? Does the Do No Harm effect apply as powerfully to economic harms as it does to physical harms? Apparently so. Another Do No Harm experiment asked research subjects if, as the trade negotiator for a nation of wheat growers and bean growers, they would accept a final offer of a trade agreement that would decrease the income of one group but increase the cost of the other. Research subjects responded by requiring much larger gains to the one group in exchange for the losses to the other—in exchange for a $10,000 increase in the income of one group, subjects rejected losses greater than $4,000. In order to answer the objection that these losses would be more painful than the gains would be beneficial, research subjects were also asked if they thought the harms were "greater" than the gains. They generally acknowledged that the losses were not as significant as the gains. Baron contends that people were "knowingly nonutilitarian."[13] Apparently, Do No Harm includes a Do No Economic Harm effect.

That a carbon tax is unpopular because it harms people was most directly tested by Baron and James Jurney in 1993. They hypothesized that voter support for certain reforms might be reduced by the presence of certain norms against coercion. Using six different hypothetical reform proposals, one of which was a gasoline tax to "combat global warming," Baron and Jurney not only asked survey respondents whether they would vote for a gas tax that would double the price of gasoline, but also asked them if they thought it was a reform that would actually make things better. In different experiments, they found that substantial numbers of respondents believed that the proposal would make things better, but opposed it anyway, because they feared that the proposal would harm people, and thought the proposal unfair.[14] Exactly why respondents thought this and whether they would think this about other climate instruments are subjects for further research, but the implication for carbon taxes seems quite compelling.

Another facet of the analysis of the Do No Harm effect is highly relevant to the climate policy debate: the effect is particularly acute when people think of trading off harms and benefits *among groups*. Even more than singling out people for harm, people hate to impose harm on specific groups, even if the harm is economic or probabilistic.

In the vaccination problem, Ritov and Baron varied the basic scenario to include possibilities that children could be at particular risk of dying from the flu, or dying from the side effects of the vaccine, or both. The findings suggested that when risk groups are identified, people are especially reluctant to make tradeoffs that add to that risk. In the public policy scenario, 57 percent of the respondents answered with a number from one to eight, indicating that they demanded a vaccine with greater safety than the flu itself; 23 percent answered zero, indicating that they would do absolutely no harm in vaccinating; only 9 percent responded with nine of ten, indicating true neutrality.[15] Interestingly, when it was posed that the risk groups for both dying from the flu and dying from the vaccine *were the same*, subjects became more willing to vaccinate; 47 percent responded with a maximum tolerable vaccine death rate of nine or ten, as compared to the 9 percent when there were separate risk groups. It is as if people were willing to do a cost-benefit analysis *within* one group, but not across groups. People show an even stronger desire to Do No Harm to identifiable groups. This Do No Harm to groups effect has particular salience to the climate policy instrument choice problem because of concerns over regressiveness (as discussed in the previous section, potentially misplaced concerns). The problem of economic inequality has a well-developed discourse that has led to a rule of thumb that holds sway over public policy: there are "poor people" and policies with economic consequences should not exacerbate income inequalities. This may be why, in the Baron and Jurney study that hypothesized an increased gasoline tax to "combat global warming," many respondents opposed the gasoline tax increase even if it would make things better, because it was "unfair." But even if this is common perception, what is the basis for this perception? If there is a norm against coercive reform, as Baron and Jurney posit, what if the underlying facts of the thought experiment are based upon a grand mistake? Does that undermine such a norm? This is food for further thought and research. But in the meantime, carbon taxes, like most consumption taxes, are commonly thought to be regressive, even if this is not necessarily so. Thus, a carbon tax has two things going against it: the fact that it apparently penalizes one group disproportionately, and that the group happens to have a strong moral claim against economic hardship.

Again, the possibility that a Do No Harm effect may bias people away from taking action on climate change entirely should be separated from the climate policy instrument choice problem. Doing no harm may cause people to avoid supporting any policy that causes economic hardship, even if the benefits are greater. But the argument made here is that the Do No Harm effect negatively impacts carbon taxes more than it does other instruments.

Carbon taxation's disadvantage from the Do No Harm effect looms largest when it is juxtaposed with government subsidy programs. Even though public opinion polls seem to show, over the last decade, an increase in public concern for climate change, people remain vigorously opposed to anything with the word "tax" in it.[16] People remain enthusiastic about subsidies to encourage homeowners to replace old and inefficient appliances.[17] Of course, I have argued *ad nauseum* that there are strong doubts that subsidy programs are broadly effective. But in the eyes of the general public, if there is a Do No Harm influence, the choice could not be more stark: help somebody do something positive for climate change, or penalize a disadvantaged group for not being more efficient. The latter may not be a fair characterization of carbon taxes, but it is a fairly ubiquitous one. And it is almost certain that for those that even bother to think about the costs of government subsidies, the cost seems so diffuse and such a tiny fraction of government outlays, that it is easy to slip into thinking that there is no cost at all. So not only do government subsidies avoid doing harm, they help people! Small wonder, then, that subsidies to assist consumers are so popular; a recent study jointly conducted by OPEC, the US Energy Information Administration, OECD, and the World Bank estimated that worldwide, fossil fuel-related consumption subsidies amounted to more than $550 billion dollars (US) in 2008,[18] nearly 1 percent of 2008 world GDP.[19]

A Do No Harm way of thinking also helps sustain, in smaller groups of environmentalists, a command-and-control approach to regulating greenhouse gas emissions. In fact, the command-and-control approach makes most intuitive sense if one taps into biases to Do No Harm. With command-and-control regulation, pain is visited upon those that are "causing" the harm—large industrial polluters. There is a very nice sense of corrective justice there, a "polluter pays" principle at work.[20] By contrast, a carbon tax seems to punish the little guy—consumers, all the rest of us, who do not seem as blameworthy for the climate problem as large industries. Some environmental organizations have thus continued to push EPA to regulate under the Clean Air Act, under its command-and-control template, earlier and more aggressively.[21] It is possible, as a strategic matter, that environmental organizations view the Clean Air Act as a worst-case method of reducing emissions, as a form of regulation that is better than nothing. But if these environmental organizations are playing to their base support, it would also be perpetuating two delusions: that only large industrial polluters are responsible, and that costs will not get passed down to consumers.

Given the Do No Harm effect, it becomes possible to interpret public opinion poll results a little more critically. Experienced pollsters like the *New York Times* and CBS will ask the following question:

> In order to cut down on energy consumption and reduce global-warming, which would you prefer—requiring car manufacturers to produce cars that are more energy efficient OR imposing an increased federal tax on gasoline?

It should surprise no one that the answer to this question is lop-sidedly in favor of "more energy efficient cars" (87 percent) over "increased federal gasoline tax." (8 percent) Gallup will ask people if they would prefer that the federal government "increase, decrease, or not change the financial support and incentives it gives for producing energy from [alternative energy sources such as wind and solar]. People will overwhelmingly respond favorably (77 percent), even as they express a preference that "support and incentives" for "traditional sources such as oil and gas" either increase or stay the same (a total of 67 percent). But do these truly reflect policy preferences?

Asked without any price tags, or any way to equalize the information across policy instruments, the responses suggest themselves. And yet survey after survey asks the general public these loaded questions. Table 5-1 below shows some questions from some other surveys that have attempted to elicit respondents' preferences for climate change policy instruments.

Not everything points incontrovertibly to the conclusion that transparency of costs is fatal to a proposal. For example, the question shown above asking if people would support requiring utilities to generate 20 percent of their electricity from "wind, solar, or other renewable energy sources, even if it cost the average household an extra $100 a year," seems to suggest people would be willing to absorb some costs to reduce emissions after all. It is possible that the modest cost of the proposal—$100 per year is about $8 per month—helps respondents feel better about the proposal. A follow-up study found support

TABLE 5-1

	Strongly favor or somewhat favor	Somewhat oppose or strongly oppose
Nathan Cummings Foundation Global Warming Survey, August 2007[i]:		
Making clean energy sources such as solar and wind energy cost less	92	7
Funding a massive federal research and development effort to develop new clean energy technologies that can meet our energy needs without polluting	83	16
Providing federal subsidies to clean energy producers	74	23
Establishing a carbon tax on electricity, gasoline, and other products	37	58
Yale/George Mason University, Global Warming's Six Americas, 2010[ii]:		
Fund more research into renewable energy sources, such as solar and wind power	86	10
Provide tax rebates for people who purchase energy-efficient vehicles or solar panels	83	12
Increase taxes on gasoline by 25 cents per gallon and return the revenues to taxpayers by reducing the federal income tax	35	65
Yale University/Gallup/ClearVision Institute, American Opinions on Global Warming, 2007[iii]:		
Requiring electric utilities to produce at least 20 percent of their electricity from wind, solar, or other renewable energy sources, even if it cost the average household an extra $100 a year.	82	17
Requiring that any newly constructed home, residential, or commercial building meet higher energy efficiency standards	89	11
Increasing taxes on electricity so people use less of it	29	71
Increasing taxes on gasoline so people either drive less or buy cars that use less gas	34	67

TABLE 5-1. Continued

	Strongly favor or somewhat favor	Somewhat oppose or strongly oppose
Public Opinion and Climate Change: Analysis of the Virginia Climate Survey (2009)[iv]:		
Creation of Renewable Portfolio Standard	55	
Increased Support for Clean Coal Technology	51	
Increased Fossil Fuel Taxes	13	
Increased Gasoline Taxes	10	

i. Nathan Cummings Foundation Global Warming Survey p. 3, (August 2007), online: www.nathancummings.net/news/NathanCummingsFoundationGlobalWarmingSurvey.pdf (accessed February 8, 2011).
ii. Anthony Lieserowitz, Edward Maibach, Connie Roser-Renouf, and Nicholas Smith, *Global Warming's Six Americas* 44–46 (June 2010) online at http://environment.yale.edu/climate/files/SixAmericasJune2010.pdf (accessed February 8, 2011).
iii. Anthony Lieserowitz. American Opinions on Global Warming, A Yale University/Gallup /ClearVision Institute Poll   (2007).
iv. Barry Rabe and Christopher Borick, *Public Opinion and Climate Change: Analysis of the Virginia Climate Survey*, 27 VA. ENVTL. L.J. 177, 196 (2009).

for other proposals that would cost small amounts of money—on the order of two to five dollars per month.[22] This is speculation, of course, and warrants some testing. In general, however, the overall pattern is unmistakable: people do not like policies that significantly harm people by imposing costs, and generally prefer policies in which the costs are either invisible or somehow bounded and small enough to be manageable. The way that policies are presented feed into this heuristic. Words like "funding," "providing," and "supporting" seem to put respondents in one frame of mind, while words like "tax" and "taxing" place them in another frame of mind. In this regard, the Do No Harm principle seems to be a very widely used cheat sheet for respondents.

Finally, the Do No Harm effect would even seem to play a role in positioning cap-and-trade more favorably than carbon taxes. While the theoretical debate and the lengthy analysis earlier in this book would point to fairly subtle differences between the two instruments, the public perception is likely to be much less refined: cap-and-trade imposes costs on large industrial polluters, carbon taxes impose costs on ordinary consumers, and on poor ones the most. Carbon taxes *scream* of increases in the cost of things, most notably energy. Of course, cap-and-trade programs *should* increase the costs of electricity, but the murky details and the uncertain economic effects render the costs much less clear than in the case of a carbon tax. Will the costs be passed down to consumers and will energy prices go up? Even when they will, it is made unclear. In both the Waxman-Markey bill, which passed the US House of Representatives in 2009, and the American Power Act (Kerry-Lieberman), which was proposed in 2010 (but did not come up for a floor vote), contained provisions that attempted to protect electricity consumers from higher prices by setting aside allowances that would be dedicated to helping low-income consumers pay energy bills.[23] The Kerry-Lieberman bill even negotiated a tortuously concocted "carbon fee," which would levy a fee on oil producers, with revenues from the fee earmarked for assisting consumers in dealing with higher gasoline prices.[24] It is an amazing attempt to cabin off the oil industry from what would otherwise be broad cap-and-trade program, all in the interests of blunting the impact of higher gasoline prices on consumers, and thereby missing opportunities for people to reduce consumption. Still, opponents decried Kerry-Lieberman as creating a new "gas tax."[25] In Canada, greenhouse gas regulation proposals from the last two federal governments—one from the centrist Liberal Party and one from the Conservative Party—have both involved an emissions trading program (not quite a cap-and-trade program, but an emissions intensity program, as briefly described above) for the same group of about 700 "large industrial emitters." These proposals both seemed to draw upon a perception that people still commonly perceive that regulatory costs imposed by cap-and-trade would largely stay where they are imposed. Most obviously, in campaigning against the governing British Columbia Liberal Party that enacted the carbon tax, the opposition New Democratic Party proposed a cap-and-trade program that would have ineffectively focused upon a small number of large emitters within the province.[26] The fact that these provisions are aimed at helping people afford higher energy costs completely misses the point that price signals are needed to spur "ordinary" people into conserving energy.

In short, the Do No Harm effect likely influences both ordinary voters that participate in public opinion polls, and policymakers that are asked to consider tradeoffs. As several climate policy instruments make their way to the fore, some will weather public and policy maker opinion better than others, and the Do No Harm effect will ensure that the carbon tax faces a harder road than the others. Even if carbon tax revenues are recycled in such a way as to provide some progressive tax relief, the nature of the redistribution is difficult to sell unless it is made abundantly clear and its redistribution is clearly connected to the carbon tax. The British Columbia government's redistribution of $100 checks to BC residents as part of the BC carbon tax was labeled a "climate action dividend," and was accompanied by an explanation of how this was part of the BC carbon tax program.[27] Even then, the checks were mocked. Interestingly, for many taxpayers, the checks were greater than any costs that they would feel at the gasoline pump and elsewhere, but the perception was that they were much smaller. British Columbia residents did not feel compensated.[28] The lesson here appears to be that if revenues are being recycled to overcome hostility toward a carbon tax, an explanation of how some have been made better off would be worthwhile.

The Identifiability Effect

Psychological researchers have found that people tend to have stronger emotions about people that they can better identify than for people they cannot. This *identifiability effect* makes people more sympathetic to other people that they can visualize, or see, or otherwise relate to in some sense.[29] Conversely, it also makes people more punitive when they can visualize, see, or otherwise know a perpetrator.[30] If there are people who have been harmed by say, climatic events such as a hurricane or a tsunami or an earthquake, donations pour forth, so that the marginal benefit of each contributed dollar becomes miniscule. To be able to say, "I am helping the unfortunate people of Japan/Haiti/Indonesia/New Orleans" seems to make people more inclined reach into their wallets. The problem with this is that it fools people into incorrectly prioritizing certain causes over others. It is not as if the people of Japan/Haiti/Indonesia/New Orleans are unworthy of help. Rather, the point is that if people had all of the facts before them, and understood the consequences of policies, they would likely make different choices. If people could fully understand what it means for 1 million children to die of malaria each year,[31] they might reconsider if the extra money they found would be better spent supplementing US governmental efforts (however inadequate) or buying mosquito netting for African villages.[32] But the media coverage that focuses on the human interest stories emerging from these terrible tragedies mobilizes people to act. When in 1987, "Baby Jessica" McClure was trapped in a well for several days, sympathetic media-watchers sent her family over $700,000 to assist with rescue efforts—enough money to save hundreds of childrens' lives if spent on preventative health care, or perhaps thousands if employed in Africa. As a species, we are more inclined to help or favor people who can be readily seen or heard than we are for more abstract, statistical victims. As Nobel laureate economist Thomas Schelling said in 1968, "the more we know, the more we care."[33]

The identifiability effect very clearly works its influence in public policy, often serving to bias public decision making. In 2005, the *Globe and Mail* newspaper of Canada ran a front-cover story about a forty-one-year-old Ontario woman who was diagnosed with breast cancer, and was told she might benefit from treatment with a new drug, Herceptin. Herceptin was available in the United States but not in Canada, since provincial health ministries had not yet approved it for coverage under the different provincial health plans. The news story was poignant, and included a twelve-inch-square photo of the attractive woman, hugging her twelve-year-old daughter, who had written a letter to the Ontario health minister asking for help.[34] The very next day, the *Globe and Mail* reported that the Ontario Health Ministry would fast-track the review process so that Herceptin would become fundable by the province within a few months. Ontario Health Minister George Smitherman was quoted in the article as saying "I'm a human being like anybody else and I'm personally impacted by personal stories . . . I have a very, very keen personal sense of the degree to which this is a tremendously impactful decision point for some women and many families in the province of Ontario."[35]

It seems callous to take issue with the health minister's intervention. But one wonders, when George Smitherman jumped Herceptin to the top of the queue, what drugs were pushed aside. Might there have been people who might have been helped by these other drugs, and possibly even hurt by this move? It is difficult to know. But following the ministry's announcement, doubts surfaced in Ontario's medical community regarding the cost-effectiveness of Herceptin.[36] The *Canadian Medical Association Journal* published an editorial questioning the wisdom of the province's approval, given Herceptin's $148 million-per-year price tag.[37]

It is not just visibility that makes people more sympathetic. The "availability heuristic" is a separate behavioral anomaly in which people place too much emphasis on events that have recently occurred, or on events that are somehow disproportionately influential in terms of real-life risks. For example, highly publicized crimes tend to serve as availability heuristics, making people think criminal behavior is more common than it actually is.[38] But the identifiability effect is more subtle, and taps into deeper cognitive processes. One need not be attractive, sympathetic, or even visible to merit a greater weight in decision making. In identifiability experiments, even small amounts of information made research subjects significantly more likely to aid victims. In one study, a group of research subjects were given $10 to begin with. At random, the $10 was taken away from half of the subjects. The half that were able to keep their $10 were asked if they were willing to give up some of their $10 to aid those that had lost theirs. Their willingness to do so was highly correlated with the amount of information they had about the person or persons losing their $10. Even a small amount of information, such as an identification number that represented *but did not name or identify* a specific person, boosted willingness to pay, as compared with a situation in which no information at all was provided about the potential recipient.[39]

I have argued elsewhere in my work that this identifiability "bias" works systemically against greater environmental protection. This is because the tradeoffs involved with questions of environmental protection usually involve the economic benefits of identifiable individuals—those who may lose jobs because of an environmental measure—and the environmental benefits of the general populace, who are considerably less specific and less identifiable.[40] Consider, for example, the tens of thousands of people that can be statistically shown to die prematurely from fine particulate matter air pollution emitted by power plants every year—at least 24,000 per year![41] True, there are error bars associated with such estimates, but how certain does one need to be when the estimates are so large? What if we could *name* even half, or a quarter, of the 24,000 people that would die in any given year, and put them in a searchable database? One could hardly doubt the policy alternatives for energy would change overnight. But again, in this chapter, the identifiability effect is used to explain why *carbon taxation* is unpopular, not climate policy or environmental policy generally.

The identifiability effect operates in a similar fashion as the Do No Harm effect by playing on the relative certainty presented by carbon taxes, as opposed to the uncertainty posed by other climate instruments. The identifiability effect biases people against carbon taxes because they can better identify people who are harmed by carbon taxes than by other climate instruments. For example, a carbon tax most viscerally affects people who must commute by driving, which many people can at least identify with; a cap-and-trade program is likely, given incentives facing politicians, to obfuscate such effects, as the American Power Act (Kerry-Lieberman) did by excluding oil refineries from their cap to avoid raising gasoline prices. However, while the Do No Harm effect and the identifiability effect overlap, they do exert separate and distinct influences on the instrument choice problem. The identifiability effect *only* works because some person or group can be identified; the Do No Harm effect would work equally strongly whether a group was identifiable or not—it is the thought of harming *anybody* that makes people balk. The identifiability effect, which works to make people more punitive as well as more sympathetic; the Do No Harm effect only makes people more sympathetic.

Again, thinking about gasoline prices helps us understand the identifiability effect and how it might be distinguished from the Do No Harm effect. One type of human interest story invariably follows a period in which gasoline prices rise sharply: how hard it is for a specific person, in a certain type of occupation, to make ends meet. In the summer of 2006, when gasoline prices rose for a second consecutive year (after the spike caused by Hurricane Katrina), the *New York Times* ran a series of articles on the impact of high gasoline prices on various individuals throughout the country, highlighting the hardships imposed upon cabdrivers ("'Compared to a year ago, I pay $15 more a day in gas,' said Miguel Gonzalez, 67, of Queens. 'I only take home $100 a day, so that's my lunch and dinner right there.'"), immigrants ("Lesly Richardson, 50, a Haitian immigrant from Brooklyn, nodded in agreement. 'That's $100 a week,' he said. 'That's your grocery bill.'"), lovestruck college students ("Mr. Cole, who studies computers at Lakeland Community College and earns $8.18 an hour working in a factory that heat-treats metal, did not have money for gas. So he stayed home. 'I won't be able to see her [his girlfriend] till I get paid,' he said. 'Ever since gas prices went up, it's like I'm barely able to see her.'"), single mothers ("In an adjoining gas lane, Cindy Wright spoke of the pain high gas prices cause the single mothers who make up many of the clients at the public health clinic in Torrington, where she is a nurse.").[42]

Although it was not the intent of the *New York Times* to perpetuate a bias against carbon taxes, this series of articles only reinforced the storyline that runs throughout the carbon tax debate: higher gasoline prices (which would increase under a carbon tax) disproportionately hurt the working poor, the lunch-bucket and hard-hat laborer, the student, for whom an increase in transportation costs would be especially painful, maybe even crippling. Even in wake of the Arab Oil Embargo of the 1970s, frantic American efforts to reduce reliance on imported oil did not include a gasoline tax, despite the widely accepted proposition that increased gasoline prices would reduce driving and oil consumption, and increase energy independence. In arguing against a 1975 gasoline tax proposal, Democratic congressman Bill Alexander of Arkansas, railed:

> [i]f this tax is enacted, we will be requiring the people of the heartland of America to carry this burden on both shoulders. It is unfair; it is inequitable; it is grossly discriminatory against the people of this country who do not have access to public transportation. . . . Did you ever hear of anybody catching a subway in Osceola, Arkansas, or a bus in Bugtussle, Oklahoma?[43]

Few people actually know anybody from Osceola, Arkansas, or Bugtussle, Oklahoma. But knowledge or familiarity are not required for the identifiability effect to influence a decision. It is enough that one can imagine a person hailing from such a place, to make the economic pain of higher gasoline prices (real or not) feel more significant.

Note these do not have to be *extreme* hardships that are visited upon ordinary working folk, so it may not be much of a harm to not do. They just have to seem more trouble than the modest good that a carbon tax would do. The identifiability effect works to make the pain *seem* more real, because it operates on people that seem more real.

The identifiability effect also works in favor of climate policy instruments that appear to be directing punishment at "others," such as large industrial emitters. That has always been the populist appeal of command-and-control regulation, which can be easily spun as a "punishment" for polluters for polluting. Recall that the identifiability effect also works to increase punitive instincts when people somehow have in mind a perpetrator. Combine that with the deceptively commonsense notion that if there is a large emitter of carbon dioxide (or some other greenhouse gas), then there should be some direct regulation of that emitter. One survey asked the following question:

> Carbon dioxide is the primary greenhouse gas said to be causing global warming and is produced by electric power plants and motor vehicles (e.g., cars, trucks and sport utility vehicles). Currently, carbon dioxide is not regulated as a pollutant. How much do you support or oppose the regulation of carbon dioxide as a pollutant?[44]

Seventy-seven percent were in favor of this proposal. But when the following question was asked, only 17 percent said they were in favor:

> How much do you support or oppose a 60-cent per gallon gasoline tax, over and above existing gas taxes, to encourage people to drive less and thus reduce carbon dioxide emissions?[45]

So, although political elites seem to be favoring cap-and-trade over command-and-control, some environmental organizations have continued to support command-and-control regulation under the command-and-control-styled Clean Air Act. In particular, as the EPA advances greenhouse gas emissions regulations for large emitters, industry groups opposing EPA regulations have fought pitched public relations battles with environmental organizations, which have spent heavily to preserve EPA's authority to regulate greenhouse gas emissions.[46] The debates are clearly fought with identifiability in mind: for the industry groups, it's "jobs," (read humans), and for the environmental organizations, it's "emitters," (those industrial polluters). The 2007 Nathan Cummings Foundation study that found concern over global warming and support for action, but opposition to carbon taxes, also found, by a margin of 81 percent to 17 percent that respondents supported "[r]equiring American industries to reduce their carbon emissions," but supported by a smaller margin of 68 percent to 30 percent "[r]equiring American consumers to reduce their carbon emissions."[47]

Along the same lines, the identifiability effect has also subtly helped cap-and-trade appear palatable. With a cap-and-trade program, it is difficult to tease out a link between economic hardships and individual identifiable people, and the connection is not strong enough to make for compelling journalism. So political proponents of cap-and-trade enjoy some protection from sympathy entrepreneurs in the popular media. Moreover, because cap-and-trade usually targets industrial emitters as the point of regulation, they play on the punitive side of identifiability: the greater propensity for people to want to punish people they can identify as perpetrators. Again, people need not be *very* identifiable to exert an identifiability effect. And again, people are unlikely to be considering the possibility that costs imposed upon industrial emitters will be passed onto consumers.

In British Columbia, the opposition NDP's criticism of the provincial carbon tax was accompanied by an NDP proposal to regulate the emitters by imposing a cap-and-trade system in the province. The NDP's strategy was rooted in identifiability: focus on how the carbon tax would affect "ordinary" British Columbians, while using the cap-and-trade idea to demonstrate that they would regulate the big bad large industrial emitters instead of ordinary folk. The NDP website advertised that the NDP plan places "[r]eal caps on greenhouse gas emssions from BC's largest polluters," while the Premier Campbell plan has "[n]o caps on greenhouse gas emissions. Polluters can pollute as much as they want."[48] Again, it does not seem to be of any consequence that neither command-and-control nor cap-and-trade can isolate the pain on emitters while sparing ordinary folk; all that seems to matter is that the programs can be spun that way, and that the impressions created thereby can be very durable.

One could be forgiven for confusing the identifiability effect with ordinary political economy effects, or even public choice effects. The people who dangle campaign contributions in front of elected lawmakers, and even the agency officials that work for a political executive, ignore political power at their peril; by definition, these people and groups are more identifiable and more salient than others. In fact, the identifiability effect could be considered the operationalization of representative democracy. Only *real people* get to vote, sue in court, and otherwise avail themselves of the instrumentalities of government. Identifiability is the *essence* of representative democracy.

But if that is true, then representative democracy has an undesirable bias. The flaw lies in the failure to uphold the rights of those that are not identifiable, but still deserve protection from lawmakers. Future generations of Americans will be stuck with the indebtedness that the current generation accumulates. Is there nothing wrong with borrowing from the accounts of future generations to fund current actions?

In the climate policy instrument problem, the identifiability effect doubly penalizes carbon taxation. It makes carbon taxes seem less desirable than other instruments because they more visibly hurt people, and also makes other instruments seem better because they appear to punish visible emitters. Neither of these perceptions is accurate for comparison purposes, but they still powerfully affect public perceptions.

The Endowment Effect

A third way people bias themselves against carbon taxes is the *endowment effect*. One the most studied and well-known of all of the anomalous behavioral effects, the endowment effect is the reluctance of people to part with objects within their possession, as compared with their eagerness to obtain the same objects when they are not in their possession. Economic theory posits, and a layperson would reasonably assume, that a specific object has a certain single objective value to an individual, regardless of whether she possesses it or not. The endowment effect, however, suggests otherwise. Repeated experiments have shown that the value may be higher if the individual has possession over the object than when she does not. In economic terms, a person's *willingness to accept* a price for selling an object is demonstrably larger than the same person's *willingness to pay* for the same object. This has also been thought of as a *status quo bias*, a bias against change.[49]

Some versions of the endowment effect have been the subject of experimental research for a long time, but the most definitive demonstrations were carried out in 1990 by Daniel Kahneman, Jack Knetsch, and Richard Thaler. In a series of experiments, they distributed a random object to half of a pool of research subjects, who were told that they "now own the object." In the first experiment, a token was given to half of the subjects, and everyone was told what their valuation of a token should be, whether they had one or not. A trading session was then carried out in which those that were assigned high valuations of the token bought them from those with lower valuations. In a second experiment, coffee mugs were distributed to half the subjects, and in a third, boxes of pens. The null hypothesis, and one that would comport with economic theory (and probably common intuition) is that about half of the tokens/mugs/pens would be sold—assuming that the distribution of valuations for tokens/mugs/pens were similar in the two halves, which, statistically speaking, they should be. Taking the mug experiment, for example, a random distribution of people should place half of the people with a high valuation of the object—the "mug-lovers"—in the pool given a mug, and half in the pool not given a mug. One would also think that those that had the tokens/mugs/pens would have an average selling price quite similar to the average bidding price for those that didn't, and wished to have obtain a token/mug/box of pens.

The stunning result was that for objects with no intrinsic ownership value—the tokens, which were meant to simulate an "induced-value" market—about half of the tokens were indeed sold. For coffee mugs and pens, however, *fewer* trades took place than expected. Perhaps even more importantly, the stated willingnesses to accept and willingnesses to pay were markedly different for mugs and pens, but not for tokens. The median willingness to accept was consistently higher than the median stated willingness to pay for mugs and pens, but not tokens. These stated prices were not bogus responses, since trades were actually executed on the basis of these stated prices. Repeated rounds of trading were conducted, so as to allow the subjects an opportunity to learn and think about and update their willingness to pay or accept. Every time, willingness to accept came out higher than willingness to pay for mugs and pens, but not tokens. A number of variations on this basic experimental design were conducted to counter several peer reviewers' objections, but the nature of the results remained robust. In a final experiment of this series, subjects in one group were given coffee mugs, and were then shown a chocolate bar and asked if they wanted to exchange their mug for the chocolate bar. Those in a second group were given chocolate bars and then shown a coffee mug and asked if they wanted to exchange their bar for a mug. A third group was simply offered a choice between a coffee mug and a chocolate bar. In the group offered a choice, 55 percent chose the coffee mug. But of those given a coffee mug, 89 percent decided to keep theirs, and of those given the chocolate bar, only 10 percent chose to exchange for the mug.[50] This last variation should have put to rest any suspicions that there was anything artificial about the monetary aspects of this series of experiments. The endowment effect has generally been borne out in experimental simulations for a variety of goods.[51]

What does this mean for carbon taxes? At its core, the endowment effect is a general reluctance to exchange. Climate policy must ultimately, if it is to succeed in reducing greenhouse gases, require an exchange of our existing way of life for a different one—probably not a poorer one, as the expected environmental benefits of avoiding or mitigation climate change are likely to swamp the costs. But certainly tradeoffs will have to be made by virtually everyone on the planet. These will be large and profound exchanges, at both the individual and societal level. The endowment effect, if it applies to the way that people view climate policy, would bias people against carbon taxes, because of all of the climate policy options, a carbon tax most clearly communicates the fact that climate policy will involve an exchange, and a compulsory one at that. Everyone will be forced to deal with higher energy prices, and some may be well aware that there will be higher commodity prices, and job loss.

A carbon tax, more clearly than other climate policy instruments, signals that there is a *price* for an exchange. The price is the increased cost of goods that people will have to absorb, in exchange for the environmental benefit of reducing the risk of climate change. In fact, people are likely to *overestimate* their costs from a carbon tax. People are sometimes able to quickly make some rough calculations about how much an increase in gasoline prices will cost them, and perhaps even calculate increases in home heating costs, but are much less likely to consider what they might do in response to rising costs. Economists study this consumption behavior and know that energy is price-elastic, and so are better able to make a full accounting of the costs of an increase in energy and other goods with a carbon footprint. But this is not what ordinary consumers and voters do. The rough first-order calculation is all most ordinary consumers and voters will bother with in forming their opinions on carbon taxes, and in our collective (but perhaps rational) apathy, we have accepted this.

It is not, by the way, necessarily inaccurate to view government policy as a series of exchanges. Government policy can often be thought of as a change in status that involves some sort of an *exchange* for some or all of the population. The problem is that the more obvious the exchange is, the more hardened the opposition will be. Some exchanges will be clearly more favorable for some than others, generating resentment. One of the pitfalls of American federal health care legislation, insofar as it sought to "contain" health care costs, was the effect that legislation would have on the wide variety of stakeholders that prospered under the incumbent health care system. A central point of contention in debates leading up to the recent passage of federal health care legislation was whether or not the US government would get into the business of directly providing health care insurance, which almost every economically advanced country does, as well as some very poor ones—even Rwanda has a health care system with a $2 premium that prevents and treats the most costly illnesses, including malaria. The "public option" of having Americans buy their health care insurance from the US government was apparently a huge threat to the American health insurance industry, such that this aspect of it was dropped from the legislation. Health care legislation was such a huge challenge in part because it involved such a large and profound exchange for many Americans and, perhaps more importantly, some critical industries.

The problem is that among the climate policy instruments, carbon taxation is the option that most clearly signals an exchange. At least the way that other instruments are packaged by politicians and the policy community, there is a very strong hint that these policies are not exchanges, and are, to borrow a dreadful policy phrase, a "win-win." This is misleading. Environmental policy is inherently an exchange. Regulating and reducing pollution involves costs, typically higher costs for all kinds of consumer goods, and sometimes (not nearly as frequently as critics claim) it costs jobs. These costs are incurred in exchange for benefits like a cleaner and safer environment. It may be a good trade to many, and it may actually be a good trade for *everybody*, but it is a trade nonetheless. Electricity has historically cost more because of a variety of environmental requirements imposed upon power plants. The vast majority of these requirements have been well worth imposing, and the resulting exchanges well worth making, but *ex ante*, they have been exchanges. So it would be with climate policy. Because such profound changes are required to wean the world economy from a predominantly fossil fuel-powered one, the exchanges will be large and profound.

It is true that other instruments would, like carbon taxes, also result in some price being imposed. But what makes carbon taxation as a policy so unpopular is the obviousness of the cost. Contrast this with cap-and-trade: as noted earlier, the cap-and-trade proposals before the US Congress contained provisions explicitly aimed at *not* raising the price of energy for some consumers. Of course, it is silly to make a claim that carbon would be priced, and emissions curtailed, without making energy more expensive. But if this little bit of three-card-monte can be slipped past the wavering attention of enough rationally apathetic voters, then the policy can appear to be something for nothing, and not an exchange at all.

This is what is tricky about cap-and-trade: rules for allocating emissions allowances are intentionally made complicated in part to obfuscate the otherwise obvious truth that if carbon dioxide emissions are to decrease to a cap, fossil fuel energy prices are going to have to go up. It is not clear that a cap-and-trade program involves a *trade*. Little wonder, too, that political opponents of cap-and-trade have astutely labeled cap-and-trade programs as a hidden "tax," in the hopes of presenting the cap-and-trade program more obviously as a close cousin of a carbon tax.[52] Opponents have good reason to try and emphasize the costs of cap-and-trade. In the 2007 Nathan Cummings Foundation survey, a cap-and-trade program was described to respondents in the following way:

> The Global Warming Act of 2007 would establish a cap on US carbon emissions. It would require business and industry to reduce their emissions by 80% by the year 2050 and it would allow businesses that could not reduce their emissions as much as required to purchase pollution credits from businesses that had reduced their emissions below the level required by the cap.[53]

Sixty-six percent of respondents either "strongly supported" or "somewhat supported" this cap-and-trade program. Next, respondents were further told about the cap-and-trade program:

> This proposal would likely result in much higher gasoline and energy costs over the next several decades, potentially doubling or tripling the price of gasoline, heating oil, and electricity in order to reduce carbon dioxide emissions.[54]

After receiving this information, 52 percent of respondents who said they would support the program subsequently said they were "much less likely to support" the cap-and-trade program, and 23 percent said they were "somewhat less likely to support" the program. The fact that this information—that cap-and-trade would cost money (who knew?!) would actually sway three-quarters of respondents, and strongly sway over half—suggests that in the first instance respondents did not fully appreciate that a cap-and-trade program would cost money.

Put another way, the cost of climate policy appears *more certain* under a carbon tax than it does under other instruments. Psychologists and economists from the same Kahneman-Knetsch-Thaler school of behavioral economics have long understood that people make inconsistent decisions under uncertainty. When faced with the task of weighing certain information against uncertain information, people systemically overweight the certain information and underweight the uncertain information.[55] If, on a spectrum of certainty, carbon taxes convey the costs of climate policy in a more certain manner than do other instruments, people are likely to overweight the costs of a carbon tax, even if a cap-and-trade program would cost exactly the same.

Even less so do government subsidies or command-and-control regulation communicate the idea that tradeoffs are involved. In fact, that is what is politically appealing about these forms of government policy: most people would suppose these policies do not cost them anything. For government subsidies, what is a few extra million or billion dollars when government stimulus packages and bailouts now routinely cost hundreds of billions of dollars? What is the likelihood that taxpayers believe they would ever personally see concrete costs stemming from government subsidy programs to address climate change? This is the specious nature of government subsidy programs: they appear cheap, even costless. Note the endowment effect offers an alternative explanation for why respondents in public opinion polls are so broadly supportive of government subsidy programs. Returning to the 2007 Cummings Foundation survey, a subsidy program was described in the following way:

> The Apollo Energy Act would invest $300 billion over 10 years to develop new, low-cost clean energy technologies and industries. The goal of the project would be to eliminate America's dependence on foreign oil within ten years, create jobs in new clean energy industries, and dramatically reduce US carbon emissions."[56]

Eighty-four percent of respondents either "strongly supported" or "somewhat supported" this program. But after being told that

This proposal would cost hundreds of billions of dollars yet there is no plan for how to pay for it. That means that either our taxes will go up or the federal deficit will increase.[57]

Forty-one percent of respondents said they were "much less likely to support" the program, and 31 percent said they were "somewhat less likely to support" the program. Again, the fact that subsidy programs cost money seems to have been important but missing information for many respondents, suggesting that these people did not begin with an assumption that subsidies cost money.

As for command-and-control, if politicians are any gauge, most people seem to have either consciously or unconsciously bought into economic doctrine on markets: market-based instruments minimize compliance costs. In Washington, in Ottawa, and even in Brussels, cap-and-trade dominates command-and-control. But pockets of populists still have a preference for command-and-control regulation, because they *appear* to impose costs on polluters (them), but not consumers (us). Command-and-control regulation always carries with it a price tag for regulated industries, but it is never apparent that it costs consumers anything. Returning to a survey result mentioned earlier, the wide public support for the policy "regulate carbon dioxide as a pollutant"—77 percent either "strongly supporting" or "somewhat supporting" suggests that the general public still likes command-and-control regulation, and perhaps fails to realize the costs.[58]

The endowment effect suggests that revenue recycling may not be as effective as might be hoped in building public support for carbon taxation. Even if carbon tax revenues come back to carbon taxpayers in some other way, like reduced income taxes or some other governmentally funded benefit, it is still overtly an exchange. The thinking behind revenue recycling is that people would approach the exchange without any biases. Money is money, after all, and spending more on some goods but getting more back elsewhere could be seen as a wash. Not so. Recall that when asked about essentially exchanging payment of a payroll tax or an income tax for a carbon tax, most respondents declined. There is no good reason that would be obvious to a typical survey respondent that a carbon tax should *not* be exchanged for the US payroll tax, which is a much more regressive policy than a carbon tax.

Consider also a policy that, if enacted, would be a part of a carbon tax: an increased gasoline tax. This is certainly the biggest part of the

British Columbia carbon tax, as transportation accounts for 40 percent of British Columbia's carbon dioxide emissions.[59] Even with revenues recycled, a gasoline tax attaches viscerally to an extremely important consumption good: driving. A gasoline tax would clearly threaten consumption of that good. Even if revenues from a gasoline tax were recycled, cognitively, the proposed trade would look something like, "drive less, get some money back so that you can buy . . . something." That sounds fine to an economist, because the economist would argue that the driver could just use the recycled money to buy gasoline, if that's the driver's preference. But for those unaccustomed to thinking about government policy as tradeoffs, and not inclined to think of climate policy as involving some exchange, a gasoline tax sounds much less appealing than simply having the government go away and fix the problem. In a survey I have conducted, a proposed gasoline tax increase to reduce emissions from motor vehicles was, as expected, unpopular. When revenue recycling was introduced, opposition to the gasoline tax increase abated, but not by as much as one would expect. As noted earlier, one explanation would lie in the continuing suspicion that even when government says it will return the revenues, it will find an accounting trick to not actually return the revenues.[60] But another explanation may lie in the fact that survey respondents simply don't feel like giving up their driving habits, even in an exchange that could leave them better off in the end.

Gasoline is an illustrative case because a gasoline tax evokes perhaps even more visceral reactions than a carbon tax. People seem to be able to make some heroic calculations about how much a gasoline tax increase would cost them, and this calculation sticks in their minds as a price tag. Filling up at the pump is a common activity, and drivers pay close attention to gas prices. Because of the frequency of the chore, drivers also seem to be able to map a per-gallon or per-liter price onto a fill-up cost. In this context, a proposal to increase gasoline taxes is a proposal that carries with it a very clear price tag.

A carbon tax may be a little less or a little more vulnerable than a gasoline tax increase. While a carbon tax is not easily translatable into a cost increase at the gasoline pump, it affects more forms of consumption, most notably home heating. It would be no exaggeration to say that a carbon tax would increase the cost of almost everything—that is a large part of the point of a carbon tax—and this could have a more frightening impact on a household budget than a gasoline tax does. A carbon tax carries with it a somewhat less calculable price tag than does a gasoline tax, but is clearly much larger.

The endowment effect makes carbon taxes seem most painful because they present climate policy most obviously as an *exchange*. That is fundamentally what so much of government policy is about—paying for some things that may be worth having, or perhaps giving up things that were previously paid for, but no longer worth paying for. The problem is that political discourse has changed so that politicians have no incentive to present policies as imposing any kind of harm on anyone. It is rare for any government policy to openly require anything from anyone.

Note that the endowment effect is a different biasing effect from the Do No Harm argument. Although in both cases it is the visibility of the price that works against carbon taxation, the endowment effect makes people balk for selfish reasons. People oppose carbon taxes because they do not wish to exchange their current situation for a different one that includes a carbon tax. Do no harm makes people oppose carbon taxes because they do not wish to harm *other people*. Although the Do No Harm effect also makes people want to refrain from harming themselves, the Do No Harm effect primarily operates in the public policy realm to make people averse to harming others, particularly groups of other people.

Environmental policy is usually a trade in which the benefit side of the ledger is environmental quality. What other climate policy instruments get away with is either hiding the costs of emissions reduction or simply being ineffective. The perception problem suffered by carbon taxation is that relative to other climate policy instruments, it most clearly presents the price tag. It is not in politicians' interests to present alternative instruments as having a price tag, so they wind up sounding like "win-win" policies. This is not possible with a carbon tax. Even with revenue recycling, the individual is being asked to suffer a known cost, albeit in exchange for some tax benefit *and* some environmental benefit. But given the importance and prevalence of energy usage, the idea of paying more for energy presents itself very clearly as an important loss. For small trades such as coffee mugs for chocolate bars, the endowment effect tilts against trading; for large trades involving the energy bill, the effect is likely greater. The carbon tax, by proposing an exchange to nudge fossil fuel consumers off of the status quo, and in a fairly intrusive way, is a victim of the endowment effect.

Conclusion

People are conflicted about what to do about climate change. On the one hand, a solid majority of people, even Canadians and Americans, favor action on climate change.[61] Even though the public continues to trail scientists and probably even politicians in their understanding of climate change, they seem to have an intuitive understanding that catastrophic things *could* happen if greenhouse gases continue to increase, and that avoiding this *risk* would be good policy.[62] On the other hand, climate change is usually trumped by other issues, most prominently economic ones, when people are asked to rank them in importance.[63] So how does one reconcile these two somewhat contradictory public positions? The path of least cognitive dissonance is to be in favor of some grand-sounding, and yet not obviously painful measures to address climate change. Hence, there is appeal to "launching a Manhattan Project" to perfect carbon capture and storage, or the government launch of a hydrogen fuel cell automobile project, or a supposedly "economy-wide" cap-and-trade program that covers all polluters. These all sound grand enough to match the size of the climate change problem, and yet do not *obviously* cost the taxpayer, the consumer, or the voter anything. Politicians that stand to gain political support from proposing climate policy are happy to nurture these misperceptions, and public opinion polls unwittingly assist them by supplying survey results that perpetuate these misperceptions.

If one takes a hard look at the climate policy instrument choice problem, the differences between carbon taxes and cap-and-trade are, in the grand scheme of things, relatively small. Based on the arguments and the analysis in this book, the nod should go to carbon taxes, as the climate policy instrument of choice, although it is true that many of the differences can be eliminated with clever policy design. But cap-and-trade enjoys an advantage in terms of public perceptions, although some of them have been revealed as being superficial. Similarly, on the merits, the advantages of carbon taxes over government subsidy programs and command-and-control are much greater, but as in the comparison with cap-and-trade, carbon taxes *look* worse. Because government subsidies seem to pale in comparison with the enormous amounts of money that federal governments take and spend, sometimes on outrageously silly things such as bridges to nowhere, subsidies *seem* costless, even if people might not admit they perceive it that way. Command-and-control, too, does not overtly impose a cost on consumers, but instead costs society in some nonobvious ways. Both of these instruments, however, are alive and well and would seem to enjoy cosmetic advantages over carbon taxation.

As keen observers of what people say they want, politicians have no incentive to bring up a carbon tax. There is no reason to propose a carbon tax if one can propose a cap-and-trade program. Ask the federal Canadian Liberal Party, which campaigned in 2008 on a "Green Shift," a thoughtful plan with a carbon tax that would return the revenues in the form of reduced income taxes, in the style of the BC carbon tax.[64] And because the Green Shift sought to merely harmonize taxes across fossil fuels, it would not even have increased gasoline prices. The Green Shift, the federal Liberal Party, and Liberal leader Stéphane Dion were defeated decisively in the 2008 federal elections, leading Dion's resignation as leader of the federal Liberal Party. Politicians who seek the affection of environmentally minded voters might be better advised to instead propose one of these other better-sounding-but-less-effective programs.

All of the behavioral effects that work against carbon taxation and in favor of other instruments stem from the transparency of carbon taxes and the opaqueness (at least in the forms that have been developed by legislators and regulators) of the alternative instruments. This root cause operates in a variety of different ways to make carbon taxation seem like an inferior option. Thus, while a carbon tax may represent the best policy option, it loses the popularity contest. And in the current climate, few are willing to champion a political loser.

Chapter 6

Changing Political Fortunes?

Cognitive biases and the reinforcement of these biases—inadvertent by pollsters, to some extent purposeful by politicians—have seemingly created a deep political pit from which carbon taxes will never emerge to see the light of day. Carbon taxes mean higher energy prices, and it is easy for anti-tax groups to tap into consumers' fears and squeeze out other considerations.[1] But although these biases are widespread, they are fragile and fixable. Misperceptions and errant decision-making processes can be corrected, and information can be supplied to help citizens evaluate different policy instruments.

What if public opinion polls weren't so loaded against the idea of carbon taxes? One survey by the Center for Local, State and Urban Policy at the University of Michigan actually asked respondents their willingness to pay for climate policies, automatically signaling to respondents that climate policies cost money.[2] Also, this study asked respondents about their support for cap-and-trade programs and for carbon taxes, if (i) cost was not specified, (ii) at a cost of $15 per month, and (iii) at a cost of $50 per month.[3]

This is better than those surveys noted in the previous chapter, which pretend that these kinds of policies are free. But they can be made better. For one thing, there is still no indication of effectiveness included in the policy proposals. Put forth as if they were equal policies, a respondent could be forgiven for thinking that all of these policies accomplish the same thing.

A study conducted at MIT to measure the public's acceptance of carbon capture and storage technology seems to reveal a very prominent role for information about costs. In split samples, people were asked what they thought was the way to "best address the issue of global warming as it relates to electricity production." The potential responses included "do nothing . . . [w]e can live with global warming," but also several alternatives including these two: carbon capture and storage, and increasing use of renewable energies. Generally, using renewable energy was more popular, but in one subsample, respondents received information that carbon capture and storage would reduce emissions by 90 percent and double the average household cost of electricity from $1,200 to $2,400 per year; they were also told that using renewable energies would increase electricity costs to $4,000 per year. Not surprisingly, the effect of this information was to make carbon capture and storage more popular than renewable energies.[4]

Given these results, consider instead of the question formats in the public opinion polls reviewed above, the following (the numbers in table 6-1 are for illustrative purposes only, and do not reflect economic modeling results):

Of course, there would be considerable debate over exactly what to put in the different boxes. But having an argument over the costs and estimated emissions reductions of each climate policy option would be a *vast* improvement over current practice, which is to ignore them when they are difficult to calculate. Just debating how to put all of the climate policy instruments on even footing would improve the instrument choice process.

Of course, we can only speculate about the effects or even the feasibility of conducting public opinion polls on climate policy in a balanced way. But certainly the misperceptions about carbon taxes vis-à-vis other climate policy instruments are partially the result of the haphazard (and sometimes consciously misleading) descriptions (or lack thereof) of policy instruments and their effectiveness. Just attempting to cure these defects would be a very important step toward neutralizing the bias against carbon taxes.

Even if the misperceptions are fixed, the politics of carbon taxes will have to change. But already, the potential for change is palpable. If the former chief economic adviser to President Clinton (Stiglitz) and the former chief economic adviser to President George W. Bush

TABLE 6-1

Please take a moment to review the following proposals that are being considered by the US Congress to reduce carbon dioxide emissions that cause global warming.

Please indicate whether, given the costs and the estimated tons of emissions reduced, whether you would strongly support, somewhat support, somewhat oppose, or strongly oppose these policies.

	Costs	Estimated tons of CO_2 emissions reduced	Would you . . .
The Carbon Tax Act would impose a tax of $30 per ton of carbon dioxide on all wholesale purchases of coal, natural gas, or crude oil, or imports of coal, natural gas, or crude oil, and increasing up to about $100 per ton of carbon dioxide.	About 30 cents per gallon of gasoline, and about $15 per month on the average monthly home heating and electricity bill, increasing to about $1 per gallon of gasoline and $50 per month for heating and electricity, as well as other energy cost increases.	Starting at about 900 megatons annually, or about 15 percent of total annual US emissions, and going up to about 4,800 megatons and 80 percent of total.	Strongly support? Somewhat support? Somewhat oppose? Strongly oppose?
The Apollo Energy Act would invest $300 billion over 10 years to develop new, low-cost clean energy technologies and industries. The goal of the project would be to eliminate America's dependence on foreign oil within ten years, create jobs in new clean energy industries, and dramatically reduce U.S. carbon emissions.	An increase in personal income taxes of about 2 percent per year or about $2,000 per year for an average taxpayer.	About 300 megatons annually, or about 5 percent of total annual US emissions.	Strongly support? Somewhat support? Somewhat oppose? Strongly oppose?

TABLE 6-1. Continued

Please take a moment to review the following proposals that are being considered by the US Congress to reduce carbon dioxide emissions that cause global warming.
Please indicate whether, given the costs and the estimated tons of emissions reduced, whether you would strongly support, somewhat support, somewhat oppose, or strongly oppose these policies.

	Costs	Estimated tons of CO_2 emissions reduced	Would you . . .
The Global Warming Act of 2007 would establish a cap on US carbon emissions. It would require business and industry to reduce their emissions by 80 percent by the year 2050 and it would allow businesses that could not reduce their emissions as much as required to purchase pollution credits from businesses that had reduced their emissions below the level required by the cap.	About 20 cents per gallon of gasoline, and about $10 per month on the average monthly home heating bill, and increasing to about $1 per gallon and $50 per month for heating and electricity, as well as other energy cost increases. Cost increases could be more or less.	Starting at about 500 megatons annually, or about 8 percent of total annual US emissions, and going up to about 4,200 megatons, or 70 percent of total.	Strongly support? Somewhat support? Somewhat oppose? Strongly oppose?

(Mankiw) can agree on the need for carbon taxes, one suspects other surprising alliances are possible. A surprising variety of public figures and groups have either come out in support of carbon taxes, or even more controversially, in favor of gasoline taxes: Leon Panetta, the former Democratic congressman and President Clinton's former budget director[5]; Nobel laureate and University of Chicago economist Gary Becker[6]; the very liberal environmental organization Friends of the Earth[7]; Charles Krauthammer, the very conservative *Washington Post* columnist[8]; the very controversial Obama economic adviser and former Treasury secretary Lawrence Summers[9]; economist Arthur Laffer, a member of President Reagan's economic advisory team, and the original "supply-side" economist[10]; and most prominently to environmentalists, NASA atmospheric scientist James Hansen, one of the first and most forceful scientists to speak of the urgency of climate change, a hero to environmentalists.[11] Carbon taxes and gasoline taxes thus have supporters at both ends of the political spectrum, as well as places in between. Capitol Hill figures that have supported carbon taxes include former Democratic senator Christopher Dodd of Connecticut[12]; recently defeated Republican congressman Robert Inglis of South Carolina[13]; and Democratic congressmen Pete Stark of California and Jim McDermott of Washington, who proposed carbon tax legislation in 2007.[14] And who could make up stranger bedfellows than the rancorous *New York Times* columnist (and also Nobel laureate) Paul Krugman, and über-libertarian Grover Norquist, the founder of the aggressive anti-tax lobbying group Americans for Tax Reform, both of whom support higher gasoline taxes (but Norquist only if the proceeds are returned in the form of cuts in other taxes)?[15]

Others have also now spoken out in favor of carbon taxes. Anticipating that greenhouse gas regulation of one sort or another is coming soon, some industries have tried to get in front of public opinion by supporting carbon taxes. Oil industries have led the call, perhaps reckoning that a carbon tax would be less obnoxious and costly to their industries than alternatives. Executives in the Canadian oil sands business now support a carbon tax, possibly calculating that the legal and economic certainty it could provide would be worth the cost (or that carbon tax revenues might fund their carbon capture and storage technology).[16] So, too, has ExxonMobil CEO Rex Tillerson come out in favor of a carbon tax.[17]True, much of the cost of a carbon tax would be absorbed by consumers, but given the elasticity of gasoline consumption, it is clear that oil companies stand to sell less gasoline if a carbon tax is imposed. Some environmentalists may shudder at these kinds of allies, but it must be an advantage when pushing for climate policy to have at least the acquiescence, if not support, of some fossil fuel industries.

And as noted earlier, economists other than Stiglitz and Mankiw have typically favored carbon taxes, at least those that have weighed in on climate policy. Although they disagree vehemently about the magnitude of a carbon tax, William Nordhaus, Nicholas Stern, and Martin Weitzman have all expressed agreement on the desirability of a carbon tax.[18] While critical of the Stern Review, Weitzman also wrote in his critique:

> To its great credit, the [Stern] Review supports very strongly the politically unpalatable idea, which no democratic politician planning to remain in office anywhere wants to hear, that (however it is packaged and whatever spin is put on it) substantial carbon taxes must be levied because energy users need desperately to start confronting the expensive reality that burning carbon has a significant externality cost that ought to be taken into account by being charged full freight for doing it.[19]

Few economists would disagree with either Weitzman's point that carbon taxes are politically dangerous, or that carbon taxes are effective. In his blog, Professor Mankiw wrote:

> So here are three votes for a carbon tax: [*New York Times* columnist John] Tierney, [William] Nordhaus, and Mankiw. The first is a journalist who leans libertarian, the second is an economist who worked in a Democratic administration, and the third is an economist who worked in a Republican administration. What do we all have in common? None of us is planning to run for elected office.[20]

Economists have thus been stumping fairly consistently for carbon taxes, while complaining that politicians have been resistant. The previous chapter offers some explanations as to why economists and other carbon tax advocates have been unsuccessful in convincing the general public of the usefulness of carbon taxes.

The lack of success has been gauged by public opinion polls, which, as argued above, have been biased. But in 2006, a public opinion poll in Canada found that 52 percent of all Canadians agreed with this statement: "Canada needs a special carbon tax to increase the cost of burning fossil fuels like oil, gas and coal for consumers and industry. This tax would promote energy efficiency and help the environment."[21] Canada has never been substantially different from the United States in terms of its environmental attitudes, so this survey is almost as surprising as if it had been conducted in the United States. Perhaps the most astonishing result was that more than half of respondents from the province of Alberta agreed with the statement. Much of Alberta's prosperity is tied up in its vast reserves of hydrocarbons, and the province has historically been as conservative as possible in its regulation of greenhouse gases. Although this is not the sort of result that survives economic downturns—this poll marked the first time since 1990 that Canadians placed the environment in their list of concerns—it is still surprising that a broad Canadian population actually supported a policy clearly labeled as a carbon *tax*. It's just possible that the conventional wisdom—carbon taxes are politically toxic—could be wrong.

Canada is also where North America's first real carbon tax has been implemented, in British Columbia. Although British Columbia is a small jurisdiction—a province of about 4.5 million people—the political lessons from the BC carbon tax are significant. It is true that some believe the governing Liberal Party that passed the carbon tax was punished for it at the polls, winning the subsequent provincial election less handily than it otherwise might have.[22] But the political damage was greatly mitigated by a flow of support from environmental voters, who were traditionally more likely to vote with the opposition New Democratic Party and against the Liberal Party. The BC Liberal Party, having only one rival party and having it on its political left, deftly outflanks the New Democratic Party, challenging it to either agree with the Liberals and support the carbon tax, or split its constituency by opposing the carbon tax. The NDP chose the latter course, and lost out on much environmental support. Notable environmental groups and figures scolded the NDP for its position, and clearly helped the Liberals to siphon off some traditional NDP voters.[23]

Is it possible that the politics of carbon taxes are changing, the advocacy a work in progress? The seeds of a movement running counter to conventional wisdom are certainly present. Pigouvian taxes have always had some appeal to those inclined toward libertarian views. For those frustrated with the oppressiveness of environmental regulation, Pigouvian taxation has always represented an alternative to giving an agency like the EPA power and resources. For libertarians, Pigouvian taxation can *replace* or supplant environmental law. Seeing the kind of regulation that may be required to curb greenhouse gases, libertarian advocates of limited environmental regulation could seize on carbon taxes as a way of preempting a lot of what they see as heavy-handed regulation. On the other end of the spectrum, some environmentalists familiar and comfortable with economic concepts readily see that Pigouvian taxation *is* environmental regulation. And for environmentalists and environmental organizations exasperated with American federal inaction on climate policy, a carbon tax would certainly be a step in the right direction. Although different interest groups want different things from carbon taxes, there is no need for them to agree on *why* carbon taxes are desirable, only that they would be desirable. In light of the recent failures in the US Congress to pass cap-and-trade legislation, it seems more plausible now that carbon taxes would receive a fair hearing.

The evolution of cap-and-trade from a strange, wonky economists' idea to the presumptive climate policy instrument of choice also holds some lessons and some hope for carbon taxes. Like carbon taxes now, cap-and-trade was in the political hinterlands for a long time, until environmental economists managed to convince all economists of its usefulness, which managed to sway a broader policy audience. And just as it took a Republican president to bring cap-and-trade into the mainstream of environmental discourse, it has taken a relatively conservative British Columbia premier to bring carbon taxes to North America. Like cap-and-trade, a small number of environmental organizations have begun to champion carbon taxes, though their idea of the appropriate price may differ quite a lot from that of many conservatives that also champion carbon taxes.

Unlike cap-and-trade, however, the political economy of carbon taxes—while not as toxic as commonly believed—will never be a selling point. Part of what made cap-and-trade so palatable to regulated industries was the grandfathering of emissions allowances, the ability of Congress to make a transfer payment to regulated industries in exchange for their acquiescence. The fact that the 111th Congress failed to pass climate legislation does not mean that future legislators cannot find a more winning formula. Carbon taxes do not offer the same prospects for Congress to print money and buy acquiescence. The political drive for carbon taxes will have to be a grassroots one. That would appear to be difficult, since getting people worked up about carbon taxes sounds like quite a challenge.

It is beyond the scope of this book to suggest the political strategies and messaging that might bring about change in the way that people commonly perceive carbon taxes. Suffice it to say, the arguments made in this book point only to the overlooked potential for the politics and psychology of carbon taxes to change, not the specifics of how that is to be accomplished. This is left to more capable marketers and political strategists than this author.

Chapter 7

Conclusion

Given the complications surrounding the implementation of many other greenhouse gas reduction programs, a carbon tax—despite its apparent blemishes—emerges as the simplest, easiest, and most straightforward approach. There is obviously no magic bullet in the fight against climate change. Rather, a policy instrument must enable a large number of potential greenhouse reduction strategies to emerge. To ferret out all of these strategies—from large-scale construction of transmission lines and nuclear power plants to swapping out incandescent light bulbs for energy-efficient ones—a very broad carbon price must be imposed. An incentive must exist in every nook and cranny of everyday life in which fossil fuels are burned, to empower literally everybody in the world to find ways to reduce or eliminate the amount of carbon dioxide emitted.

Climate policy should not be wedded to the popular notion that government must undertake some grand project to prevent catastrophe. While technological innovation is necessary, we must not fall into the trap of thinking that only huge, expensive "game-changers" can save us from climate change. Many years from now, if one summed up the emissions reductions from a large number of small contributions like the Vegawatt, there is a strong possibility that they could add to more than the potential "game-changers." It would be a mistake to conflate the need for action with the need for government to spend

191

money or undertake an elaborate regulatory scheme for the sake of doing something. Fundamentally, one must have faith that markets will bring forth the innovations necessary to find ways to reduce greenhouse gas emissions. One has reason to question whether government projects currently considered for funding would produce as much innovation.

A carbon tax is also the best first step because it does not preclude any future alternative policies. A carbon tax can peacefully coexist with cap-and-trade, command-and-control, and even government subsidies. Almost everyone agrees that pricing carbon is important. The fact that other market distortions exist that may counter the effect of a carbon price does not detract from the need to have one. A carbon tax represents the quickest way to introduce such a price. Some limited, targeted subsidies and perhaps some limited, targeted command-and-control-style regulation may be warranted in some circumstances. For example, controlling the flaring of natural gas may call for something other than a carbon tax. But the central policy that should serve as the platform on which other climate policies can be added is the carbon tax.

For once, economists are right in advocating for the simplest way to reduce carbon dioxide emissions—impose a price, and impose it on *all* carbon dioxide emissions from fossil fuel combustion. The fundamental problem with carbon dioxide emissions is the lack of a price, and while other policy instruments try to impose a price under certain specified conditions, they do not impose it across the entire carbon-emitting economy.

Perhaps most importantly, the carbon tax offers the best chance of getting that elusive international buy-in. Complexity has proven to be a problem in forging international agreement on how to reduce greenhouse gas emissions. The most important stumbling block is a clash of perspectives on how, under a global cap-and-trade program, to allocate emissions among nations. The view of the United States (shared by Canada and most other developed countries) is that while developed nations should reduce more emissions than developing countries, current emissions must serve as *some* baseline for allocating global emissions. It would be unfair to disproportionately punish developed countries for emitting when it was not yet known that emissions were harmful. The view of China, India, and most other developing countries is that the developed countries have created this problem, and should be the ones to clean it up; and that any allocation of global emissions would have to take into account historical emissions. Although it would seem that some reconciliation of these two views is possible, there has been little movement on either side. The internal politics in the United States, China, and India do not appear to allow for much compromise on the problem of allocating global emissions.

Given this impasse over how to set up a global cap-and-trade program, the simplicity of a carbon tax presents an attractive alternative. Far from claiming that a carbon tax would be easy to harmonize across countries, this book simply argues that a global carbon tax presents fewer obstacles to international agreement. While cap-and-trade theoretically has the value of allowances as a potential means of making transfer payments from developed to developing countries, carbon taxation generates revenues that can be used to pay developing countries to participate.

The obstacles to implementing a carbon tax are not trivial, but nor are they, as conventional wisdom would have it, insurmountable. In fact, when one carefully considers the perception problems of carbon taxes, the solutions seem downright manageable. The psychological issues and misperceptions surrounding carbon taxation can be addressed by simply paying attention to framing issues, something to which even economists have learned to be sensitive. And the political economy argument against even trying for a carbon tax is that those interest groups that oppose it have more concentrated interests and therefore will devote more resources toward defeating a tax than advocates could possibly muster in favor of it. For some policy issues, this could well be an insurmountable obstacle. But the general public, though still trailing climate scientists in concern about climate change, have actually long been aware of and at least mildly concerned. This concern can be mobilized. A reasonable carbon tax, if explained properly and in the context of how it stacks up against alternative policy instruments, will not be the political third rail it has been thought to be. Besides, the resources may be available to mobilize this concern; already, tremendous resources have been devoted to climate change science, and many environmental organizations have swung the considerable weight of their staffing and attention toward climate change advocacy. If just a fraction of those resources were devoted toward better communications strategies, it is very possible that the perception of carbon taxes could change.

The disappointing international climate negotiations in Copenhagen in 2009 indicate how difficult it remains to find common ground among diverse nations to address climate change. And the subsequent collapse of negotiations in the US Congress over American climate legislation underscores how difficult it is to find a domestic legislative solution. In the midst of all this disappointment, carbon taxes are an overlooked alternative to the dominant cap-and-trade paradigm. A carbon tax large enough to internalize the currently expected social damages of emissions would be ideal. But even a small one would be an important step, for all of the reasons set out in this book. And with the right communications strategies, a small carbon tax could find enough converts to augment the core group of current advocates, which include several Nobel Laureates and other distinguished experts. If we examine our options carefully, looking beyond apparent political blemishes, it becomes abundantly clear that a carbon tax is the most effective policy, and a critical first step to stopping global climate change.

Chapter 1

1. There have been many scientists deeply involved with the development of global climate change theory, but perhaps none as influential as the late climatologist Stephen H. Schneider, who wrote *The Genesis Strategy: Climate and Global Survival* in 1976 and *Global Warming* in 1989.

2. Traditional economic modeling would predict that the world will, as it has for centuries, continue to grow richer. This is an assumption as well as an explicit part of economic modeling, including the three dozen or so *integrated assessment models*, combined climate and economy models that have played a prominent role in climate debate and policy. They include the PAGE2002 model that was heavily relied upon by Nicholas Stern and his modeling team in producing the *The Stern Review on the Economics of Climate Change* (Cambridge Press, 2007), as well as models that call for much more modest action, such as the RICE and DICE models created by economist William Nordhaus and his associates. On the other hand, some economists warn that future generations will not necessarily be richer, either because natural and environmental capital will be depleted, undermining economic growth (Cameron Hepburn and Nicholas Stern, "The Global Deal on Climate Change" Ch. 3 in *The Economics and Politics of Climate Change* [D. Helm and C. Hepburn, eds., Oxford Press, 2009]), or because traditional economic models do not accurately model large changes in marginal values of environmental goods, which will become much more scarce in a climate-changed future (Thomas Sterner and U. Martin Persson, "An Even Sterner Review: Introducing Relative Prices into the Discounting Debate," 2 *Review of Environmental Law and Policy*, 61, 63 [2008]).

3. World Resources Institute, "Climate Analysis Indicators Tool, Yearly Emissions," online at http://cait.wri.org/cait.php?p. (accessed March 18, 2010, on file with author). Carbon dioxide is not the only greenhouse gas, but it is by far the most abundant.

4. World Resources Institute, "Climate Analysis Indicators Tool, Yearly Emissions," online at http://cait.wri.org/cait.php?p. (accessed March 18, 2010, on file with author).

5. National Development and Reform Commission, "People's Republic of China, China's National Climate Change Program" (2007), online at http://en.ndrc.gov.cn/newsrelease/P020070604561191006823.pdf.

6. World Resources Institute, "Climate Analysis Indicators Tool, Yearly Emissions," online at http://cait.wri.org/cait.php?p. (accessed March 18, 2010, on file with author).

7. World Resources Institute, "Climate Analysis Indicators Tool, Yearly Emissions," online at http://cait.wri.org/cait.php?p. (accessed March 18, 2010, on file with author).

8. See, e.g., Evan Lehman, "Eight House Republicans, after Carrying Climate Effort Last Year, Fend off Attacks" *ClimateWire*, August 5, 2010 ("'I would not vote for it again in its current form because of the lack of progress in Copenhagen,' [Representative Leonard] Lance of New Jersey said of the cap-and-trade bill. 'I don't think we can do this alone. China and India have to come aboard.'"); "GOP: US Should Reject Climate Pact," *Seattle Times*, December 12, 2009, online at http://seattletimes.nwsource.com/html/politics/2010488118_apclimaterepublicans.html (accessed August 10, 2010).

9. US Department of Defense (2008) "National Defense Strategy," at 4–5.

10. Department of Defense, "Quadrennial Defense Review Report," February 2010.

11. This argument was first and most eloquently made by Nobel Laureate economist Thomas Schelling, in "Intergenerational Discounting," 23 *Energy Policy* 395 (1995).

Chapter 2

1. Nicholas Stern, *The Stern Review on the Economics of Climate Change* (2007).

2. Shi-Ling Hsu, "A Game-theoretic Model of International Climate Negotiations." 19 NYU. *Environmental Law Journal*, in publication.

3. Carolyn Kousky, Olga Rostapshova, Michael Toman, and Richard Zeckhauser, *Responding to Threats of Climate Change Mega-Catastrophes*, Resources for the Future Discussion Paper 09-45 (November 2009).

4. US Environmental Protection Agency, 2010. "US Greenhouse Gas Inventory Report," available online: www.epa.gov/climatechange/emissions/downloads10/US-GHG-Inventory-2010_Report.pdf (accessed February 10, 2011).

5. Gilbert Metcalf and David Weisbach, "The Design of a Carbon Tax," (January 8, 2009). University of Chicago Law & Economics, Olin Working Paper No. 447. Available at SSRN: http://ssrn.com/abstract=1324854.

6. US Department of the Interior, National Park Service, *Spanning the Gap: Newsletter of the Delaware Water Gap National Recreation Area*, Summer

1998 (reporting that the average ph of the Delaware Water Gap, between New Jersey and Pennsylvania, was 4.5, the same as for Coca Cola).

7. A 1997 cost-benefit analysis of the first twenty years of the Clean Air Act found that benefits outweighed the costs to industry and consumers by almost two orders of magnitude. While compliance costs over the years 1970 to 1990 totaled $523 billion, the benefits totaled $22.2 *trillion*. *United States Environmental Protection Agency, Executive Summary, Final Report to Congress on Benefits and Costs of the Clean Air Act 1970 to 1990,* ES-2 to ES-8 (1997), available online at www.epa.gov/air/sect812/812exec2.pdf. Since this estimate was a measure of just the benefits of reduced air pollution over twenty years, it is clear that the total damages of pollution over longer time scales would well exceed $22.2 trillion dollars. And since the largest component of damages from air pollution comes from sulfur dioxide, it is not an adventurous guess to say that the damages from sulfur dioxide over the nearly century of coal-fired power plant operations is very easily into the trillions of dollars.

8. It is now widely recognized that earlier estimates of damages from sulfur dioxide pollution were likely underestimates as they did not take full account of the effect of sulfur dioxide as particulate matter pollution, which has now emerged as the greatest threat to human health. See, e.g., Francine Laden et al., "Reduction in Fine Particulate Air Pollution and Mortality: Extended Follow-up of the Harvard Six Cities Study," 173 *American Journal of Respiratory and Critical Care Medicine* 667 (2006); C. Arden Pope III et al., "Lung Cancer, Cardiopulmonary Mortality, and Long-term Exposure to Fine Particulate Air Pollution," 287 *Journal of the American Medical Association* 1132 (2002); C. Arden Pope III et al., "Particulate Air Pollution as a Predictor of Mortality in a Prospective Study of US Adults," 151 *American Journal of Respiratory and Critical Care Medicine* 669 (1995); Douglas W. Dockery et al., "An Association Between Air Pollution and Mortality in Six US Cities," 329 *New England Journal of Medicine* 1753 (1993); "Health Effects Institute, Special Report: Reanalysis of the Harvard Six Cities Study and the American Cancer Society Study of Particulate Air Pollution and Mortality," available at http://pubs.healtheffects.org/view.php?id=6 (July 2000).

9. The century-old case *Georgia v. Tennessee Copper* 237 US 474 (1907), involved a dispute between the two states over sulfur dioxide pollution that resulted in massive destruction of tree and plant life on the Georgia side. It was alleged in the complaint, and not disputed, that "great quantities of sulphur dioxid [sic] are formed; if allowed to escape into the air this becomes sulphurous acid, a poisonous gas destructive of plant life."

10. 40 C.F.R. §76.6 & §76.7 (1996).

11. Ontario Regulation 419/05—Local Air Quality (December 22, 2009).

12. Clean Air Act §§ 401–416; 42 U.S.C. §§ 7651a–7651o (1990).

13. In its initial phase, the program imposed a somewhat hard nation-wide "cap" of 8.90 tons of SO_2 per year. Subsequent years have incorporated more facilities and also raised the cap. Clean Air Act § 403, 42 U.S.C. § 7651b (1990).

14. US Environmental Protection Agency, National Emissions Inventory, Air Pollutant Emission Trends Data, online at www.epa.gov/ttn /chief/trends/trends06/nationaltier1upto2006basedon2002finalv2.1.xls (Excel spreadsheet format, tabbed SO_2 Nat'l) (2003).

15. Kyoto Protocol, Article 12.

16. Kyoto Protocol, Article 6.

17. Internal Revenue Code §45 (2009).

18. I.R.C. § 45(c)(7) (2009).

Chapter 3

1. Alfred C. Pigou, *The Economics of Welfare*, 131–135 (1928). Taxes that reflected the extent of negative externality thus became known as "Pigouvian" taxes. William J. Baumol and Wallace E. Oates, *The Theory of Environmental Policy* 21–23 (2d ed., 1988).

2. A tax on carbon dioxide and a tax on carbon accomplish the same thing, but they are keyed, respectively, to the entire carbon dioxide molecule and to only the carbon atom, the weight ratio being 44/12. A tax on carbon of $12/ton thus has the same effect of a tax on carbon dioxide of $44/ton.

3. Richard S. J. Tol, "The Marginal Damage Costs of Carbon Dioxide Emissions: An Assessment of the Uncertainties," 33 *Energy Policy* 2064, 2068–69 (table 2) (2005). Based on his evaluations of the studies, Tol declared that "it is unlikely that the marginal damage costs of carbon dioxide emissions exceed $50/tC and are likely to be substantially smaller than that."

4. William D. Nordhaus, *A Question of Balance* 90 (Table 5-4) (2008).

5. Nicholas Stern, *The Stern Review on the Economics of Climate Change* 287 (2007).

6. Nicholas Stern, *The Stern Review on the Economics of Climate Change* 143 (2007).

7. Nicholas Stern, *The Stern Review on the Economics of Climate Change* 287 (2007).

8. William D. Nordhaus, *A Question of Balance* 95 (2008).

9. Nicholas Stern, *The Stern Review on the Economics of Climate Change* (2007).

10. William D. Nordhaus, *A Question of Balance* 95 (2008).

11. William D. Nordhaus, "A Review of the Stern Review on the Economics of Climate Change," 45 *Journal of Economic Literature* 686, 688 (2007).

12. Simon Cox and Richard Vadon, "Running the Rule Over Stern's Numbers," BBC News, January 26, 2007, online at http://news.bbc.co.uk/2/hi/science/nature/6295021.stm.

13. Martin Weitzman "A Review of the Stern Review on the Economics of Climate Change," 45 *Journal of Economic Literature* 703, 710 (2007).

14. Thomas Sterner and U. Martin Persson, "An Even Sterner Review: Introducing Relative Prices into the Discounting Debate," 2 *Review of Environmental Economics and Policy*, 61–76 (2008).

15. US Department of Agriculture, Natural Resources Conservation Service, Energy Estimator, online at: http://nfat.sc.egov.usda.gov/.

16. US Environmental Protection Agency, EPA Lifecycle Analysis of Greenhouse Gas Emissions from Renewable Fuels (May, 2009).

17. Allison Winter, "Peer review of EPA lifecycle rules fails to quell debate," E&E News PM, August 7, 2009.

18. 74 Fed. Reg. 66496 (December 15, 2009).

19. 139 *Canada Gazette* No. 36, Order Adding Toxic Substances to Schedule 1 to the Canadian Environmental Protection Act, 1999 (September 3, 2005) (citing section 64 of the Canadian Environmental Protection Act).

20. McKinsey & Co., *Unlocking Energy Efficiency in the US Economy* iii (2009).

21. McKinsey & Co., *Pathways to a Low-Carbon Economy* 7 (2009).

22. Henry Chu, "Carbon Tax is Sensible, and Perhaps Inevitable," *L.A. Times*, November 21, 2009.

23. See, for example, Steven Stoft, *Renewable Fuel and the Global Rebound Effect*, Global Energy Policy Center, Research Paper 10-06, 6 (Table 1) May 19, 2010 (discussing rebound effects of renewable fuel standards, which would also occur with subsidized renewable fuel production).

24. McKinsey & Co., *Pathways to a Low-Carbon Economy* 116 (2009).

25. Martin L. Weitzman, "Prices vs. Quantities," 41 *Review of Economic Studies* 477 (1974).

26. World Resources Institute, Climate Analysis Indicators Tool, Yearly Emissions, online at http://cait.wri.org/cait.php?p. (accessed April 7, 2010, on file with author).

27. European Commission, Environment, Climate Change, Emissions Trading, Questions and Answers on Emissions Trading and National Allocation Plans, http://europa.eu/rapid/pressReleasesAction.do?reference=MEMO/05/84&format=HTML&aged=1&language=EN&guiLanguage=en.

28. David Weisbach, "Instrument Choice Is Instrument Design," (October 23, 2009). University of Chicago Law & Economics, Olin Working Paper No. 490. Available at SSRN: http://ssrn.com/abstract=1493312.

29. 26 I.R.C. §§ 1001 et seq. (2010).

30. 26 I.R.C. § 1031 (2010).

31. American Council for Capital Formation, online at: www.accf.org /home.php.

32. I.R.C. § 631(c) (2007).

33. I.R.C. § 613(c) (2007).

34. For a review of the health and environmental effects of coal, see, Committee on Health and Environmental Effects of Increased Coal Utilization, "Report on Health and Environmental Effects of Increased Coal Utilization," 36 *Environmental Health Perspectives* 135 (1980); see also Jonathan I. Levy, Lisa K. Baxter, and Joel Schwartz, "Uncertainty and Variability in Health-Related Damages from Coal-Fired Power Plants in the United States" 29 *Risk Analysis* 1000, 1007–8 (2009). For a history of the utilization of coal, including the environmental and health effects, see, Barbara Freese, *Coal: A Human History* (2003).

35. The carbon intensity of various fuels was reviewed in Daniel Weisser, "A guide to life-cycle greenhouse gas (GHG) emissions from electric supply technologies" 32 *Energy* 1543. He found that presently operating coal plants have carbon emissions of between 800 and 1000 g CO_2eq/kWh. When cumulative emissions were taken into account, including emissions relating to plant construction, coal mining and transportation, the figure rose to between 950 and 1250 g CO_2eq/kWh (at 1550). This compares to natural gas, which has a range of 360 to 575 g CO_2eq/kWh relating to the actual operation of the plant, and cumulative emissions of between 440 and 780 g CO_2eq/kWh (at 1550). On the other hand, life cycle GHG emissions from wood based biomass electrical generation is estimated as being between 35 and 99 g CO_2eq/kWh (at 1553).

36. I.R.C. § 45(c)(7) (2009).

37. Elisabeth Rosenthal, "Solar Industry Learns Lessons Under the Spanish Sun," *New York Times*, March 8, 2010, at A1.

38. Wind Turbines UK, About Wind Energy, online at: www .windturbinesuk.co.uk/aboutwindenergy.htm#17.

39. Sergio Pacca, Deepak, Sivaraman, Gregory A. Keoleian, "Paramters Affecting the Lifecycle Performance of PV Technologies and Systems," 35 *Energy Policy* 3316 (2007).

40. Concentrating solar power plants could potentially generate electricity at between 3.5 and 6.2 cents per kilowatt hour by 2020, US Department of Energy, Report to Congress on Assessment of Potential Impact of Concentrating Solar Power for Electricity generation, (February 2007) online < http://www.nrel.gov/csp/troughnet/pdfs/41233.pdf >

41. Settlement Agmt (on file with author); Darren Samuelson, "Court Settlement Fails to Still Debate over IGCC in Permitting," *Greenwire*, October 13, 2006 (on file with author).

42. A number of recent cases in the US Supreme Court have curtailed federal jurisdiction to regulate water pollution. See, e.g., *Rapanos v. United*

States, 547 US 715 (2006), and *Solid Waste Agency of Northern Cook County v. Army Corps of Engineers*, 531 US 159 (2001).

43. It would be an open question as to whether a cap-and-trade program with auctioned allowances would be similar enough to a carbon tax to be deemed a revenue-raising mechanism, and therefore within the ambit of the revenue-raising powers of a state, province or national government. Since taxes do not *tend* to vary in amount, there would be significant legal obstacles to overcome in characterizing such a cap-and-trade program as a *tax*.

44. Regional Greenhouse Gas Initiative: www.rggi.org/home.

45. Western Climate Initiative: www.westernclimateinitiative.org/ewebeditpro/items/O104F19871.PDF.

46. Canadian Environmental Protection Act, Part 5, R.S.C. (1999).

47. Canadian Environmental Protection Act, Part 5, R.S.C. (1999), section 64(a).

48. Canadian Environmental Protection Act, Part 5, R.S.C. (1999), section 64(b).

49. Canadian Environmental Protection Act, Part 5, R.S.C. (1999), section 64(c).

50. Shi-Ling Hsu and Robin Elliot, "Regulating Greenhouse Gas Emissions in Canada: Constitutional and Policy Dimensions," 54 McGill Law Journal 463 (2009).

51. Western Climate Initiative, WCI Design Recommendations for the Cap-and-Trade Program Summary, online at www.usclimatepolicy.com/documents//CPIS/WCI/WCI_Design_Recommendations_Summary.pdf (accessed August 1, 2010).

52. US Conference of Mayors Climate Protection Center, "About the Mayors Climate Protection Center," online at www.usmayors.org/climateprotection/about.htm (accessed August 1, 2010).

53. California Global Warming Solutions Act, AB 32 (Ch. 488, Statutes of 2006).

54. B.C. Carbon Tax Act, S.B.C., 2008.

55. California Global Warming Solutions Act, AB 32 (Ch. 488, Statutes of 2006).

56. Numerous papers have contained variations of this statement. A recent paper incorporating this statement is by Richard E. Baldwin and Frederic Robert-Nicoud, "Entry and Asymmetric Lobbying: Why Governments Pick Losers," online at www.nber.org/papers/w8756.pdf.

57. The Presidency Project, Address Before a Joint Session of the Congress and a State of the Union, January 28, 2003, online at www.presidency.ucsb.edu/ws/index.php?pid=29645.

58. Id.

59. McKinsey & Co., *Pathways to a Low-Carbon Economy* 96 (2009).

60. US Department of Energy, 2010 Congressional Budget Request:

Budget Highlights 14 (2009), online at ww.cfo.doe.gov/budget/10budget /Content/Highlights/FY2010Highlights.pdf.

61. US Department of Energy, "2010 Congressional Budget Request: Budget Highlights 14" (2009), online at www.cfo.doe.gov/budget/10budget /Content/Highlights/FY2010Highlights.pdf.

62. Todd Zaun, "Ford to Use Toyota's Hybrid Technology," *New York Times*, 10 March 2004, online http://www.nytimes.com/2004/03/10 /business/ford-to-use-toyota-s-hybrid-technology.html.

63. US Senator Lamar Alexander, Floor Statements, April 22, 2009, online at http://alexander.senate.gov/public/index.cfm?FuseAction=Speeches .Detail&Speech_id=6e0de357-4757-49bb-adb1-3b5e795a81d4&Month= 4&Year=2009 (also on file with author).

64. Using an exchange rate of 1.4637 Euro per US dollar, the average rate for 2008. Bank of Canada, Financial Markets Department, Year of Average Exchange Rates, online at www.bank-banque-canada.ca/pdf/nraa08.pdf. More recent reports suggest that the current estimates are still too low. Mohammed Al-Juaied and Adam Whitmore, "Realistic Costs of Carbon Capture," Discussion Paper 2009-08, Energy Technology Innovation Research Group, Belfer Center for Science and International Affairs, Harvard Kennedy School, July 2009.

65. McKinsey & Co., *Carbon Capture and Storage: Assessing the Economics* 6 (2008), online: www.mckinsey.com/clientservice/ccsi/pdf/CCS _Assessing_the_Economics.pdf. A more favorable report concludes that the cost of capturing, transporting, and storing carbon is closer to $30/ton of CO_2. James Katzer et al., The Future of Coal: Options in a Carbon Constrained World, A Massachusetts Institute of Technology Interdisciplinary Study xi (2007) online at http://web.mit.edu/coal/The_Future_of_Coal.pdf.

66. McKinsey & Co., *Pathways to a Low-Carbon Economy* 7 (2009) (on file with author).

67. Dr. James Katzer et al., "The Future of Coal: Options in a Carbon Constrained World, A Massachusetts Institute of Technology Interdisciplinary Study" (2007) online http://web.mit.edu/coal/The_Future_of_Coal.pdf (Hereinafter "MIT Coal Study") at ix.

68. Id.

69. Jessica Leber, "Energy-Saving Process 'Scrubs Emissions without Water," *ClimateWire*, August 18, 2009.

70. Mark Chediak and Katarzynska Klimasinska, "AEP to exit clean coal project," *Tulsa World*, June 25, 2009.

71. Jason Plautz, "States See Rebirth in Battery Manufacturing," *Greenwire*, July 12, 2010 ("This is a game-changer for Michigan. It's the birth of an industry").

72. Lea Radick, "Some Energy Storage Solutions May Be 'Game-Changers' Industry Leaders Say," *ClimateWire*, March 13, 2009.

73. Nathan Gronewold, "Industry Needs Federal Help to Avoid Continued Slump," *Greenwire*, June 29, 2010; Mike Soraghan, "Shale Plays Create 'New World' for Energy Industry," *Greenwire*, March 11, 2010 ("Nearly every presenter at the conference has found a way to describe shale as a 'game changer.'"), Mike Soraghan, "US Shale Boom Could Go Global, Shifting Geopolitics," *Greenwire*, March 9, 2010 ("Shale gas in Ukraine could be a game-changer").

74. Katherine Ling, "House Panel to Focus on Small Reactors, Future R&D at DOE," *Energy & Environment Daily*, May 17, 2010.

75. Peter Behr, "A Reactor That Burns Depleted Fuel Emerges as a Potential 'Game-Changer'," *ClimateWire*, February 23, 2010.

76. Paul Voosen, "Researchers Explore 'Coal without Mining' in Bid to Slash CO_2-Storage Price Tag," *Greenwire*, April 16, 2010.

77. Saqib Rahim, "Is 'Ocean Thermal' Power Ready for Its Day in the Sun?" *ClimateWire*, February 11, 2009.

78. Peter Behr, "Proposal to Link Nation's Grid Sparks a Debate," *ClimateWire*, February 3, 2010; Peter Behr, "Electric 'Game-Changer' Gets FERC Scrutiny," *ClimateWire*, December 23, 2009.

79. Josh Voorhees, "Plug-in Hybrids Likely to Stay Expensive for Decades—Report," *Greenwire*, December 14, 2009.

80. Peter Behr, "A Reactor That Burns Depleted Fuel Emerges as a Potential 'Game-Changer'," *ClimateWire*, February 23, 2010 ("Politicians and scientists speak of them hopefully as "home runs" and "game changers," the long-shot technology breakthroughs that could produce a major advance toward the nation's future climate policy goals.").

81. For a review of energy and low-carbon subsidies, see Gilbert E. Metcalf, "Tax Policies for Low-carbon Technologies," National Bureau of Economic Research Working Paper 15054 (June 2009).

82. The weight of the empirical evidence seems to indicate that the turnover of capital stock brings environmental improvements that exceed that of regulation with grandfathered standards. It is impossible to prove this with respect to the scrubber mandate, in the absence of two counterfactuals: the amount of turnover that would have occurred without the grandfathering, and the amount of emissions reductions that would have occurred with the natural turnover of capital. See, John A. List, Daniel L. Millimet, and Warren McHone, "The Unintended Disincentives in the Clean Air Act," 4 *Advances in Economic Analysis & Policy* Issue 2, Article 2. Available at: www.bepress.com /bejeap/advances/vol4/iss2/art2; Howard Gruenspecht, " Differentiated Regulation: The Case of Auto Emissions Standards," 72 *American Economic Review* 328 (1982); Randy A. Nelson, Tom Tietenberg, Michael R. Donihue, "Differential Environmental Regulation: Effects on Electric Utility Capital Turnover and Emissions," 75 *Review of Economics and Statistics* 368 (1993); Randy Becker and Vernon Henderson, "Effects of Air Quality Regulation on

Polluting Industries," *Journal of Political Economy* 108:379 (2000); Michael T. Maloney and Gordon E. Brady, "Capital Turnover and Marketable Pollution Rights," *Journal of Law and Economy* 32:203 (1988).

83. Bruce A. Ackerman and William T. Hassler, *Clean Coal/Dirty Air* (1981).

84. Clean Air Act §404(a)(3); 42 U.S.C. §7651c(a)(3).

85. H.R. 2454, The American Clean Energy and Security Act of 2009, online at http://energycommerce.house.gov/Press_111/20090515/hr2454.pdf.

86. Breakthrough Institute, Breakthrough Blog, First Analysis of Waxman-Markey Allowance Allocation, online at http://thebreakthrough.org/blog/2009/05/analysis_of_waxman_markey.shtml.

87. John M. Broder, "Climate Bill Clears Hurdle, But Others Remain," *New York Times*, May 21, 2009, A13.

88. Timothy Gardner, "Lobbyists Elbow for Influence on US Climate Bill," Reuters, August 12, 2009.

89. Jessica Leber, "Chu Predicts That Energy Efficiency Will Bring the Fastest Reductions," *E&E News*, June 16, 2009 (on file with author).

90. David Duff and Shi-Ling Hsu, "Carbon Taxation in Theory and Practice," 261–74 (Ch. 15) in *Critical Issues in Environmental Taxation*, Vol. VIII (forthcoming, 2010).

91. Valentina Bosetti, Carlo Carraro, Romain Duval, Alessandra Sgobbi, and Massimo Tavoni, "The Role of R&D and Technology Diffusion in Climate Change Mitigation: New Perspectives Using the WITCH Model," Fondazione Eni Enrico Mattei, *Nota Di Lavoro* 14.2009 (February, 2009).

92. NO_x emissions regulation under the Acid Rain Program has subsequently been largely supplanted by a number of federal and regional directives that create a cap-and-trade program for NO_x emissions, covering the Midwestern and Eastern states. See, US Environmental Protection Agency, NO_x Budget Trading Program/NO_x SIP Call, 2003–2008, online at: www.epa.gov/airmarkets/progsregs/$NO_x NO_x$/sip.html.

93. Natur Vardsverket (Swedish Environmental Protection Agency), The Swedish Charge on Nitrogen Oxides 1–2 (2006) online: www.swedishepa.com/Documents/publikationer/620-8245-0.pdf.

94. Using an exchange rage of 0.1045 Euros per Swedish kroner and 0.1280 US dollars per Swedish kroner in effect on June 14, 2010.

95. Natur Vardsverket (Swedish Environmental Protection Agency), The Swedish Charge on Nitrogen Oxides 2 (Fig. 1) (2006) online: www.swedishepa.com/Documents/publikationer/620-8245-0.pdf.

96. US Environmental Protection Agency, National Emissions Inventory (NEI) Air Pollutant Emissions Trends Data, 1970–2008 (June 2009) downloadable from: www.epa.gov/ttn/chief/trends/index.html.

97. Kalle Määttä, "Finnish Energy Taxation: How Well Has It Worked?"

in *Critical Issues in Environmental Taxation*, 177 (Janet Milne, Kurt Deketeleare, Larry Kreiser, and Hope Ahsiabor, eds. 2002).

98. Carolyn Fischer, "Rebating Environmental Policy Revenues: Output-Based Allocations and Tradable Performance Standards," *Resources for the Future Discussion Paper 01-22* (2001).

99. Dallas Burtraw, "Innovation Under the Tradable Sulfur Dioxide Emission Permits Program in the US Electricity Sector," *Resources for the Future Discussion Paper* 00-38 (2000).

100. Nathaniel Keohane, "Cost Savings from Allowance Trading in the 1990 Clean Air Act: Estimates from a Choice-Based Model," in Charles E. Kolstad and Jody Freeman, eds., *Moving to Markets in Environmental Regulation: Lessons from Twenty Years of Experience* (New York: Oxford University Press, 2006).

101. A. Denny Ellerman, *Markets for Clean Air* (1951).

102. Dallas Burtraw, "Innovation Under the Tradable Sulfur Dioxide Emission Permits Program in the US Electricity Sector," *Resources for the Future Discussion Paper 00-38* (2000).

103. Shi-Ling Hsu, "Fairness Versus Efficiency in Environmental Law," *Ecology Law Quarterly* 31:303 (2004).

104. David Popp, "Pollution Control Innovations and the Clean Air Act of 1990," *Journal of Policy Analysis and Management* 22:641 (2003).

105. David Popp, Richard G. Newell, and Adam B. Jaffe, "Energy, the Environment, and Technological Change," NBER Working Paper 14832 (2009).

106. Adam B. Jaffe and Karen Palmer, "Environmental Regulation and Innovation: a Panel Data Study," *Revie. of Economics and Statistics* 79:610 (1997); Smita B. Brunniemer and Mark A. Cohen, "Determinants of Environmental Innovation in US Manufacturing Industries," *Journal of Environmental Economics & Management* 45:278 (2003); Mitsusugu Hamamoto, "Environmental Regulation and the Productivity of Japanese Manufacturing Industries," *Resource and Energy Economics* 28:299 (2006).

107. Ellerman, supra, note, at 174.

108. Ellerman, supra, note, at 172–73.

109. Michael Grubb & Karsten Neuhoff, "Allocation and Competitiveness in the EU Emissions Trading Scheme: A Policy Overview," *Climate Policy* 6:7–30 (2006).

110. Nathaniel Gronewald, "Prices Take a Sharp Dip in Fifth RGGI Auction," *Greenwire*, September 11, 2009.111. US Energy Information Administration, US Carbon Dioxide Emissions in 2009: a Retrospective Review, May 6, 2010, online at www.eia.doe.gov/oiaf/environment/emissions/carbon/index.html.

112. Sandbag, Press Release, April 1, 2010, EU Emissions Fall Dramatically Leaving Carbon Trading High and Dry, online at http://sandbag.org.uk/press_releases.

113. Peter Cramton and Suzi Kerr, "Tradeable Carbon Permit Auctions: How and Why to Auction not Grandfather," *Energy Policy* 30:333, 340 (2002).

114. Daron Acemoglu, Philippe Aghion, Leonardo Bursztyn, David Hemous, "The Environment and Directed Technical Change," National Bureau of Economic Research Working Paper 15451 (2009); David Popp, "Innovation and Climate Policy, " National Bureau of Economic Research Working Paper 15673 (2010); Valentina Bossetti, Carlo Carraro, Romain Duval, Massimo Tavoni, "What Should We Expect From Innovation? A Model-based Assessment of the Environmental and Mitigation Cost Implications from Climate-based R & D," *Nota Di Lavoro* 42.2010 (2010).

115. US Energy Information Administration, Net Generation by Energy Source, online: www.eia.doe.gov/cneaf/electricity/epm/table1_1.html.

116. Paolo Garrone and Luca Grilli, "Is There a Relationship Between Energy R&D and Carbon Emissions Per GDP? An Empirical Investigation," *Energy Policy* 38:5600 (2010).

117. I.R.C. §45(c).

118. 2013 for some facilities. Publ. L. 111-5, §1101; 123 Stat. 115 (Feb. 17, 2009).

119. www.powerauthority.on.ca/Page.asp?PageID = 122&ContentID = 7136.

120. This phrase has become so often used that its origin is difficult to determine. It was invoked in a recent speech by Canadian Environment Minister Jim Prentice (online at www.ec.gc.ca/default.asp?lang = En&n = 6F2DE1CA-1&news = E110AAE9-B810-4F07-ADEC-2A4C245D67D9) as well as in a recent interview by Australian Minister for Climate Change and Water Penny Wong (www.environment.gov.au/minister/wong/2008 /tr20081207.html).

121. University of British Columbia, Climate Action Plan, Emissions Sources, online at: http://climateaction.ubc.ca/category/emission-sources /energy (accessed April 19, 2010, on file with author).

122. University of British Columbia, Climate Action Plan, Overview viii (2010) online at www.sustain.ubc.ca/sites/default/files/uploads/pdfs /UBC%20Vancouver%20CAP_summary.pdf; on file with author).

123. David Weisbach, "Instrument Choice is Instrument Design," (October 23, 2009). University of Chicago Law & Economics, Olin Working Paper No. 490. Available at SSRN: http://ssrn.com/abstract = 1493312; Robert Stavins, "Addressing Climate Change With a Comprehensive US Cap-and-Trade System," *Oxford Review of Economic Policy* 24:298 (2008), Gilbert Metcalf and David Weisbach, "The Design of a Carbon Tax," (January 8, 2009), University of Chicago Law & Economics, Olin Working Paper No. 447; University of Chicago, Public Law Working Paper No. 254. Available at SSRN: http://ssrn.com/abstract = 1324854.

124. Nicholas Institute, "Size Thresholds for Greenhouse Gas Regulation: Who Would Be Affected by a 25,000 ton Emissions Rule?" 6 (2009) online at www.nicholas.duke.edu/institute/ni.report.09.05.pdf.

125. US Energy Information Administration, Average Retail Price of Electricity to Ultimate Customers, by End-User, by State, www.eia.doe.gov /cneaf/electricity/epm/table5_6_a.html (accessed April 19, 2010, on file with author).

126. Assuming a CO_2 emissions rate of about 2 lbs./kwh, which has been a typical emissions rate for coal-fired power plants. US Energy Information Administration, Carbon Dioxide Emissions from the Generation of Electric Power in the United States 8 (July 2000), online at www.eia.doe.gov/cneaf /electricity/page/co2_report/co2emiss.pdf (accessed April 19, 2010, on file with author).

127. American College and University Presidents Climate Commitment, online at: http://acupcc.aashe.org/.

128. American College and University Presidents Climate Commitment, "GHG Report for American University" (April 2, 2010), online at: http:// acupcc.aashe.org/ghg/824/ (accessed August 7, 2010).

129. Sharon Donnell, "AU Aims for Carbon Neutrality by 2020," NBCWashington.com (May 14, 2010) online at: www.nbcwashington.com /news/green/AU-Carbon-Neutral-by-2020-93778929.html (accessed August 8, 2010).

130. McKinsey & Co., *Unlocking Energy Efficiency in theUS Economy* iii (2009).

131. Valentina Bosetti, Carlo Carraro, Romain Duval, Alessandra Sgobbi & Massimo Tavoni, "The Role of R&D and Technology Diffusion in Climate Change Mitigation: New Perspectives Using the WITCH Model," Fondazione Eni Enrico Mattei, *Nota Di Lavoro* 14.2009 (February, 2009).

132. For a discussion of these and other measures, see, McKinsey & Co., *Pathways to a Low-Carbon Economy* 7 (2009) (on file with author).

133. Clean Air Act § 173(a)(2), 42 U.S.C. § 7503(a)(2).

134. Clean Air Act § 165(a)(4), 42 U.S.C. § 7475(a)(4).

135. Clean Air Act § 172(c)(1), 42 U.S.C. § 7502(c)(1).

136. Clean Air Act §412(a), 42 U.S.C. §7651k(a).

137. Clean Air Act §412(b) & (c), 42 U.S.C. §7651k(b) & (c).

138. Clean Air Act §412(d), 42 U.S.C. §7651k(d).

139. Nathaniel Gronewold and John J. Fialka, "European Commission Halts Transfers of Carbon Emissions Allowances Until Thefts Are Sorted Out," *ClimateWire*, January 20, 2011.

140. Congressional Budget Office, Cost Estimate, S. 2191, America's Climate Security Act of 2007 16 (April 10, 2008), online at www.cbo.gov /ftpdocs/91xx/doc9120/s2191.pdf.

141. American Clean Energy Leadership Act, S. 1462 (July 16, 2009).

142. John M. Broder, "Climate Bill Clears Hurdle, But Others Remain," *New York Times*, May 21, 2009, at A13.

143. Michael W. Wara, "Measuring the Clean Development Mechanism's Performance and Potential," *U.C.L.A. Law Review* 1759, 55:1783-86 (2008); see also Michael W. Wara and David G. Victor, "A Realistic Policy on International Carbon Offsets," Working paper, online at http://iis-db.stanford.edu /pubs/22157/WP74_final_final.pdf.

144. William Irving and Martin Branscombe, "2006 Good Practice Guidance and Uncertainty Management in National Greenhouse Gas Inventories, HFC-23 Emissions From HCFC-22 Production," Intergovernmental Panel on Climate Change (2006), online at www.ipcc-nggip.iges.or.jp/public /gp/bgp/3_8_HFC-23_HCFC-22_Production.pdf.

145. Wara, supra, note; Michael W. Wara and David G. Victor, "A Realistic Policy on International Carbon Offsets," Stanford University Program on Energy and Sustainable Development Working Paper #74 (2008), online at http://iis-db.stanford.edu/pubs/22157/WP74_final_final.pdf.

146. The concept of a public good has a long history, and it is difficult to pinpoint any time or credit any economist with its definition. But in the 1960s Mancur Olson's "The Logic of Collective Action: Public Goods and the Theory or of Groups" (Harvard, 1965) is considered seminal, and a famous exchange in the *Journal of Law and Economics* between Paul Samuelson, James Buchanan, and Jora Minasian played an important role in the development and diffusion of the concept. Jora R. Minasian, "Television Pricing and the Theory Public Goods," *Journal of Law and Economics* 7:71 (1964); Paul A. Samuelson, "Public Goods and Subscription TV: Correction of the Record," *Journal of Law and Economics* 7:81 (1964); James Buchanan, "Public Goods in Theory and Practice: a Note on the Samuelson-Minasian Discussion," *Journal of Law and Economics* 10:193 (1967); Paul A. Samuelson, "Pitfalls in the Analysis of Public Goods," *Journal of Law and Economics* 10:199 (1967); Jora R. Minasian, "Public Goods in Theory and Practice Revisited," *Journal of Law and Economics* 10:205 (1967).

147. Mitigation will require action from both developed and developing countries. See, e.g., Nichoals Stern, *The Stern Review on the Economics of Climate Change*, 205–6 (2007).

148. Scott Barrett, *Environment and Statecraft* 393–96 (2003).

149. Embassy of the People's Republic of China in the United States of America, China Announces Targets on Carbon Emissions Cuts, online at: www.china-embassy.org/eng/xw/t629651.htm (November 26, 2009).

150. Eward Wong and Jonathan Ansfield, "China Insists That Its Steps on Climate Be Voluntary," *New York Times*, January 29, 2010, at A5.

151. Steven Stoft, "The Cause of the War Over Caps and How to End It," Global Policy Energy Center (December, 2009) (on file with author).

152. Trevor Houser, Rob Bradley, Britt Childs, Jacob Werksman, and Robert Heilmayr, "Leveling the Carbon Playing Field: International Competition and US Climate Policy Design" (Peterson Institute, 2008).

153. For an analysis, see, Joost Pauwelyn, "US Federal Climate Policy and Competitiveness Concerns: the Limits and Options of International Trade Law," Working paper, Nicholas Institute for Environmental Policy Solutions (April 2007), online at www.nicholas.duke.edu/institute/internationaltradelaw.pdf.

154. General Agreement on Tariffs and Trade, Article II:2(a) (1948).

155. This was the term that seemed important in Appellate Body Report, "Mexico—Taxes on Soft Drinks," WT/DS308/AB/R, para. 8.42. (October 7, 2005).

156. GATT, BISD 34S/136, para. 2.5 (June 17, 1987).

157. Comprehensive Environmental Response, Compensation, and Liability Act, 42 U.S.C. §§ 9601 et seq. (2002).

158. Internal Revenue Code, 26 U.S.C. §§ 4681, 4682 (1997).

159. Internal Revenue Code, 26 U.S.C. § 4682 (d)(2) (1997).

160. Gary Clyde Hufbauer, Steve Charnovitz, and Jisum Kim, "Global Warming and the World Trading System" 96 (Peterson Institute, 2009).

161. B.C. Carbon Tax Act, S.B.C, 2008, s. 5.

162. Shi-Ling Hsu, Joshua Walters & Anthony Purgas, "Pollution Tax Heuristics: an Empirical Study of Willingness to Pay Higher Gasoline Taxes," *Energy Policy* 36:3612 (2008).

163. See, e.g., Graeme Morton, "No Money Available for New Schools," *Calgary Herald,* March 23, 2006; David Olive, "Dubious Dividend: Despite a Laundry List of Items Demanding Fiscal Attention, Alberta Premier Klein Plans to Send a $400 'Resource Rebate' to All 3.2 Million Albertans," *Toronto Star,* October 23, 2005.

164. Shi-Ling Hsu, Joshua Walters & Anthony Purgas, "Pollution Tax Heuristics: An Empirical Study of Willingness to Pay Higher Gasoline Taxes," *Energy Policy* 36:3612 (2008).

165. Ian Parry, "Revenue Recycling and the Costs of Reducing Carbon Emissions," Resources for the Future, *Climate Issues Brief No. 2,* (1997), online at www.rff.org/rff/documents/rff-ccib-02.pdf; Govindar R. Timilsina, "The Role of Revenue Recycling in Environmental Tax Schemes," World Bank Policy Research Working Paper 4438 (2007), available online at http://papers.ssrn.com/sol3/papers.cfm?abstract_id=1069478; Ian W. H. Parry and Antonio Bento, Revenue Recycling and the Welfare Effects of Road Pricing, Resources for the Future Discussion Paper 99-45 (1999), online at www.rff.org/Documents/RFF-DP-99-45.pdf; Winston Harrington, Alan Krupnick, & Anna Alberni, "Overcoming Public Aversion to Congestion Pricing," *Transportation Research* 35:A87 (2001).

166. Martin L. Weitzman, "A Review of the Stern Review of the Economics of Climate Change," *Journal of Law and Economics* 45:703, 723 (2007).

167. Martin L. Weitzman, "Prices vs. Quantities," 41 *Review of Economic Studies* 477 (1974).

168. E&ETV, "Pew's Claussen Compares Cap-and-Trade and Carbon Tax Approaches for Emission Reduction," *On Point*, July 16, 2008 (transcript on file with author).

169. Gernot Wagner and Nathaniel Keohane, "There's Certainty in the Environmental Outcome," *Bulletin of the Atomic Scientists, Carbon Tax vs. Cap and Trade Blog*, September 11, 2008; Nathaniel Keohane, "Environmental Policy Design and the Distribution of Pollution Control Techniques in a Regulated Industry," (May 26, 2006) Yale SOM Working Paper, available at SSRN: http://ssrn.com/abstract=907292; Nathaniel Keohane, "Cap and Trade, Rehabilitated: Using Tradable Permits to Control Greenhouse Gases," *Review of Environmental Law and Policy* 3:42 (2009).

170. See, e.g., Intergovernmental Panel on Climate Change, Third Assessment Report, Climate Change 2001: Synthesis Report, 20 (2001).

171. Intergovernmental Panel on Climate Change, Fourth Assessment Report, Climate Change 2007: Synthesis Report, 47, 54 (2007).

172. Saqib Rahim and Evan Lehmann, "Companies Search for Energy Savings, with Mixed Results," *ClimateWire*, May 16, 2010.

173. See, e.g., William Pizer, "Climate Policy Design Under Uncertainty," Resources for the Future Discussion Paper 05-44 (2005).

174. Woods Hole Research Center, Understanding the Global Carbon Cycle, Global Flows of Carbon. online at: www.whrc.org/carbon/index.htm.

175. Global Carbon Project, Carbon Budget, Summary Highlights (November 17, 2009). online at: www.globalcarbonproject.org/carbonbudget /08/hl-brief.htm.

176. McKinsey & Co., *Pathways to a Low-Carbon Economy* 7 (2009).

177. Environmental Protection Agency, Comparison of the Economic Impacts of the Acid Rain Provisions of the Senate Bill (S. 1630) and the House Bill (S. 1630). Report prepared by ICF Resources Inc. Washington: Environmental Protection Agency, July 1990.

178. US Environmental Protection Agency, 1999 Progress Report on the EPA Acid Rain Program 4 (1999), online www.epa.gov/airmarkt /progress/docs/1999report.pdf.

179. US Environmental Protection Agency, 1999 Progress Report on the EPA Acid Rain Program 4 (1999), online www.epa.gov/airmarkt /progress/docs/1999report.pdf.

180. Winston Harrington, Richard D. Morgenstern, and Peter Nelson, "On the Accuracy of Regulatory Cost Estimates," Resources for the Future

Discussion Paper 99-18 (1999), online: www.rff.org/documents/RFF-DP
-99-18.pdf.

Chapter 4

1. David Duff and Shi-Ling Hsu, "Carbon Taxation in Theory and in
Practice," ch. 15 in *Critical Issues in Environmental Taxation*, Vol. VII. (2010).

2. "France drops carbon tax plans," *ClimateWire*, March 23, 2010.

3. Henrik Hammar, Asa Lofgren, and Thomas Sterner, "Political Economy Obstacles to Fuel Taxation," 25 *Energy Journal* 25:1 (2004).

4. Darren Samuelson and Katherine Ling, "Fragile Compromise of
Power Plant CEOs in Doubt as Senate Debate Approaches," *E&E News*, August 5, 2009.

5. John M. Broder, "Senate Gets a Climate and Energy Bill, Modified by
a Gulf Spill That Still Grows," *New York Times*, May 12, 2010, at A18 ("The
leader of the main utility industry trade group, Thomas R. Kuhn of the Edison Electric Institute, stood with Mr. Kerry and Mr. Lieberman on Wednes-
day and endorsed their bill.")

6. Monterey Bay Aquarium, Review of Public Opinion Surveys on
Climate Change (August 4, 2008) (online at http://itconf.mbayaq.org
/climatechangesummit/ReviewofClimateChangesurveysfor2010FINAL.pdf.

7. While compliance costs over the years 1970 to 1990 totaled $523 bil-
lion, the benefits totaled $22.2 *trillion*. United States Environmental Protec-
tion Agency, *Executive Summary, Final Report to Congress on Benefits and Costs
of the Clean Air Act 1970 to 1990*, ES-2–ES-8 (1997), available online at
www.epa.gov/air/sect812/812exec2.pdf.

8. The Carbon Limits and Energy for America's Renewal Act, S. 2877,
downloadable from: http://thomas.loc.gov/cgi-bin/query/z?c111:S.2877:.
(accessed August 4, 2010).

9. Jim Snyder, "AARP Prefers Cantwell-Collins Climate Bill," *E2 Wire*,
March 10, 2010, online at http://thehill.com/blogs/e2-wire/677-e2-wire
/85959-aarp-prefers-cantwell-collins-climate-bill (accessed August 4, 2010).

10. Joanna Smith, "Carbon Tax Would Hurt the Poor, NDP Says,"
TheStar.com, May 23, 2008, online at www.thestar.com/printarticle/429174.

11. New Democratic Party, "Axe the Tax," *New Democrat*, June 16, 2008.
online at: www.bcndpcaucus.ca/en/axethegastax (accessed August 4, 2010).

12. Sarah E. West and Roberton C. Williams, "Estimates from a Consumer Demand System: Implications from the Incidence of Environmental
Taxes," *Journal of Environmental Economics and Management* 47:535, 547
(table 2) (2004).

13. For 2009, the average weekly retail price of a gallon of gasoline in
California was $2.68 per gallon, with refiners realizing an average weekly

profit of $1.47 per gallon, and distributors (gas stations) realizing an average weekly profit of about 14 cents. These figures are derived from data from the California Energy Commission, Energy Almanac, Estimated 2009 Gasoline Price Breakdown Margins and Details, http://energyalmanac.ca.gov/gasoline /margins/2009.html.

14. Lans A. Bovenberg and Lawrence Goulder, "Neutralizing the Adverse Industry Impacts of CO_2 Abatement Policies: What Does It Cost?" *Distributional and Behavioral Effects of Environmental Policy*, pp. 45–85 (Univ. of Chicago Press, C. Carraro and G. E. Metcalf, eds., 2001).

15. Sarah E. West and Roberton C. Williams, "Estimates from a Consumer Demand System: Implications from the Incidence of Environmental Taxes," *Journal of Environmental Econimics and Management* 47:551, 553 (Table 3) (2004). See also, James M. Poterba, "Is the Gasoline Tax Regressive?" *Tax Policy and the Economy* 145–60 (D. Bradford, ed., 1991).

16. Kevin A. Hassett, Aparna Mathur, and Gilbert Metcalf, "The Incidence of a US Carbon Tax: A Lifetime and Regional Analysis," National Bureau of Economic Research Working Paper 13554 (2007) (on file with author).

17. This hypothesis has many authors, but a leading one is Milton Friedman, in Milton A. Friedman, A Theory of the Consumption Function (Princeton Univ. Press, 1957).

18. Nicholas Bull, Kevin A. Hassett, and Gilbert E. Metcalf, "Who Pays Broad-Based Energy Taxes? Computing Lifetime and Regional Incidence," *Energy Journal* 15:145 (1994).

19. Kevin A. Hassett, Aparna Mathur, and Gilbert Metcalf, "The Incidence of a US Carbon Tax: A Lifetime and Regional Analysis," National Bureau of Economic Research Working Paper 13554 (2007) (on file with author).

20. Kevin A. Hassett, Aparna Mathur, and Gilbert Metcalf, "The Incidence of a US Carbon Tax: A Lifetime and Regional Analysis," National Bureau of Economic Research Working Paper 13554 (2007) (on file with author).

21. Dallas Burtraw, Rich Sweeney, and Margaret Walls, "The Incidence of US Climate Policy: Where You Stand Depends on Where You Sit," Resources for the Future Discussion Paper 08-28 (2008); Corbett A. Grainger and Charles D. Kolstad, "Who Pays for a Carbon Tax?" working paper, Department of Economics, University of California at Santa Barbara, online at http://econ.ucsb.edu/~grainger/GK_Carbon_10-2.pdf.

22. B.C. Carbon Tax Act, S.B.C, 2008, s. 5.

23. Government of British Columbia, Ministry of Finance, Budget and Fiscal Plan 2008/09–2010/11 at 103-06 (February 19, 2008) online at: www .bcbudget.gov.bc.ca/2008/bfp/2008_Budget_Fiscal_Plan.pdf.

24. Government of British Columbia, Ministry of Finance, Budget and

Fiscal Plan 2008/09–2010/11 at 105 (February 19, 2008) online at: www
.bcbudget.gov.bc.ca/2008/bfp/2008_Budget_Fiscal_Plan.pdf.

25. Marc Lee and Toby Sanger, "Is BC's Carbon Tax Fair?" Canadian Centre for Policy Alternatives 13–14 (2008) online at www
.policyalternatives.ca/sites/default/files/uploads/publications/BC_Office_Pubs
/bc_2008/ccpa_bc_carbontaxfairness.pdf.

26. Marc Lee and Toby Sanger, "Is BC's Carbon Tax Fair?" Canadian Centre for Policy Alternatives 14 (2008) online at www
.policyalternatives.ca/sites/default/files/uploads/publications/BC_Office_Pubs
/bc_2008/ccpa_bc_carbontaxfairness.pdf.

27. Marc Lee and Toby Sanger, "Is BC's Carbon Tax Fair?" *Canadian Centre for Policy Alternatives* 21 (2008) online at www
.policyalternatives.ca/sites/default/files/uploads/publications/BC_Office_Pubs
/bc_2008/ccpa_bc_carbontaxfairness.pdf. ("The paper also did not take into
account behavioural change as a result of the carbon tax.")

28. Marc Lee and Toby Sanger, "Is BC's Carbon Tax Fair?" *Canadian Centre for Policy Alternatives* 21 (2008) online at www
.policyalternatives.ca/sites/default/files/uploads/publications/BC_Office_Pubs
/bc_2008/ccpa_bc_carbontaxfairness.pdf.

29. Sarah E. West and Roberton C. Williams, "Estimates from a Consumer Demand System: Implications from the Incidence of Environmental
Taxes," *Journal of Environmental Econimics and Management* 47:535 (2004).

30. Sarah E. West and Roberton C. Williams, "Estimates from a Consumer Demand System: Implications from the Incidence of Environmental
Taxes," *Journal of Environmental Econimics and Management* 47:535, 551
(Table 3) (2004) (showing that the policy which returns gas tax revenues lump
sum to households yields a net positive welfare gain for the poorest quintile).

31. Dallas Burtraw, Richard Sweeney, and Margaret Walls, "The Incidence of US Climate Policy: Alternative Uses of Revenues from a Cap-and-
Trade Auction," Resources for the Future Discussion Paper 09-17 REV
(2009).

32. There would still be a difference in that a carbon tax maintains a price,
while the cap-and-trade program maintains a quantity of emissions.

33. Sebastian Rauch, Gilbert Metcalf, John Reilly, and Sergey Paltsev,
"Distributional Implications of Alternative US Greenhouse Gas Control
Measures," NBER Working Paper 16053 (June 2010).

34. Don Fullerton, Garth Heutel, and Gilbert Metcalf, "Does the Indexing of Government Transfers Make Carbon Pricing Progressive?," NBER
Working Paper 16768 (February 2011).

35. B.C. Carbon Tax Act, S.B.C, 2008, s. 5.

36. Shi-Ling Hsu, Joshua Walters, and Anthony Purgas, "Pollution Tax
Heuristics: An Empirical Study of Willingness to Pay Higher Gasoline Taxes,"
Energy Policy 47:3612, 3618 (2008).

37. Government of Sweden, Ministry of Finance, "20 Years of Carbon Taxation in Sweden" 3 (June 21, 2010) (on file with author) (using an exchange rate of 9.625 Swedish Krona per Euro in effect as of July 6, 2010).

38. David Duff and Shi-Ling Hsu, "Carbon Taxation in Theory and Practice," *Critical Issues in Environmental Taxation,* Vol. VIII, 261–74 (forthcoming, 2010).

39. Government of Sweden, Ministry of the Environment, "Sweden and the Challenge of Climate Change" (January 2007).

40. Government of Sweden, Ministry of Finance, "20 Years of Carbon Taxation in Sweden" 5 (Table 1) (June 21, 2010) (on file with author).

41. Government of British Columbia, Ministry of Finance, Budget and Fiscal Plan 2008/09–2010/11 at 18–20 (February 19, 2008) online at: www.bcbudget.gov.bc.ca/2008/bfp/2008_Budget_Fiscal_Plan.pdf.

42. BCGasPrices.com, www.bcgasprices.com/retail_price_chart.aspx.

43. A review of empirical studies of energy elasticities is in Kenneth Gillingham, Richard G. Newell, and Karen Palmer, "Energy Efficiency Economic and Policy," Resources for the Future Discussion Paper 09-13 6 (Table 1) (April 2009).

44. The National Academies, What You Need to Know about Energy, How We Use Energy, online at: http://needtoknow.nas.edu/energy/energy-use/.

45. Richard G. Newell, Adam Jaffe, and Robert Stavins, "The Induced Innovation Hypothesis and Energy-Saving Technological Change," *Quarterly Journal of Economics* 114: 941 (1999).

46. Adam Jaffe and Robert Stavins, "The Energy Efficiency Gap: What Does It Mean? " *Energy Policy* 22:804 (1994).

47. Kenneth Gillingham, Richard G. Newell, and Karen Palmer, "Energy Efficiency Economic and Policy," Resources for the Future Discussion Paper 09-13 6 (Table 1) (April 2009).

48. Carl Blumstein, Betsy Kreig, Lee Schipper, and Carl York, "Overcoming Social and Institutional Barriers to Energy Efficiency," *Energy* 5:355 (1980).

49. Richard G. Newell, Adam Jaffe, and Robert Stavins, "The Induced Innovation Hypothesis and Energy-Saving Technological Change," *Quarterly Journal of Economics* 114:941 (1999).

50. Richard G. Newell, Adam Jaffe, and Robert Stavins, "The Induced Innovation Hypothesis and Energy-Saving Technological Change," *Quarterly Journal of Economics* 114:941 (1999).

51. Uri Gneezy and Aldo Rustichini, "A Fine is a Price," *Journal of Legal Studies* 29:1 (2000).

52. Catherine C. Eckel, Philip J. Grossman, and Rachel M. Johnston, "An Experimental Test of the Crowding Out Hypothesis," *Journal of Public Economics* 89:1543 (2005).

53. Timo Goseschl and Grischa Perino, "Instrument Choice and Motivation: Evidence from a Climate Change Experiment," Centre for Behavioural and Experimental Social Science (June 9, 2009).

54. The widely used market metaphor to support legal arguments for the First Amendment right to freedom of expression is attributed to a dissenting opinion by Justice Oliver Wendell Holmes, in *Abrams v. United States*, 250 US 616 (1919), but was never actually used by Holmes. In *Keyishian v. Board of Regents*, another US Supreme Court case, this one involving the constitutionality of university requirement that it's faculty members certify that they were not communists, Justice Brennan wrote that "[t]he classroom is peculiarly the 'marketplace of ideas.' The Nation's future depends upon leaders trained through wide exposure to that robust exchange of ideas which discovers truth 'out of a multitude of tongues, [rather] than through any kind of authoritative selection.'" 385 US 589, 603 (1967).

55. Nicholas Stern, *The Stern Review on the Economics of Climate Change* (2007).

Chapter 5

1. Joseph Stiglitz, "A New Agenda for Global Warming," *Economists' Voice* 3:7, Article 3 (2006), online at www.bepress.com/cgi/viewcontent .cgi?article=1210&context=ev); Gregory Mankiw, "Three Votes for a Carbon Tax," Gregory Mankiw's Blog, May 23, 2006, online at: http:// gregmankiw.blogspot.com/2006/05/three-votes-for-carbon-tax.html.   See also, Gregory Mankiw, "Raise the Gasoline Tax," *Wall Sreet Journal*, October 20, 2006, online at http://online.wsj.com/article/SB116131055641498552 .html, republished on Gregory Mankiw's blog, at http://gregmankiw .blogspot.com/2006/10/pigou-club-manifesto.html).

2. Woods Institute for the Environment, Global Warming Poll (June 9, 2010) online at: http://woods.stanford.edu/research/americans-support-govt -solutions-global-warming.html (accessed March 25,2011).

3. Nathan Cummings Foundation Global Warming Survey (August 2007).

4. Anthony Lieserowitz, Edward Maibach, Connie Roser-Renouf, and Nicholas Smith, "Global Warming's Six Americas" 44–46 (June 2010) online at http://environment.yale.edu/climate/files/SixAmericasJune2010.pdf (accessed August 7, 2010).

5. Edward J. McCaffery and Jonathan Baron, "Isolation Effects and the Neglect of Indirect Effects of Fiscal Policies ," *Journal of Behavioral Decision Making* 19:289 (2006); Edward J. McCaffery and Jonathan Baron, "Thinking About Tax," *Psychology & Public Policy* 12:106 (2006).

6. Mark Spranca, Elisa Minsk, and Jonathan Baron, "Omission and Comission in Judgment and Choice," *Journa. of Experimental Social Psychology*

27:76 (1991); Ilana Ritov and Jonathan Baron, "Status-quo and Omission Bias," *Journal of Risk and Uncertainty* 5:49 (1992); Jonathan Baron, "Heuristics and Biases in Equity Judgments: a Utilitarian Approach," *Psychological Perspectives on Justice: Theory and Applications* 135–36 (B. A. Mellers and J. Baron, eds., 1993); Ilana Ritov and Jonathan Baron, "Reluctance to Vaccinate: Omission Bias and Ambiguity," *Journal of Behavioral Decision Making* 263, 3:275–77 (1990).

7. Jonathan Baron, "Heuristics and Biases in Equity Judgments: a Utilitarian Approach," *Psychological Perspectives on Justice: Theory and Applications* 135–36 (B. A. Mellers and J. Baron, eds., 1993).

8. Jonathan Baron, "Nonconsequentialist decisions," *Behavioral and Brain Sciences* 17:1 (1994).

9. Abt Associates, Power Plant Emissions: Particulate Matter-Related Health Damages and the Benefits of Alternative Emission Reduction Scenarios 6-2 (2004), applying analysis from Francine Laden et al., "Reduction in Fine Particulate Air Pollution and Mortality: Extended Follow-up of the Harvard Six Cities Study," *American Journal of Respiratory & Critical Care Medicine* 173:667 (2006). Air pollution probably causes more deaths in the United States than radon gas, but not by causing lung cancer.

10. National Cancer Institute, Radon and Cancer: Questions and Answers, online at: www.cancer.gov/cancertopics/factsheet/Risk/radon (accessed July 19, 2010).

11. Jonathan Baron, "Blind Justice: Fairness to Groups and the Do-No-Harm Principle," *Journal of Behavioral Decision Making* 8:71 (1995).

12. Edward J. McCaffrey, "Cognitive Theory and Tax," *UCLA Law Review* 41:1862, 1868 (1994).

13. Jonathan Baron, "Blind Justice: Fairness to Groups and the Do-No-Harm Principle," *Journal of Behavioral Decision Making* 8:71 (1995).

14. Jonathan Baron and James Jurney, "Norms Against Voting for Coerced Reform," *Journal of Personality and Social Psychology* 64:347 (1993).

15. Ilana Ritov and Jonathan Baron, "Reluctance to Vaccinate: Omission Bias and Ambiguity," *Journal of Behavioral Decision Making* 3:263, 275–77 (1990).

16. David Hardisty, Eric Johnson, and Elke Weber, "A Dirty Word or a Dirty World? Attribute Framing, Political Affiliation, and Query Theory," *Psychological Science* 2:86 (2010).

17. Monterey Bay Aquarium, Review of Public Opinion Surveys on Climate Change (August 4, 2008) (online at http://itconf.mbayaq.org/climatechangesummit/ReviewofClimateChangesurveysfor2010FINAL.pdf.

18. Analysis of the Scope of Energy Subsidies and Suggestions for the G-20 Initiative, Joint Report of IEA, OPEC, OECD, and the World Bank, June 16, 2010, prepared for submission for the 2010 G-20 Summit Meeting.

19. World Bank, World Development Indicators and World Global Finance, online at: http://databank.worldbank.org/ddp/home.do.

20. "Polluter pays" refers to a widely popular if loosely defined norm, accepted more prominently in international legal circles, that holds that the costs of pollution should be borne by those causing the pollution. Acceptance of this principle has been formalized in a few contexts, most notably the OECD. See, e.g., Environment and Economics: Guiding Principles Concerning International Economic Aspects of Environmental Policies, May 26, 1972, annex para. 1 Doc. No. C(72)128.

21. Robin Bravender, "Sierra Club, States File Challenges to EPA 'Tailoring' Rule," *Greenwire*, August 3, 2010; "CBD's Snape says Clean Air Act Good Tool for Emissions Regulation," *Greenwire*, March 31, 2010; Robin Bravender, "CBD among 18 Groups Challenging 'Johnson Memo' in Federal Court," *Greenwire*, June 2, 2010.

22. Edward Maibach, Connie Roser-Renouf, and Anthony Lieserowitz, "Global Warming's Six Americas 2009: An Audience Segmentation Analysis" –93-94 (May 2009) online at http://environment.yale.edu/uploads/6Americas2009.pdf (accessed March 25, 2011).

23. H.R. 2454, §321, amending the Clean Air Act by adding section 782(a), (c) & (d) (2009). American Power Act, S. 1733 § 2101, amending the Clean Air Act by adding section 781.

24. Darren Samuelson, "Senate Trio Hopes to Hit Paydirt with 'Carbon Fee' on Transportation Fuels," *Energy & Environment Daily*, March 3, 2010.

25. Alex Kaplun, "Conservatives Aim to Sink Kerry-Lieberman with 'Gas Tax' Claims," *Energy & Environment Daily*, May 13, 2010.

26. New Democratic Party, "Carole James and the NDP: A Better Climate Change Plan," www.bcndp.ca/climatechange (accessed July 19, 2010).

27. Government of British Columbia, LiveSmart BC, BC's Carbon Tax Shift, www.livesmartbc.ca/government/carbon_tax.html (accessed July 19, 2010); Government of British Columbia, Ministry of Finance, Budget and Fiscal Plan 2008/09–2010/11 at 103-06 (February 19, 2008) online at: www.bcbudget.gov.bc.ca/2008/bfp/2008_Budget_Fiscal_Plan.pdf.

28. See, e.g., Michelle Hoar, "How Will You Spend Your $100?" *The Tyee*, February 25, 2008, http://thetyee.ca/Views/2008/02/25/100GreenDollars/.

29. Karen Jenni and George Loewenstein, "Explaining the "Identifiable Victim Effect,"" *Journal of Risk & Uncertainty* 14:235, 236–37 (1997); Richard Nisbett and Lee Ross, *Human Inference: Strategies and Shortcomings of Social Judgment* 43–62 (1980).

30. Deborah A. Small and George Loewenstein, "The Devil You Know: The Effects of Identifiability on Punishment," *Journal of Behavioral Decision Making* 18:311 (2005).

31. World Health Organization, "Malaria, Key Facts," online at: www
.who.int/mediacentre/factsheets/fs094/en/.

32. Advocated by economist Jeffrey Sachs as a low-cost way of reducing
malaria cases and deaths. Jeffrey D. Sachs, "Ending Malaria Deaths in Africa,"
Scientific American (October 2007).

33. Thomas C. Schelling, "The Life You Save May Be Your Own," in
Problems in Public Expenditure Analysis 127, 129–30 (S. Chase, ed., 1968).

34. Lisa Priest, "Breast Cancer Survivors Fighting for New Drug," *Globe
and Mail*, June 23, 2005, at A1.

35. Lisa Priest, "Ontario Will Fast-Track Breast Cancer Drug," *Globe and
Mail*, June 24, 2005, at A9.

36. Elaine Carey, "Do Politics Affect Drug Coverage?; Herceptin Cited
by CMAJ Editorial Taxpayers Must Foot Costly Bill Treatment Costs for Few
Are Being Borne by Many; Herceptin Case Cited by CMAJ Editor," *Toronto
Star*, August 19, 2005, at D2.

37. Editorial, "Genomics and Economics," *Canadian Medical Association
Journal* 173(4):329 (Aug. 2005).

38. See, e.g., Christine Jolls, Cass R. Sunstein, Richard Thaler, "A Behavioral Approach to Law and Economics," *Stanford Law Review* 50:1471, 1509–
10 (1998).

39. Deborah A. Small and George Loewenstein, "Helping 'A' Victim or
Helping 'THE' Victim: Altruism and Identifiability," *Journal of Risk and Uncertainty* 26:5, 7 (2003).

40. Shi-Ling Hsu, "The Identifiability Bias in Environmental Law,"
Florida State University Law Review 35:433 (2008).

41. Abt Associates, "Power Plant Emissions: Particulate Matter-Related
Health Damages and the Benefits of Alternative Emission Reduction Scenarios" 5-5 (2004), applying analysis from Health Effects Institute, "Special Report: Reanalysis of the Harvard Six Cities Study and the American Cancer
Society Study of Particulate Air Pollution and Mortality" (July 2000), reana-
lyzing Douglas W. Dockery et al., "An Association Between Air Pollution and
Mortality in Six US Cities," *New England Journal of Medicine* 329:1753
(1993). More recent estimates are actually higher, as much as three times
higher. Abt Associates, "Power Plant Emissions: Particulate Matter-Related
Health Damages and the Benefits of Alternative Emission Reduction Scenarios" 6-2 (2004), applying analysis from Francine Laden et al., "Reduction in
Fine Particulate Air Pollution and Mortality: Extended Follow-up of the Harvard Six Cities Study," *American Journal of Respiratory & Critical Care Medicine* 173:667 (2006).

42. "As Gas Prices Go Up, Impact Trickles Down," *New York Times*, April
30, 2006, at A1.

43. *Congressional Record* June 11, 1975, 18435.

44. Anthony Lieserowitz, "Climate Change Risk Perception and Policy Perception: the Role of Affect, Imagery, and Values," *Climatic Change* 77:45, 68 (2006).

45. Anthony Lieserowitz, "Climate Change Risk Perception and Policy Perception: the Role of Affect, Imagery, and Values," *Climatic Change* 77:45, 68 (2006).

46. Robin Bravender, "Groups launch $2M ad campaign as Senate sprints to July floor debate," *Greenwire*, June 30, 2010; Anne C. Mulkern, "Green groups fight to keep EPA's power over emissions," *Greenwire*, April 6, 2010; "CBD's Snape says Clean Air Act good tool for emissions regulation," *Greenwire*, March 31, 2010.

47. Nathan Cummings Foundation Global Warming Survey (August 2007).

48. New Democratic Party, Carole James and the NDP: A Better Climate Change Plan, www.bcndp.ca/climatechange (accessed July 19, 2010).

49. William Samuelson and Richard Zeckhauser, "Status Quo Bias in Decision-making," *Journal of Risk and Uncertainty* 1:7 (1988).

50. Daniel Kahneman, Jack L. Knetsch,, and Richard H. Thaler, "Experimental Tests of the Endowment Effect and the Coase Theorem," *Journal of Political Economy* 98:1325 (1990).

51. For a review of the many various experiments in this area see John K. Horowitz and Kenneth E. McConnell. "A Review of WTA / WTP Studies," *Journal of Environmental Economics and Management* 44:426 (2002).

52. Robin Bravender, "GOP Hosts Sympathetic Panel to Blast Cap-and-Trade," *Energy & Environment Daily*, July 31, 2009.

53. Nathan Cummings Foundation Global Warming Survey (August 2007).

54. Nathan Cummings Foundation Global Warming Survey (August 2007).

55. Amos Tversky and Daniel Kahneman, *Judgment under Uncertainty: Heuristics and Biases*, *Science* 185:124 (1974); Daniel Kahneman and Amos Tversky, "Prospect Theory: An Analysis of Decisions Under Risk," *Econometrica* 47:313 (1979).

56. Nathan Cummings Foundation Global Warming Survey (August 2007).

57. Nathan Cummings Foundation Global Warming Survey (August 2007).

58. Anthony Lieserowitz, Edward Maibach, Connie Roser-Renouf, and Nicholas Smith, "Global Warming's Six Americas," 44–46 (June 2010) online at http://environment.yale.edu/climate/files/SixAmericasJune2010.pdf (accessed August 7, 2010).

59. Environment Canada, "Canada's 2005 Greenhouse Gas Inventory,

National Inventory Report 1990–2005: "Greenhouse Gas Sources and Sinks in Canada," Table A11-10 through A11-21, 2005 GHG Emission Summaries by province, www.ec.gc.ca/pdb/ghg/inventory_report/2005_report/a11_eng .cfm.

60. Shi-Ling Hsu, Joshua Walters & Anthony Purgas, "Pollution Tax Heuristics: an Empirical Study of Willingness to Pay Higher Gasoline Taxes," *Energy Policy* 36:3612 (2008).

61. See, e.g, Woods Institute for the Environment, Global Warming Poll (June 9, 2010) online at: http://woods.stanford.edu/research/americans -support-govt-solutions-global-warming.html.

62. See, e.g., Gallup, "Americans' Global Warming Concerns Con-tinue to Drop" (March 11, 2010) online at www.gallup.com/poll/126560 /americans-global-warming-concerns-continue-drop.aspx.

63. See, e.g., Gallup, "Americans: Economy Takes Precedence over Environment" (March 19, 2009) online at: www.gallup.com/poll/116962 /Americans-Economy-Takes-Precedence-Environment.aspx.

64. For a description and analysis of the unsuccessful plan, see Michael Mercer and Laura Wagner, Blakes, "Liberal Party of Canada Introduces "Green Shift" Carbon Tax Plan," (July 4, 2008) online at www.blakes.com /english/view.asp?ID = 2418 (accessed August 10, 2010).

Chapter 6

1. Anne C. Mulkern, "New Coal Ads Emphasize Energy Costs in Bid for 'Hearts and Minds,'" *Greenwire*, August 14, 2009.

2. Center for Local, State, and Urban Policy, "Climate Compared: Public Opinion on Climate Change in the United States and Canada" 10 (2011), online: http://closup.umich.edu/publications/reports/pr-15-climate-change -public-opinion-report.pdf (accessed March 25, 2011).

3. Center for Local, State, and Urban Policy, "Climate Compared: Public Opinion on Climate Change in the United States and Canada" 10 (2011), online: http://closup.umich.edu/publications/reports/pr-15-climate-change -public-opinion-report.pdf (accessed March 25, 2011).

4. Knowledge Networks, "Carbon Sequestration Survey 2009," Field Re-port (September 24, 2009).

5. Steve Mufson, "Talk of Raising Gas Tax Is Just That," Washingtonpost.com, October 18, 2006 ("I don't think there's any question that as a matter of policy it makes a lot of sense to move in that direc-tion," he said. "But politically it's a very high hurdle to get over."), on-line at: www.washingtonpost.com/wp-dyn/content/article/2006/10/17 /AR2006101701327.html.

6. Gary S. Becker, "Want to Cut Gasoline Use? Raise Taxes," *Business Week*, May 27, 2002, 26.

7. Friends of the Earth, "Support the Carbon Tax," http://action.foe
.org/dia/organizationsORG/foe/content.jsp?content_KEY=3303.

8. Charles Krauthammer, "Decline Is a Choice," 2009 Wriston Lecture,
Manhattan Institute, online on Liberty's Army, October 19, 2009, online at:
www.libertysarmy.com/2009/10/12/iraq/dr-charles-krauthammer-decline
-is-a-choice-the-new-liberalism-and-the-end-of-american-ascendancy/ ("We
have it in our power to institute a serious gasoline tax [refunded immediately through a payroll tax reduction] to curb consumption and induce
conservation.").

9. Lawrence Summers, "Practical Steps to Climate Control," *Financial
Times*, May 28, 2007.

10. Bob Inglis and Arthur B. Laffer, "An Emissions Plan Conservatives
Could Warm To," *New York Times*, December 28, 2008, at WK10.

11. James Hansen, "Cap and Fade," *New York Times*, December 6, 2009,
at A29; Testimony of James E. Hansen, Committee on Ways and Means, US
House of Representatives, February 25, 2009; online at www.columbia.edu
/~jeh1/2009/WaysAndMeans_20090225.pdf (accessed August 6, 2010).

12. Alex Kaplun, "Campaign 2008: Sen. Dodd's Energy Plan Focuses on
Carbon Tax, Makes Room for Reactors," *E&E News PM*, April 19, 2007.

13. Bob Inglis and Arthur B. Laffer, "An Emissions Plan Conservatives
Could Warm To," *New York Times*, December 28, 2008, at WK10.

14. H.R. 2069, Save Our Climate Act of 2007, available online
at http://frwebgate.access.gpo.gov/cgi-bin/getdoc.cgi?dbname=110_cong
_bills&docid=f:h2069ih.txt.pdf (Library of Congress, Thomas Bills and Res-
olutions).

15. Paul Krugman, "Gasoline Tax Follies," *New York Times*, March 15,
2000, at A27. Economist Robert Frank reported Norquist's agreement with a
gasoline tax, provided that the proceeds were completely returned to taxpayers in other ways. Robert H. Frank, "A Way to Cut Fuel Consumption That
Everyone Likes, Except the Politicians," *New York Times*, Feb. 16, 2006, at C3.

16. Shaun Polczer, "Suncor CEO Back Carbon Tax Concept," *Edmonton
Journal*, June 23, 2010, online at www.edmontonjournal.com/technology
/Suncor+backs+carbon+concept/3189609/story.html. Matthew Burrows,
"Petro-giants Will Accept Carbon Tax," Straight.com, December 7, 2007, online at www.straight.com/article-123594/petro-giants-will-accept-a-carbon
-tax; Gordon Jaremko and Jason Markusoff, "Oilsands Backs Carbon Tax: All
Polluters Must Help Pay for Carbon-Capture Scheme, Industry," *Edmonton Journal*, March, 11, 2008, online at www.uofaweb.ualberta.ca/CMS
/printpage.cfm?ID=75017.

17. Russell Gold and Ian Talley, "Exxon CEO Advocates Emissions Tax,"
Wall Sreet Journal, February 9, 2009.

18. William D. Nordhaus, *A Question of Balance* 90 (Table 5-4) (2008),
Martin Weitzman "A Review of the Stern Review on the Economics of

Climate Change," *Journal of Economic Literature* 45:703, 710 (2007); Nicholas Stern, *The Stern Review on the Economics of Climate Change* 470 (2007).

19. Martin Weitzman "A Review of the Stern Review on the Economics of Climate Change," *Journal of Economic Literature* 45:703, 723 (2007).

20. Greg Mankiw's blog, "Three Votes for a Carbon Tax," (May 23, 2006) online at: http://gregmankiw.blogspot.com/2006/05/three-votes-for -carbon-tax.html.

21. Ipsos Reid, Press Release: "Environment Tops the List of Priorities for Canadians—First Time Since 1990" (November 6, 2006) (on file with author).

22. David G. Duff, "Carbon Taxation in British Columbia," *Vermont Journal of Environmental Law*" 10:87, 102 (2008).

23. CBCNews.ca, "Environmental Groups Disagree With NDP's Stand on Carbon Tax," April 13, 2009, online at: www.cbc.ca/canada/bcvotes2009 /story/2009/04/13/bc-ndp-carole-james.html.

INDEX

Figures/photos/illustrations are indicated by an "f" and tables by a "t."

AARP, 124
abatement
  marginal abatement benefit curves,
    105–107, 107f, 109f
  of pollution, 105
  technology, 34
Acid Rain Program, 18
Ackerman, Bruce, 60
ACUPCC. *See* American College and
    University Presidents Climate
    Commitment
adaptation, 14
adjustments, 140–141
  border tax, 96, 98
  of consumption, 128–129
administrability, 84, 87
aggregate, 140–141
agriculture, 129
air pollution, 84–85
Alberta, 187
Alexander, Bill, 167
Alexander, Lamar, 57
allowances, 15, 20–21, 39, 72, 120
  allocation of, 61–62
  auctioned, 71
  bonus, 61
  borrowing of, 114
  prices for, 71
  theft of, 86
American Clean Energy and Security
    Act, 48
American College and University Pres-
    idents Climate Commitment
    (ACUPCC), 80

American Council for Capital Forma-
    tion, 41
American Electric Power Company,
    58, 144
American Power Act, 114, 123, 162,
    166
American University, 80
Americans for Tax Reform, 185
analysis, cost-benefit, 29
Apollo Energy Act, 175, 183t
Arab Oil Embargo, 167
Arrhenius, Svante, 1
auctioning, 61, 71
auto industry
  General Motors, 53, 55, 58, 138
  Japanese, 54–55
availability heuristic, 165

bailouts, 138
Ballard, Geoffrey, 54
Baron, Jonathan, 153–154, 156,
    157
Barrett, Scott, 92
batteries, electric vehicle, 58
BC *See* British Columbia
Becker, Gary, 185
behavior
  consumptive, 172
  prosocial, 144
behavioral economists, 150
biases, 148
  against carbon taxes, 151, 167
  cognitive, 8, 181
  identifiability and, 165
  omission, 152, 155
  psychology and, 149, 151
  of public decision making, 164

223